De

DIARIES

of a

NORTSOIDE

TAOISEACH

1997-2008

Published by
PENFIELD ENTERPRISES LTD
T/A THE PHOENIX
44 Lwr Baggot Street,
Dublin 2, Ireland
www.phoenix-magazine.com

ISBN: 978 1 870204 03 3

Printed by ColourBooks, Dublin

De
COLLECTED
DIARIES
of a
NORTSOIDE
TAOISEACH

1997-2008

CONTENTS

INTRODUCTION

ALL GOOD tings must come to an end. And so it is dat, after more years dan I care to remember (especially if de tribunal's askin), de moment has come when I must write me final entry in de Diary of a Nortsoide Teeseach.

Today is not a day for soundbites. But, eh, I feel de hand of histry on me shoulder. I feel de udder hand of histry on de arse of me trousers. And I sense dat togedder, dey're about to feck me head-first trew de pub doorway of histry and say: "You're barred!" So I'm goin voluntarily before dat happens. Unlike Blair, I know when I'm not wanted.

I have been very lucky to lead me country for more dan a decade. Almost as lucky as de country was to have me as leader, in fact. Whatever de creepin Jesuses may say, dey were years of great achievement, durin which I transformed Oireland into one of de richest countries in de world, which could well afford to pay me tree hundred grand a year widdout feckin-well complainin about it as much as it did.

It's been a great oul' innings, all de same. Peace in de Nort. Tree election victories in de Sout. De most successful Oirish EU presidencies ever, durin which I bestrode de international stage like a colostomy. De spirit of 1916 reclaimed from de Shinners. Kevin Barry given a decent funeral. De list of me achievements goes on an on. All dat was missin, I suppose, was de Dubs winnin an All-Ireland. And unfortunately some tings in Drumcondra dat are beyond even my control (not many, dough).

But now, as Frank Sinatra said, de end is near. And so I face de final curtain. Very expensive tings, curtains. Celia spent a fortune on de soft furnishins for 44 Bercoford, which was why we used to drive around wit suitcases full of cash, in case she'd see something in a shop window she just had to have. But, eh, maybe I've done enough explainin on dat score.

Regrets? I've had a few. Me biggest single regret, lookin back, was dat I didn't manage to bring in e-votin and get rid of de stupid oul pencils. I hate pencils. We're de laughin stock of de world wit dem. Sometimes I lie awake at night listening to de world laughin at us as and sayin: "Ha, Ha! Look at the Irish. Still using pencils!"

Apart from dat, I'm sorry I didn't establish a first-class helt service in Oireland. De Bertiebowl was a big disappointment too. And did I mention de pencils?

Of course, as a socialist, I regret me failure to overtrow de international capitalist system. I apologised for dis personally to Fidel Castro when he rang a while back to ask me advice about his own resignation. But dere just wasn't enough time, especially after we lost Comrade Higgins from de struggle last year.

Even before den, as McCreevy said, dere were only tree socialists in de Dail: me, Joe, and one udder, who continues to work undercover. I will protect de turd man's identity to de last, except to say dat he's a fat lad from de midlands who is now ideally placed to carry on de struggle from widdin. My message to him is: Courage, comrade.

I don't like diggin up de past (except Kevin Barry). But obviously, in retraspect, I also regret ever settin up de bleedin tribunals. Dey seemed like a good idea back in 1997. Evrytime dere was a problem, I just launched anudder inquiry and den told de opposition to shut up and let it get on wit its work. But de more money I put in lawyers' pockets, de less gratitude de bastards showed. And as I said recently, what dey did to Grainne Caroot was real Westlife stuff. Er, I mean low-life stuff. (In case Nicky's reading dis, I love Westlife. Honestly.)

At dis point, I'd like to tank a few people for deir help down de years. De first and most important are me two daughters, for standin by me trew tick and tin. Dey were only young ones when I became Teeseach, and I hope deir oul lad didn't embarrass dem too much. Needless to say, I'm proud of deir achievements. Celia wit her bukes. And Georgina wit her glamorous pop-star husband and her beautiful, perfectly-timed twins.

I'd like to tank de udder wimmin in me life too, even if me relationships wit dem were more complex. Dey enriched me life in different ways (none of dem financial, obviously), and I hope I did deirs too. As one of dem said once: "You'll always be part of my personal brand, Bertie."

I'd also like to tank de media for deir help over de years. We had our differences from time to time. But I always accepted dey had a job to do and dey did it well. It's not a real job, obviously. Not a job any self-respectin person would do. But I wish dem well even so, and I'm confident dat some of dem will get a life eventually if dey work hard enough.

I'd like to express me gratitude to de main opposition parties too, for carryin on de futile but important task of tryin to annoy me over de past 11 years. De leaders of Fine Gael and Labour kept changin, so dey're far too numerous to mention individually. But dey remember who dey are, even if me and de electrit don't. So wherever yiz are now, lads, tanks.

Tanks are due too to me make-up girls for all deir heroic work. Especially durin pressurised periods like de EU presidency. And on Ash Wednesday every year, when dey had to touch me forehead up regularly, so I looked me penitential best all day.

Finally, I'd like to tank all de coalition partners dat served wit me. If me years in office proved anyting, it's dat Fianna Fail can work well wit udder parties, not like when Mr Cat-food was in power. Our junior partners can now be confident dat dey will have de full five years in Government, before bein blamed for everyting by de electrit. I tank de Greens for deir cooperation over de past year and I wish dem well when dey too lose all deir seats in 2012.

Lookin ahead, who knows what de next chapter of me life will hold? I have absolutely no ambition to be EU president but, eh, if Europe needs me, I'm prepared to reconsider. Apart from dat, dere's de international lecture circuit. Clinton says dat wit me great ornithological powers *("oratorical"? – Ed)*, I could make a hundrid grand a night, just for talking shite like he does.

As I've said before, a career in sports management would intrest me too. If tings don't work out wit Trappatony, maybe I could yet lead Oireland in anudder way. I'll say dis for de FAI: at least dey see nuttin wrong wit deir top man being part-funded by de private sector.

De udder ting about de FAI job dat would suit me is dat I wouldn't have to make many substitutions. Reshuffles were never me strong point: I hate disturbin de status quo. But de Oirish soccer management has even less talent on de bench dan Feena Fail, so dere'd be no hard choices.

I can't imagine what it'll be like not workin a 16-hour day. But one of de tings I definitely hope to catch up on is gardenin. I wasn't able to do much of dis in recent years, because of de lu-lus in de bushes. Now, I'll be free to devote meself to de hangin baskets: de secret passion of me life.

One of me most enjoyable periods in power was de time I spent up de trees of Nort Dublin. I was supposed to be searchin for de goods on Ray Burke. And aldough I found nuttin, in de process I fell in love wit dis densely forested area and its rich wildlife, which includes sevral species dat are found nowhere else on ert. I hope to spend much more time now explorin dis great wilderness. Dere's even talk of a possible TV documentry, with yer man David Battenburg.

As he leaves office, every Taoiseach worries about his leprosy *(er "legacy"? – Ed)*. But I have no worries about my leprosy, which I know will be carried on successfully by Brian Cowen, and in due course passed to de next Fianna Fail leader. I heard Biffo on de radio de udder day sayin he hopes he can do de job "half as well" as I did.

And I taut: he's pitchin his hopes a bit high dere, de cheeky bogger. But I suppose ye have to start out optimistic. Anyway, I wish him well.

I tink dat's about all I have to say at dis point. Except to repeat dat, whatever de tribunal claims, I did no wrong in public life, and I wronged no-one. Or if I did, I'm confident dat nobody saw me do it, and can't prove anyting. Apart from dat, I have one final message for me many friends. Whatever happens now, for Jayzus' sake, don't organise a whip-around.

TUESDAY

More talks with de independent TDs. Tony Gregory is de first in, for his Ceann Comhairle audition. Good bloke, Tony. Bit of a communist, but a real Dub, ye know? Of course, some people tink he's not Ceann Comhairle material on account of how his grammar is not de Mae West, so we have to ask him to run trew a few standard phrases.

"Order, order, yiz are all out of order, for Jayz' sake," he says. Sounds good to me, but PJ Mara tells him: "Don't call us, Tony, we'll call you." He's a bit of a snob, dat PJ.

De negotiations are takin up all my legendary deal-makin skills. I ring dis Jackie Hilly-Billy Rae fella again and lay it on de line for him. "I'm givin ye nuttin! D'ye hear me? Nuttin!" Dis is known as de softenin up process, and widdin a few minutes, sure enough, Mr Really Hay is back on sayin he'll settle for a multi-million pound investment in Sout Kerry. No mention of All-Ireland tickets, at all.

Young Mildewed is an even bigger pushover. She doesn't even try for tickets (but den, what would Wicklow be needn dem for?), only a school and a hospital wing and a couple of udder knick-knacks. I'm beginnin to enjoy meself.

WEDNESDAY

I lay it on de line to de Two Marys. "I'm de boss here. I'm de one wearin de trousers. If I say: you're Tánaiste an you're not, dat's de way it is, roite? If I say "Jump", I wanna see jumpin. I don't wanna hear any lip. If I'm interested in what eider if you tinks, I'll ask. Have I made meself clear?"

Dey bote nod meekly. Den Georgina and Celia pipe up: "Can we go now, Daddy? We've been doin dis for hours – you're goin to have to face dem yourself sooner or later."

De TV man from Donegal arrives, but I can't make him out at all. He hasn't much to say for himself, and when I ask him if he prefers tea or coffee, he abstains. Eventually, I offer him a 28-inch Mitsubishi flat screen with a year's subscription to Sky Sports, and tell him to go away an tink about it.

I'm definitely not askin dat Caoimhghín O Caoláin for his vote, I can't pronounce his bleedin name.

THURSDAY

De greatest day of me life, at least since de Dubs stuffed Meath de last time. When Bruton loses de vote for Taoiseach. I want to chant "You're not singin anymore" across at him. But I'm de Taoiseach, now, and I have to reflect de dignity of de office. So instead I get one of de ushers to bring him a note sayin "Olé, olé, olé, olé".

Afterwards, I'm dyin for a jar, but I have to go up to de Aras to have me ministers blessed by de President. I wouldn't mind, only it's de second trip up dere in one day. You'd tink a Taoiseach had nuttin else to do. "Hurry it up Missus," I tell her, "de pubs'll be closed soon."

FRIDAY

Bit of a head.

SATURDAY

Yer man is dere again dis mornin. On de way out of de house, I whisper to one of de lads: "Don't look now, but dere's dat copper again. He's been hangin round here for weeks. It's bleedin harrassment, so it is." Someone replies he's "only doin his job", but I says: "Find out who he is, and I'll arrange for him to be doin his job on Tory Island next week."

Next minute, doesn't de copper jump on some poor fella and wrestles him into de back of de cop car. De lad only wanted to clap me on de back – aldough he was carryin a knife, and he had a tattoo of de Queen on his forehead. But even so, I'm a man of de people, an dis kind of ting could get me a bad name.

MONDAY

You'd never guess. It turns out dis guard is part of a "permanent security presence" which I have to have on account of me bein de Taoiseach an dat. I'm not sure I like dis idea. I didn't realise how serious tings were until I dropped into Fagan's last night and de Garda sub-aqua unit insisted on goin trew me pint of Bass before I touched it. It put me right off me drinks, so it did.

TUESDAY

I hate dese elocution lessons too – dey're a bleedin pain in de neck. And de teacher, he's so stuck up, "Repeat after me: How now, brown cow?" he says, like he's talkin to some six-year-old.

So I says: "I'm not sayin dat, it's stupid." But he won't give up: "How now, brown cow! Say it!" So I decide on a compromise. "What are ye at now, Brian Cowen, ye bollix ye?" I says. But is he happy? No he is not.

MONDAY

Our hardline stance on de Nort has paid off. Mo Mowlam rang me on Saturday night to tell me how much she respected our position and how difficult it would be for her to ignore it completely. Which is what she was goin to do, she added.

Rambo was hoppin mad when he saw de Orangemen lined up in deir sashes and dere jackboots, an he was on for sendin in de Army. Personally, I didn't tink we should risk de Army, so we sent Eamon O Cuiv instead as an observer, on de grounds dat if he got hit in de crossfire, dat'd be one more junior ministry I'd have to give to me real friends.

I spent tonight in bed puttin de final touches to de list of juniors – all chosen because of deir special qualities, like bein over 65 and untreatenin. Anudder rule is no nortsoiders (de area is well enough represented by me and Celia). And no Lenihans eider – one of dat family is enough to be dealin wit.

TUESDAY

Celia says "dere's a man on de phone, says his name is Haughey. He claims he's an old friend of yours and he needs a big favour in a hurry". I says I don't believe I know anyone of de name Haughey, except de wee fella with de moustache. He rings twice more and each time I tell her I don't know him. Den a strange ting happens – a cock crows out in de garden. Celia says "it's like in de Gospel." I says it is de gospel. I swear I don't know de guy.

Some people were critical about givin Celia de Tánaiste's office to run me constituency, but dey don't realise de amount of work dat has to be done. You wouldn't believe de number who took me up on de offer to give everyone who voted for me a spin in de Government jet, for instance. It's a nightmare for Celia tryin to organise times for dem all.

WEDNESDAY

Oh, dat Haughey! Yes of course, now I remember Charlie. Not dat I ever called him Charlie – we were never dat close. Still, it's a pity to see de old codger caught by de short and curlies, when he used to be de most cunnin politician in de Dáil (apart from meself). What I can't understand, dough, is all dis talk about his "lavish lifestyle". In all de years I knew him, I never once seen him put his hand in his pocket in a pub.

De cabinet meetin discussed his situation and, for old times' sake, we agreed to send him a message of support as he prepares to go before de tribunal. De message reads: "You're on your own, pal. Mention any of us and you're dead." I tink dat hit de right note.

THURSDAY

De Dáil has broken up for two months, tank God. Now I can get on with runnin de country without havin to answer Dick Spring's smartarse questions about dis and dat and de udder and everything. I resisted de calls for a new, wider tribunal pendin' an internal party investigation to establish (1) wedder anybody else in de party took money and (2) wedder we can get away wit a cover-up. Den I wished Bruton and Spring an enjoyable holiday and told dem to take 6 months if dey like.

We had a crisis meetiong to discuss de Ormeau Road march. Everybody is very tense. Rambo says we should send an ultimatum to de Brits dat if de Orangemen try to march, we'll blow de bridge. Liz O'Donnell files her nails and says "why can't everybody just get along?"

We vote to send Jackie Healy Rae to Belfast as an observer, on de grounds dat he's someone who can blend in easily wherever he goes. Mansergh tells our Loyalist contacts he'll be on de six o'clock train, wearin a funny cap.

FRIDAY

De Orangemen agree to call off dere marches trew Catholic areas. Rambo tinks its a "dirty black orange trick" and he still wants to send in de Army. Gerry Adams rings me and explains dat de Orange refusal to march is typical of de unionists' unwillingness to "move de situation forward".

I don't know what to tink at all.

MONDAY

One of de reasons I always wanted to be de Taoiseach is dat I could apply me legendary cunnin and deal-makin skills to de task of achievin peace on dis oisland. So I was a very proud man yesterday when dey said the cessation was unequiv ... eh, uniquevic ... eh, when dey said it was permanent. Which dey didn't, exactly, but Mansergh says not to worry, dat's what dey tinkin. And it's de taut dat counts.

I tink what probably swung it was me personal assurance to Gerry and de boys dat we had reached an understandin wit de Brits dat dey'd be out of de Nort widdin five years, followin which we'd send in de FCA as a peace-keepin force durin de transition to a united Oirland.

TUESDAY

Of course, dere's still dose pesky unionists to deal wit. We're not even bodderin to try to get de Paisley fella into de talks, because his voice is too loud for a small room anyway. So it's vital dat de udder fella, Trimble, is dere.

On dis basis, I wrote to him today and gave him me personal assurance dat in five years time, we will drop Articles 2 & 3 and accept dat partition is permanent and dat, furdermore, we'll trow in Donegal as a goodwill gesture. Den I signed de letter as de Prime Minister of Eire. Dis is what's known in de business as a confidence-buildin measure.

WEDNESDAY

Trimble told Mansergh he loiked de sound of de letter, but he still had a problem wit de decommissionin issue. De bottom line is we have to see some weapons surrendered, he says. Mansergh offered him his Swiss pen knife, but Trimble said dere'd be no deal for de moment, anyway. President Clinton was on de phone dis evenin to inquire how it's all goin, so I told him everythin was game ball. He didn't seem to understand me – Yanks can be a bit tick like dat – but eventually he got de drift. Den I said dere was somethin I'd been meanin to ask him as de leader of de world's most powerful nation.

He says: What's that? I says: Dat Paula Jones. Did ye really drop de trousers ye dirty fecker, ye?

THURSDAY

Gerry and de boys were on to me yesterday about a plan dey had to get de UK unionists into de talks, so as to furder isolate de Paisley fella. It's crude, dey said, but we tink it's viable. Dere, I says to John Brutal when I met him in de corridor: if ye give dese fellas a chance, dere just natural politicians.

Den dis mornin I hear on de radio dat de RUC have intercepted a crude but viable parcel device sent to Robert McCartney's house. Dis is a worryin development but I decide to say nuttin for de moment.

FRIDAY

De idea for an Ettics Commission to investigate funny money to politicians has proved very popular wit everybody. People taut dere'd be no entusiasm in Fianna Fail for such a body, but I already have had several of de backbenchers on to me lookin for jobs on it.

De important ting is dat de actual commissioner will be somebody above party politics. Somebody tough and fearless who knows all de tricks and will be able to play hardball wit some of de slipperiest individuals in de country. Somebody who'll strike fear into de hearts of corrupt politicians, however mighty. Somebody like Mildred Fox, I was tinkin.

SATURDAY

Still gettin dose calls from dat Haughey man who claims he knows me. I have turned de matter over to de Gardai.

MONDAY

Dublin for de Sam Maguire, Kerry for de holidays. Dat's what we used to say, back in de good old days. Pity about de Dubs, wha? But at least de Mead boys finally got stuffed. Hard an all as it'll be to live with Biffo Cowen now, I hate nuttin more worse dan seein dose Mead farmers drivin home from Dublin in dere 4-wheel-drive tractors, wit de Sam Maguire in de trailer.

You know, Kerry is great. An by comin here for de holliers, I'm showin everybody I'm me own man. I mean, what udder Fianna Fáil leader ever took his holidays in Kerry, know wat I mean? De girls are down wit me, so it's a great family occasion. We sit around on de beach all day, listenin to: Aw da, can we not go somewhere excitin for de holidays, instead of dis borin hole – and all de udder tings dat young girls are interested in.

Ah yes. Peace in Ireland, a Fianna Fáil Taoiseach on his holidays in Kerry, an de sun shinin. Happy days, wha?

TUESDAY

De Leavin Cert results are out today and I see Mickey Martin is complainin about de standard of spoken English among school-leavers. He has a point dere, so he does. De standards have fallen a long way from when we were in school an had it beaten into us wit dem hurleys dat had de nails stuck in dem. Dere's some young ones you meet dese days and dere not able to put two gramat … grammat … two proper words togedder.

Of course, Mickey can't afford to shout too loud eider, wit his hilarious accent. I mean, dese Cork fellas can't talk roite at all – we all know dat.

WEDNESDAY

De presidential situation is gettin very complicated, wit dis Michael O'Kennedy eejit trowin his hat in de ring (he'd be better keepin it on his oul baldy head!). We still don't know wat de Hume fella's goin to do, but Albert's hell-bent on runnin eider way, and when Albert gets somethin into his tick head, it'd take a bleedin brain surgeon to remove it.

PJ says he can only win if we put my face on all de election posters, an some witty slogan like people before petfood, and even den it'd be touch and go. I agree wit PJ dat de protection of democracy is de important ting. Whatever else happens, it's vital dat we avoid an election at all costs, so dat de people don't get disillusioned by havin to vote too often.

D'ye know wat it is, but I'm nearly tempted to back Dustin for de job, radder dan Albert. One turkey's as good as annuder, and at last he's a Dub.

THURSDAY

Watchin Ireland against de Lusitanians last night. Jayzus! Were we poxy or wha? If we can't agree a candidate for de presidency, I'm tinkin maybe I'll nominate de whole Oirish soccer team. De Phoenix Park is de only place dem boys should be playin.

But at least de economy is still bright. I've been lookin at de projections for de national tax take and, speakin as a trained accountant, I reckon we're in a pigs-in-shite situation. De only problem is if I give some of dis back to de people, dey'll all spend it on bleedin imports and inflayshun will rise and dere'll be pressure on interest rates and mortgages will go trew de roof and we'll all be bollixed and John Brutal will be Taoiseach again.

Nuttin's as simple as it looks. It's because de economy is already overheatin, de economists say. But sure what wouldn't be, in dis wedder?

FRIDAY

De report on de Dunnes payments tribunal is due out on Monday, but I'm not boddered, cause I never knew de Haughey guy anyway. Still, we need to avoid a repetition of de problems de last time a major report was issued, when Dick Spring was complainin dat he was locked out of Government Buildins.

I ring de lads in Dublin an tell dem to invite Mary Harney round to de Taoiseach's office for a briefin on Monday mornin. As soon as she arrives, I tell dem, lock her inside an leave her dere until I get back.

SUNDAY

Up to dis I've been stayin neutral on Slasher's campaign for de Aras nomination. But now dat sneaky bollox Spring is after landin Eddie Roche as de Labour candidate, I'm even more neutral dan before. Dere's a lot of nonsense in de papers about me workin against Albert, but dis is all lies. De fact is he will have my full support if de party is stupid enough to choose him.

Of course, we have udder excellent candidates, like that very well-known Mary McAloon from de nort. She's a professor, so she is, an she's also someting called a pro-vice chancellor at de Queen's University. I'm not sure about dat "pro-vice" ting – it sounds like someting de Opposition could trow at us, but maybe we can keep it hushed up.

MONDAY

Dana was doin her tour of de county councils today and de backroom boys thought it'd be a good idea for us to relax de party whip. So, last night we took Seamus out for a few jars an he got very relaxed altogedder, an he had a bit of a head on him today so he stayed in bed. Dis meant dat Dana got de nomination, which de boys say is a good idea because she'll take de loony right wingers off our backs and we'll get dere number twos, so long as we have de right woman … eh, de right person runnin for us.

Dis is an historic day for anudder reason, because de all-party talks began in de Nort. Unfortunately, de Unionists didn't turn up and de only people talkin to each udder were Rambo an Mo Mowlam. But Rambo says dey had a good crack anyway, so dat's someting.

TUESDAY

A lot of hard work has gone into ensurin dat de Nordern talks take place in an atmosphere of peace. So we're very pleased dat de bomb which went off today was nowhere near Stormont. Rambo says he didn't even hear it, apart from de windows rattlin a little, so de atmosphere wasn't disturbed one bit.

Meanwhile, Dermot Ahern is havin a chat wit all de new TDs about de party's internal research which shows dat de sort of president de people want is (1) a woman and (2) not called Albert. De research also shows dat we would lose a by-election in Longford, and dat dis would be followed by de collapse of de Government an a general election, which would have to be held on December 25th. I tink it's important dat de first-time TDs make an informed decision, aldough I'm still strictly neutral on de whole matter.

WEDNESDAY

A shock result in de election, wit Professor McAleer winnin on de second count. You could have knocked me down wit a fedder when I heard de vote. And ye know, I can't help tinkin dat people have no gratitude, considerin all Albert did for de party, like collapsin de government in 1994. But at least we have a candidate who can talk proper English. An dere's also de advantage dat she's already a household name to everybody in de Republic. Yes, I tink I can hear it already – "President McAliskey".

THURSDAY

De Russians have been takin anudder look de beef situation and dis mornin we got a nice letter from dem. De letter reads: "Dear Mr Bruton, after an exhaustive investigation of your mad cow population, we are happy to announce that we are liftin de ban in Co Wexford, ie de constituency of your most excellent Minister for Agriculture, Mr Yates – nudge-nudge, wink-wink, say-no-more. Please confirm receipt of dis letter (used notes preferably)."

We don't know wat to tink about dat at all, but we're sayin nuttin for de moment.

FRIDAY

I met de Sinn Fein boys today to get clarification about de bomb, but dey were sayin nuttin about it without de presence of a solicitor. Dey did say, however, dat dey'd be happy enuff wit de idea of proxi … proxem … eh, wit talks in different rooms. And dey want to move quickly to substantive negotiations, aldough dere are certain substances dey won't negotiate about. I also met de Allowance Party leader, Lord Alder … eh Lord Elder … eh, de fella wit de beard. He seems like a nice man, but he doesn't have any votes and he doesn't have any of de semtex eider, so I don't know what he's doin in de talks at all.

SATURDAY

Professor McAllister is in to 11/8 wit de bookies, an dat's even before she gets de makeover from de fellas who did me award-winnin election poster. I tink I'll have a few bob on her meself. Each way, of course.

MONDAY

I had a historic meetin wit de Trimble fella today. Everybody expected it to be a disaster, but dey were forgettin dat I'm de most cunnin politicion dat ever lived, wit de exception of de fella dat we don't talk about any more. And like a long list of people before him, Mr Trimble discovered dat I was a man he could do business wit.

"I'll give ye articles 2 and 3," says I, "in exchange for a few cross-border bodies wit executive powers, and two years free electricity from de British grid. An as a sweetener, I'll trow in a £500 shoppin voucher in Arnott's for Missus T. What d'ye say?".

Dat's what ye call doin' business, and I could see he was impressed. "Your speakin my language, Mr Ahern," he says. And when de interpreter translated dis for me, I says: "Put it dere, Davey boy". We would have shaken on it at dat point, only when I spat on me hand, he took his away. Some fellas are funny like dat. But he's a good lad, Trimble, as black Orangeman go.

TUESDAY

Of course, de problem wit havin dese friendly meetins wit Orangemen is dat ye have de beardy fella on de next day wantin to know what concessions we gave dem. "Only de same shoppin voucher dat Missus Adams got," says I. Fortunately, he was in a good mood on account of de liberation of West Belfast, and he was lookin forward to de Brits pullin out of udder places too. "Tiochfaidh Armagh," he says, wit a beardy kind of laugh. Den he said he looked forward to de day when de Irish army would be marchin in to replace de Brits. I said we'd send dem in tomorrow only de bastards are all deaf.

WEDNESDAY

Today was anudder historic step towards national reconcilia ... reconsiliat ... towards everybody buryin de hatchet an gettin on wit each udder. I committed £150,000 of State money to de buildin of a joint monument on de Continent to commemorate all de Irishmen who fell in de first world war (not just de fellas dat fell, obviously, but de poor lads who got killed as well).

To be honest, wit de figures de way dey are, I could commit £150,000 of State money to an accumulator at Shelbourne Park, an it wouldn't be missed. But dis is a long overdue recognishen of de sacrifice made by dese soldiers. Because de ting we have to remember about dem is dat, regardless of dere politicial and religious differences, dey had one important ting in common. Dey were all traitors … er, I mean dey were all Irishmen.

THURSDAY

Dis abortion ting is gettin on everybody's nerves. We've been duckin de issue for too long and personally I tink it's time we got off de nettle and grasped de fence on dis one. Yes sir, it's definitely time to bite de bullet and butter de hot potato for once and for all. An I tink de way forward is a referendum, or legislation, or anudder Green paper, or all three. I'll have to tink about it a bit more, maybe.

Dere's also a spot of bodder for us over dis latest Department of Justice mix-up wit de drug charges, an de opposition ridiculin our "zero common sense" policy. Poor Johnny O'Donoghue – if he has to retreat much furder he'll disappear up his own hole. And den to top it all, Ivor "Biggun" Callely is shootin off about de darkies comin into Ireland. He says dey're sacrificin sheep in dere back gardens – pointin dem in de direction of Mecca and den slashin deir throats.

I'm very handy wit de knife meself, of course, an nuttin id make de Opposishen happier dan to see me sacrificin Ivor. I might have to, as well. But I'll say dis for him: he may not know de direction of Mecca, but he always knows where de next election is.

FRIDAY

An important meetin today between de EU commissioner, Monica "Wolf" Mathies, an de minister for public enterprise, Mary "She-dog" O'Rourke. Dat's a scrap I'd pay in to see, but de important ting is dat Mary saves de Luas money, even if de Luas doesn't go ahead. Most of de cabinet would like to see it diverted underground (de money, dat is) an used in marginal consituencies … er, in marginalised areas, before de next election.

But dem bloody Europeans, dey're determined to foist dese trams on us whedder we want dem or not. I asked Mary how de meetin went, but she was givin nuttin away. "Luas talk costs lives," she said. She's been listenin to Grizzly Adams too much, I'm tinkin.

SUNDAY

I was interviewed on de lunchtime news today. Bit nervous beforehand, but I had a good idea what de questions were goin to be, and I had a smart answer for everyting. A few witty comments too, and I didn't stutter on nuttin, eider.

Eh, it's only a pity I wasn't as good when dey were recordin it yesterday.

MONDAY

De economy may be boomin but dere's still no sign of an improvement in de wedder, which is, eh, shite. I phoned Noel Dempsey dis mornin and I says: "You're de Minister for de, eh, Environment. Do someting." But he says it's out of our control – like de economy, now dat de Germans are runnin everyting. De rain would be bad enuff, but it's windier dan a session of de Stormont talks as well, and dere's tousands of people tryin to get outa de country after Christmas and dey can't. I'm only worried dat if dey're here much longer, dey'll start claimin de dole and stuff and messin up de figures on us.

I see dat Radio Ireland has relaunched itself as Today FM. I could never find it on de dial meself, but dis gives me an idea for de peace process dat just might work. Maybe we could relaunch dat too, wit less talk and more music! I must suggest dis to Tony.

TUESDAY

I wasn't too pleased to hear dat Dublin Corporation voted for anudder 200 taxi plates last night. De taxi boys are well in wit us – good Dubs most of dem – an just because a few culchies can't get to Heuston Station on Christmas Eve is no reason to be floodin de market. Which is why, a while ago dere, I announced de settin up of a Taxi Forum which would debate all aspects of de issue and agree someting in time for Christmas 2005.

A nod is as good as a wink to a blind, eh, horse, I was tinkin. But now de councillors are messin wit me plan. I wouldn't mind, but de corpo is a completely undemocratic body – it doesn't even have a Fianna Fail majority, for f**k's sake! I tink it might be time to relaunch de corpo, wit less talk and more music.

WEDNESDAY

Mo was on de blower first ting dis mornin to tell me de loyalist prisoners are revolting. I know dat, I says – wit dere tattoos and dere skinhead haircuts, dey're disgustin, right enuff. But Mo says dey're threatenin to pull out of de peace process and dat drastic action is needed. I says if you have to shoot a few more of dem dat's all right wit me, but she says she's tinkin of goin in de jail to talk to dem instead!

I tink dis is a bit mad meself. Maybe it's someting to do wit bein a Fianna Failer, but I always get nervous at de idea of politicians in, eh, jail.

THURSDAY

I see dat de fella wit de big moustache is gettin dragged in to de investigation about payments to de fella we don't mention any more. I don't like de way dis is goin. I wonder what's de chances of relaunchin de terms of reference of de Moriarty Tribunal, to allow for more music?

But at least de papers reported our leak, about de two governments bein determined to "kickstart" de peace process, wit a view to havin "heads of agreement" on de table when de talks resume. Dis is not completely accurate. What we told Trimble and Adams is dat we'll have "heads on de table" or agreement when de talks resume, and if dat doesn't work, we'll "start kickin" people. But de general drift is de same, I tink.

FRIDAY

Well, Mo seems to have done de trick – de loyalist prisoners are back on board. Dis is no surprise really. Me and Tony have been reluctant to come de heavy wit de talks participants so far, but dere comes a time – and I tink it's comin soon – when we'll have to say: Stop de messin, boys. If yiz can't agree someting, we're gonna get Mo to give yiz all a big hug.

We're confident dat'll be de breaktrew. Dem unionists can't stand bein hugged.

MONDAY

I'm still a bit rattled over de, eh, Haughey leg incident. I knew nuttin about de plan to booby-trap de horse, but some of our, eh, nordern friends taut dey could do a nice clean job and dat'd be de end of dis payments-to-politicians bodder. But whatever happened, de nag only bolted an trew CJ off, so now he's still alive and even madder at us dan before. I tink I better install de bullet-proof glass in me constituency office.

Flowers were sent to de hospital yesterday, to show dere were no hard feelins. But de security boys copped dem and had dem destroyed in a controlled explosion.

TUESDAY

Still, de good news is dat de economy is still boomin. De latest signs are dat (1) de city authorities have lifted de buildin height restrictions in Dublin to cope wit demand for housin and (2) de national birt rate is dramatically up. Dis just proves what we always knew, dat dere are always more, eh, erections under a Fianna Fail government. De erection party, dat's what Fianna Fail is. In fact, tings are goin so well, I'm very tempted to call a general erection.

Which reminds me, I rang President Clinton dis mornin to give him my full support in his actions on Iraq. I expressed de hope dat de matter could be dealt with by purely diplomatic means, or by bombin de shite out of dem. Whatever works, I said. And I added dat in de event of a ground invasion, I'd be happy to commit de entire Irish Army to de effort. President Clinton said tanks very much but he'd be happier if I gave dem to Iraq instead. Dat would destroy Saddam's morale in a week, he reckoned.

I mentioned in passin to Bill dat he might revoke Jason Sherlock's visa, and stop him feckin off to play soccer in America when de Dubs are in crisis. "Is he a terrorist?" Bill asks. "Well, in a way," says I, "He, eh, terrorises defences" "I'll see wat I can do," says Bill.

WEDNESDAY

De Egyptians were on to us today tryin to enlist our support for dere attempts to revive tourism, which dey said might in turn influence (hint, hint) dere attitude to our beef exports. I assured Mr Mubarak dat Oireland was a good friend of Egypt's and dat we would stand shoulder to shoulder wit dem in de fight against Yankee imperialism in de Arab world.

Den I said, dis problem ye have wit mad Islamic militants attackin tour buses, would it help if we sent de Irish Army out to help protect dem. He said tanks all de same but he taught de tourists had enough problems as it was.

THURSDAY

My Dail speech about speedin up de nordern talks seems to have gone down well, aldough as usual people have missed de exact point. I was tinkin dat since de stationary talks in Stormont and London don't seem to have worked too well, maybe we could hold de next phase of negotiations in a speedin vehicle, like a train or a plane or, if de bastards won't cooperate, an Italian cable car.

If we got dem all into a plane, for example, and just flew around for a few days (de Yanks could refuel dem in de air), it might alter dere states of consciousness. And apart from anytin else, it might make de Shinners stop bladderin about de serious situation on de ground. I tink it's wort a shot.

FRIDAY

I held a minute's silence over me breakfast dis mornin to mark de 40th anniversary of de Munich air disaster. I was only six when it happened, but de idea of so much youtful promise wiped out has stayed wit me ever since and I never felt dat way about anytin again until 1994, when what would have been me first Government crashed on take-off because of de extreme conditions in Dick Spring's office.

Of course, I'm an ardent United fan. So as I was quietly munchin me weetabix, Celia asked me which Man Utd player I'd most like to be. I said probably David Beckham, because "I've already got me Spice Girl". Dis was de clever answer, I taught, but I should have known better. Celia says nuttin for a minute and den, casual-like, remarks: "I see David Beckham and his girlfried are gettin married".

Shite, I says to meself, I knew I should've said Roy Keane.

SUNDAY

Well, it looks like I've arrived at last. De *News of de World* reported dat I was de subject of an LVF assassination plot. Me! Just like JFK and Abraham Lincoln. Dis is a furder sign dat I'm a proper statesman now. De effin suits, de haircut, de elekution lessons, have all been worth it. Of course, havin Charlie McGreedy in as finance minister has done my own image no harm at all and with battle-axe Harney on de udder side, I'm happy as a pig in sh**e. Even Celia sez that I'm head and shoulders above de rest of party "married and all as they are".

MONDAY

I read that Tony Blair is tinkin of kickin with de udder foot. It looks like a good way to get publicity. Dere's no votes in becomin a Prod but a conversion of anudder sort might just do de trick. I could swap United for Chelsea but I've got all de gear now: Armani treads, share certificates, Ryan Giggs duvet cover (Celia picked dat one). I tink I'll just drop Articles 2 and 3 instead. Dat conversion should get me a few inches in de dailies. I hope Gerry understands.

TUESDAY

That complete barrister Whelehan is back to haunt me. Why won't he just go away? It's bringin back all de bad memories, includin that midnight chat with Dick in Baldonell where I nearly froze me nuts off for nuttin. I remember Albert givin me his opinion on Harry later: "He would make great dog food," he said. And he wasn't jokin. Where is Albert dese days anyhow? He hasn't called since I put my full weight behind his bid to become president. Of course, I had a knife in my hand at de time.

WEDNESDAY

Gerry was on de phone about Articles 2 and 3. "I'm just bein a proper statesman," I explained and he said I should stop smartarsin him and dat he knew where de anoraks were: "They haven't gone away you know," he said. He knows dat makes me nervous. Den Trimble gets on de blower and tells me dat he's puttin nuttin on de table whatsoever. It's de same with Celia: I've been gettin my own dinner for weeks now and all she does is whistle de weddin march. I'm gettin really sick of bleedin Weetabix I can tell ya.

THURSDAY

Great news. It looks like fatso Kohl is for de chop in Germany which, in my book, means I will effectively be de number one man in de EU. Blair isn't in de runnin since EMU is where is at, at least accordin to Charlie (de right one) and de Frogs will be too busy with de World Cup to worry about anytin else. Nobody takes de Mediterranean lads seriously at de council of ministers, except when we talk about de summer hols, and Finland, Sweden and Austria are still wet behind de ears. De Lowlands are even smaller dan Ireland and everyone tinks de Danes are too picky. So dat leaves me cappo dee tewty cappey. Up de Dubs!

FRIDAY

Dis Flood Tribunal is turnin out to be a right pain in de arse. If we change de terms of reference den dat will open de floodgates and Moriarty will be next. Charlie (de dodgy one) phoned to remind me dat he was watchin developments wit interest. "Remember, I've friends in de Ansbacher accounts you young pup," he said. "Sorry who's dat? I can't hear you. De line has gone dead." Am I devious or wha?

SATURDAY

Dose effers in Ryanair are messin tings up for me big time. How can I stride across Europe like a king if I can't even get out of Dublin?

SUNDAY

Back home again after securin de agreement dat ends centuries of conflict in Nordern Ireland, but Celia is in one of her moods. First, I taught she was annoyed at me for stayin out all night, negotiatin. But den she says: I tink you've forgotten someting, Mister Big-Shot Statesman. I said I didn't tink so – articles 2 & 3, nort-sout bodies, an assembly, prisoner releases, police reform, de equality agenda – no, it's all dere, says I. But she says: When are we goin to start negotiations about de wedding?

Eh, I says, dat reminds me. I'm supposed to be in Croke Park for de League semi-finals – we'll talk about de, eh, udder ting later.

MONDAY

Had a phonecall from Gerry dis mornin to say he was havin a meetin wit de hard men and it'd be a help if he had someting nice to give dem. What about an Easter Egg, says I? I was tinkin more like prisoner releases, he says. I taut about dis for a minute and I realised dat prison releases would go down very badly wit de unionists at dis time, so I decided I'd have to take a hard line. How many do ye need? I asked him. Ten, says he. Ye can have nine, says I, an dat's my final offer. Ye have to be tough in dis business.

There's a bit of a fuss over de women members of de Oireachtas Committee for Foreign Affairs visitin Iran. Apparently de birds don't want to cover deir faces as Muslim tradition requires. I'm worried about a diplomatic incident, 'cause Monica Barnes is goin on de trip and I've promised dat Arab chap we'd keep her under wraps for de duration.

TUESDAY

De Grand Orange Lodge was meetin today to discuss de agreement an we were all a bit worried about de outcome. Now dat we've ushered in a new era of understandin and mutual respect between de two traditions on de island, it'd be a terrible pity if a bunch of black orange bastards went and spoiled it. So as a bit of a sweetener, I rang de chief wizard or whatever it is dey call him an said dat if dey'd like dey can march along de River Boyne dis year. Anywhere in Meath, in fact, I said – if yez want to march trew John Bruton's sittin room, I'll arrange dat too.

I tink it worked, because de lodge postponed a final decision pendin "clarification". I must try dat one with Celia

WEDNESDAY

President Clinton is mad keen to visit Ireland, but me and Tony aren't so sure we want him. Wit all de sex scandals he has already, he might be a liability in de referendum campaign. And you couldn't trust him to keep his trousers on durin de visit eider – imagine de effect Liz O'Donnell could have on him. Jayzus dat'd be all we need!

I'll tell ye dis, I says to Tony, when ye talk about de need for decommissioning, ye could start wit, eh, Clinton's mickey!

Good news from de constituency review. I'm de biggest winner, heh heh, but poor auld De Rossa has got shafted. I'm so sorry I could cry. D'ere's also bad news for de Mitchell brothers, which upsets Celia until I explain dat it's Gay and Jim not Grant and Phil.

THURSDAY

De first opinion poll on de deal is out and it predicts de referendums will be won, nort an sout. Dis is good news, dough I would be a bit worried about de credibility of de figures. Dere's a bit in it where people in de nort were asked who deserved de most credit for de deal, an 22 per cent said Tony Blair an only 5 per cent said me. Dat looks seriously dodgy, aldough de zero ratin for Albert Reynolds seems about right. I had de press secretary fax a copy of dat bit to de Nobel Prize Commitee, just to help dem clarify de issues.

FRIDAY

As I was sayin, dese polls are completely reliable. De second part of de survey shows my personal popularity ratin at a record 84 per cent, which sounds scarily accurate. Except at home, where my personal popularity has dipped somewhat. Celia set a deadline of midnight last night for agreement on a weddin date, but I fell asleep in de middle of one of our bilaterals. It's just not de same widout George Mitchell chairin de process.

SATURDAY

De Shinners' ard-fheis has passed off peacefully an de Unionist council voted in favour of de deal. Nuttin can stop us now, I said, snugglin up to Celia in de bed tonight. I was in de mood for a bit of, eh, meaningful engagement. But Celia just turned over, and now she says dere'll be no more nort-sout cooperation until we've agreed a deal.

SATURDAY

Anudder historic breaktrough. First I help bring peace to Nordern Ireland and now I clinch de Scottish championship for Celtic, endin nine years of corrupt Unionist, eh, Rangers misrule. To be honest, I coulda done wit spendin de day at home – Celia wanted me to fix up de dog house, cos she says I'll be moving into it one of dese days – but I taught Celtic might need me. An sure enough, half way trough de second half, dey were pussy-footing round a one-goal lead, showin every sign of makin a balls of it.

So, I had to step in. I figured we could cut a deal wit St Johnstone and, by means of what de diplomatic community calls a "back channel," I let dem know dey'd have my support if dey ever wanted to relocate to Ireland. Of course, in de small print I said dey'd have to relocate to Mayo radder dan Dublin, but before any of dem copped dat it was 2-0 to de hoops, and dere was weepin an gnashin in Sandy Row.

Back to Dublin feelin tired but happy, tinkin dat a Taoiseach's work is never done

SUNDAY

Wit de Championship safely back in Parkhead, I knew de Shinners' ard-fheis would be a formality, but I sent Mansergh along to keep an eye on dem anyway. I saw him on TV pretendin to be takin notes (he told me afterwards he was doin a crossword to pass de time – dem Shinner speeches would bore de arse outta yer trousers) and I tink his presence did de trick in intimidatin dem a bit.

De main ting is dere was no undue triumphalism connected to de entry of de Balcombe Street gang. Sure dere was a bit of clappin and cheerin and Gerry Adams trew his arms around dem – de big hairy gobshite. But it was nuttin like de celebrations in Parkhead yesterday. Now, if de Shinners had run around de hall sprayin champagne and singin De Fields of Attenry, dat would have been triumphalist. It depends on de way you look at tings.

MONDAY

On de referendum trail in Cork, bored stupid an wishin it was over. Dis campaign is about as excitin as a John Bruton speech. Dere's no argument, no debate, everybody's just goin "Yes, Yes, Yes". It reminds me of de cabinet meetins when Charlie was Taoiseach. An still two weeks to go. Jayzus!

TUESDAY

I'm in a bit of trouble over de Shinners. Bruton was honkin on about it in de Dail like a donkey wit a sore leg, and de Church of Ireland sinners *(maybe "synod"? – Ed)*

are givin me grief as well. None of dem watch football – dat's dere trouble. Mansergh says we may have misjudged de mood of de unionists an we need to make a consiliatery … a concillea … a sympatetic gesture to dem. So I sent Trimble a card today sayin "Rangers for de Cup". Dat ought to do it I tink.

WEDNESDAY

A Blueshirt councillor in Mayo is callin for travellers to be implanted wit micro-chips so we can keep track on dem. Funny, I had de same idea for councillors a while back, so we could keep an eye on dem as dey criss-crossed de country, travellin six to a car and rackin up mileage from attendin conferences about de influence of French impressionism on urban refuse collection. But I was persuaded against it at de time because dere'd be serious technical difficulties: de main problem is microchips have to be placed under de skin, and councillors have some of de tickest skin known to science, apparently.

THURSDAY

Tony Blair is in de nort to help shore up de unionist Yes vote, an before he flew in, we advised him dat de man to target was Jeffrey Donaldson. Mansergh says if Donaldson's needs can be met and he declares for de Yes side, it could swing ten per cent of de UUP vote. Ok, Tony says, but what exactly does he need? We tell him we're not sure, but if he was one of ours, a m illion quid in a Swiss bank account might do for starters.

Meanwhile, Michael Stone turned up at a UDP rally tonight an got a standin ovation. It wasn't a pretty sight, to put it mildly – an dat's just his hairstyle.

FRIDAY

Grizzly finally rang me, after failin to return my calls all week. De RDS ting was all a big misunderstanding, he says. Just when de Balcombe Street boys came in, apparently, someone said dey were members of de victorious Celtic team, and dat's why dere was all de clappin and embracin. Grizzly was suspicious dat some of dem appeared to be middle-aged, but he taught de way de won de league might have put years on dem. "Honestly, Bertie, when I found out who they were afterwards, I nearly died".

"Fair enough," says I. "By de way, I see yer friend Slab is after losin his libel case". Grizzly gets huffy. "I never met that man in my life," he says and hangs up on me.

MONDAY

Tings have started off badly dis week wit Celia in a huff about not goin to de annual Fianna Fail National Women's Conference. I have explained dat she can't come because somebody has to mind de shop in case someting goes wrong. Dis is de only excuse I can tink of but dere is no way I'm lettin her cramp me style at de conference. Dose FF wimmin tink I'm de bee's knees I can tell ya. All leaders get de royal treatment from dose lassies — cakes, cream, pots of tea, de lot. But dey're a jealous bunch at de best of times and if I brought de oul ball and chain with me, dere would be daggers flyin.

De good news is Sile de Valera rang to remind me to send a telegram of congratulations to New York, where de Beauty Queen of Leenane is after winnin some big awards. I never heard of de Beauty Queen of Leenane meself – an I've been to most of dem country festivals – but whoever de girl is she's doin de country proud. It just shows ye, I said to Celia, dat Irish girls can compete wit de best. But she was pretendin to be asleep.

TUESDAY

Off to Portugal for talks wit prime minister Guterres. I had to practice de name – Guterres, not Portugal – on de plane over, because I do have problems wit me pronunci ... pronuns ... wit me words at de best of times. But Mr Gutters was an easy-goin fella an dere was no problem, except once when I tink I called him Mr Gusset and de translator had a fit of coughing. De important ting is dat Mr Gurrier and I assured each udder of mutual support at de Cardiff summit and reaffirmed Ireland and Portugal's common aim, which is to get even more money outta de Germans before dey finally cop on.

WEDNESDAY

Anudder ting we have in common wit Portugal is dat we're not in de World Cup, which starts today. Dis is a big disadvantage, because if we were in it, de Government could do whatever de feck we wanted for de next four weeks and de country would be too drunk to notice. As it is, everybody is watchin our handlin of de economy an de Garda pay and everting else.

So when David Andrews said he was announcin a major nuclear initiative today, I got excited. "Does dis mean we have de bomb?," I asked him when he came into me office to explain. I was already wonderin where we'd conduct de underground tests – maybe Rockall, to annoy de Brits. Eider way, we'd have de people out on de street celebratin like in India and Pakistan. It'd be almost as good as de World Cup. But it turns out dat his plan is only for some kind of anti-nuclear pact among de neutral countries. "A lot of feckin use dat is," I told him.

I spent tree hours, as normal, wit me make-up professional this mornin. De foundation is de biggest ting, even dough I have skin like a baby's bum. Den dere's de second coat to go on. I draw de line at wearing rouge, dough. "Don't even try," says I, when she suggested a bit. "When you're de Fianna Fáil leader, dere's nutting dat can make you blush."

While I'm assisting de tribunals to de best of my ability, I'm just sayin I may not be able to give dem all de detail dey'd like. I've explained dis to Mary Harney an, more dan anyone, she understands how long ago de 1980s were. De PDs were a serious force in Irish politics den, as I recall.

Rambo was in de firin line again today, wit news dat a couple of Mayo builders paid him £150,000 over de years from money raised at horse meetings. Horses have played a very central role in Irish public life over de past couple of decades, obviously. Dat's probably why Shergar had to die: de f**ker knew too much.

Celia says "dere's a man on the phone, says his name is Haughey. He claims he's an old friend of yours and he needs a big favour in a hurry". I says I don't believe I know anyone of de name Haughey, except de wee fella with de moustache.

I tried to reassure Blair dat de Provos pullin out of talks wit de decommissionin body meant nutting, but all he said was, "I know. I tried the withdrawal method myself and look where it got me."

Over to Downing Street for a final meetin with Blair before de holliers. It was a short meetin, partly because Celia was in de udder room with Cherie and I didn't want her gettin any ideas about babies - or, worse still, about fancy holidays in Italy.

Our hardline stance on de Nort has paid off. Mo Mowlam rang me on Saturday night to tell me how much she respected our position and how difficult it would be for her to ignore it completely. Which is what she was going to do, she added.

Nutting would do de Chinese but we go for a walk on de Great Wall, which is a bit like de Nort Wall, only longer and dere's less chance of ye bein mugged on it.

THURSDAY

Inflation has hit a tree-year high an troubles are gadderin on de industrial relations front. De guards are comin down wit anudder dose of someting an de public service craftworkers look like rejectin de Labour Court recommendation.

And den dere's de marital relations front: Celia is threatenin a series of one-day stoppages if I don't open negotiations on a marriage date. I keep tellin her dat to give in to her demands would treaten de whole marital relations structure: if she gets a marriage certificate, udder people will be lookin for a divorce, and so on. But she won't listen. As I told de Dail today, dere's some areas you can compromise on but dere's udder areas you can't. De Dail probably taught I was talkin about Garda pay.

Meanwhile, Baldy Quinn finished top of de league of donations to TDs for May to December, which at least gave us all a good laugh. I sent him a congratulations card. I believe even de top of his head was blushing.

FRIDAY

An all-day Cabinet meetin to discuss budgetary policy. Jayz! If ye tink de economy is overheatin, you want to be in a room of sweaty Fiana Fail lads all day. Some of dem country fellas can be a bit ripe, to say de least. Crafty Mickey Martin missed de whole ting, off at his sister's weddin in Cork. Dat culchie is startin to annoy me.

Charlie was doin most of de talkin, of course, layin down de law about tax an public service pay and dat. We tink he was takin a tough line, but nobody had de slightest idea what he was sayin. Redneck O'Donoghue had a bit of a speech as well about de gardai droppin us in de shite again tomorrow. He assured us dat dere would be emergency cover: de gardai have promised they'll be doin dere normal nixers as night-club bouncers and so on. So dat's someting, at least.

SATURDAY

Eighty per cent of de cops phoned in sick dis mornin. But we have de Garda trainees from Templemore on patrollin duties and de membership of Young Fianna Fail is fillin in wherever dere were spare uniforms. I also have de GAA on stand-by and if anyting happens anywhere, dey can have a squad of young lads wit hurleys at de scene within minutes.

Also, in de first of a series of hush-hush experiments in cross-border cooperation, we have a number of RUC men at our disposal in case of an emergency. If dis goes well, we'll implement de second part of de strategy next month, when selected members of de Gardai who've recovered from de flu will be enjoyin a short tour of duty in Portadown.

SUNDAY

Bit of a head on me dis mornin after Kennedy Smith's do last night. Good oul bash. In me speech, I said de country wanted to mark de cessation of her term as ambassador, provided dat it was a permanent and unequivocal cessation .... No, wait a minute, dat was anudder speech – Jayzus, I hope I didn't say dat last night! Anyway, I said we were givin her honourary citizshen ... cityzinsh ... eh, an Irish passport.

"Ye might as well have two countries, Missus – ye have de two names already," says I to her afterwards. "Thanks a million," says she, "I believe that's what Irish passports normally cost, isn't it?"

MONDAY

I had me usual session wit de voice coach today. "Repeat after me: de rain in Spain falls mainly on de plain," he says. "De rain in Portadown falls mainly on de Orangemen, wit de help of God an his blessed mudder," says I. "I don't think you're takin dis seriously, Taoiseach," he says.

Feck dat for a game of soldiers, I was tinkin. I'm also tinkin I might send de voice coach up to Drumcree, to see if he can get de Mac Cionnaith fella to say de word "yes" to anyting we suggest. We have people on de ground on bote sides, of course, and we taught we had a good compromise whereby de Orangies would go down de road at four o clock in de mornin, wearin hush puppies an walkin on dere tippy-toes so dey wouldn't wake de residents. But McKenna wouldn't have it. De guy is completely objur ... obgerat .... He's a right bollix.

TUESDAY

I can't tell ye how good it is to wake up on Tuesday mornin and not have to go into de Dail an listen to dat eejit Bruton honkin over at me all day. But I am still de Taoiseach and I still have to look after me appearance. So I spent de same tree hours as normal wit me make-up professional (£135 a day – ye can't get more professional dan dat) dis mornin.

De foundation is de biggest ting, even dough I have skin like a baby's bum. Den dere's de second coat to go on, and tings like lip gloss, which de make-up girl says brings out de natural sensousness of my mouth. I draw de line at wearin rouge, dough. "Don't even try," says I, when she suggested a bit. "When you're de Fianna Fail leader, dere's nuttin dat can make you blush."

WEDNESDAY

I don't care what anyone says, Holland were robbed. An dey still woulda won if dat waster from Arsenal had shifted his arse all night instead of baskin in de glory of his fluke goal against de Argies. Dat Jaap Stam seems like a good buy for United, dough, even if he looks old enough to be David Beckham's father. We're all hopin Croatia win tonight, so dere'll be no problem swingin tickets on Sunday. It's such a lucky coincidence dat we have to be in Paris anyway, for a highly important EU meetin about Agenda 200 or some udder shite.

THURSDAY

No luck for Croatia last night, so I had to resort to plan B. I rang Lionel Jospin dis mornin an says: "Any chance of an ould ticket?" Dere was silence for a minute: "Eh, vous etes qui?" says Lionel. "Bertie," says I, "Je suis Bertie, le grand fromage de la gouvernement Irlandaise". We shot de breeze for a while and den I made my play. "J'ai deux tickets pour le all-Ireland football final, et si vous jouez vos cartes proprement, ils sont yours. Hogan Stand, right sur le half-way line". Dere was more silence. "Je suis desole, mais je comprends rien," says Lionel, cunningly. "Allright," says I. "Vous etes un homme dur, Mr Joplin. Vous pouvez aller a le hurlin final aussi."

FRIDAY

Mansergh came up wit dis idea dat we'd invite de Orangemen and de Garvaghy roadies to "proximity" talks at a secret venue. Dey wouldn't have to be in de same room togedder (who'd want to be in de same room wit de Orangies and dem shitin in ditches for a week?). De only problem wit de plan is dat we can't suggest it or de Jaffa men won't touch it wit one of dere 40-foot poles. So I rang Tony dis mornin an told him what Mansergh says he should say. An hour later, Blair sends out de invitation and de two sides accept, an den I warmly welcome "de British initiative".

"Are we genuises, or wha?" I say to Mansergh. "De Brits are not in de same league as us at all."

SATURDAY

Labour and DL are settin up a tink-tank before dey complete de merger. What a waste of time. Eider dey're mergin or dey're not — just like me and Celia. I don't need a tink-tank to tell me dat a marriage is out of de question, er, at dis particular point in time dat is. She says we should sit down and discuss our merger like Quinn and de Rossa but I tell her dat's a take-over not a merger so Celia says I can take over de spare bed tonight. Jayzus, not again.

SUNDAY

In Croker for de hurlin final, but it's hard to take it seriously, an me off to China tonight for a week of hob-nobbin wit some of de most powerful men in de world.

On de way home, I dropped into de Golden Dragon to try out me Chinese. "I'll have de Egg Foo Yong and de Chicken Chow Mein, and a portion of Won Ton Soup an, eh, chips wit everyting," I said, wit no hesitation at all. I didn't ask for de Sasketchewan-style beef, for fear of ruinin me performance, but overall I taught I did well.

Speakin of Won Ton Soup, dough, dat reminds me: dis Fruit of de Loom situation is probably goin to come to a head in me absence. But feck it, anyway, Two Ton Harney can deal wit it herself.

MONDAY

Jayz, what a flight. I was so tired I was asleep de minute I hit me seat. Den I woke up an looked out de window and we were passin over some desolate, dimly-lit region. "It must be Afghanistan," says I, pointin at de herds of horses, an de campfires, an de flashes of what looked like gunfire. "No, Taoiseach," says one of de lads, "That's Ballymun. We've only just taken off".

Den I drifted off into a bad dream in which Celia hijacked de plane and demanded de pilot fly us to Rome to be married by de Pope. She'd started shootin de hostages when I woke up wit a start. Must be de Egg Foo Yong makin me dream like dat, I taught, but before I went back to sleep I had a quiet word wit de assistant pilot. "Don't let Celia in de cockpit, no matter what," I told him.

TUESDAY

Well, of course, when Celia heard dere was a "Forbidden City," nuttin would do but she'd hafta get into it. Just as well it was on de itinerary anyway, but I made a note dat if she picked any apples off any trees dere, I was't eatin dem. It turns out de Forbidden City is just a big collection of old deserted buildings do – a bit too much like Leinster House in de summer to be interestin.

Den dis afternoon, I met President Ziang Zemin ("You're on your own dere," said de voice coach), who praised Ireland for producin "great literary genius". I says: "Yer pronunciation is a little off Mister, eh, President. We call it 'Guinness' in Ireland. But yer right enough, it is literally great, so it is." He mentioned a few "geniuses," like Heaney and Shaw and James Joyce, but I said I didn't know any of de boys up in James's Gate dese days. "Dublin's not as small as it used to be," I told him.

I also had to address some student diplomats today on de subject of human rights. Dis was tricky, but me advisers told me to stick to generalities, like "human rights is a good ting". Whatever ye do, dey said, don't mention Tiananmen Square. "No danger of dat, I said, "I couldn't say it if I tried." One of de students asked me if I liked Tibet, and I had to tink quickly. "I do have de odd fiver on de horses, all right" I said.

WEDNESDAY

De stomach's a bit iffy dis mornin after last night's State banquet. I don't know de half of what we were eatin – I'm sayin nuttin, but you don't see many stray dogs around here. Still, Tom Kitt looks worse dan me an some of de trade delegation didn't even surface, so dat's someting. Anyway, nuttin would do de Chinese but we go for a walk on de Great Wall, which is a bit like de Nort Wall, only longer and dere's less chance of ye bein mugged on it. Me knee was a bit sore after de joggin incident in Kerry, but I held me end up and even posed for pictures wit Celia. She's relaxed into de trip at dis stage an so have de Chinese. "At first, we didn't know what to call her – your wife or your girlfriend," one of de officials told me. "Don't worry," I says, "I do have de same problem meself."

THURSDAY

On de flight to Shanghai, we heard dat Gerry Adams's pals in de Basket Country have initiated a peace process based on de Irish one. Dis can only enhance our world standin, and confirms me in de belief dat we could sort out Tibet for de Chinese. I know dat Dalai Lama fella wears a skirt, but I'd say you could talk to him. He must be half Irish, anyway, wit a name like "Daly". An wit Clinton out of de game, I could be a big player on de world scene. I could send a special envoy to Tibet – someone young and ambitious, like Dermot Ahern or Mickey Martin. Someone who'd spend three years of his life flyin back and forth, overseein de negotiations. Or ten years even – dere'd be no hurry.

FRIDAY

If it's Friday, it must be Hong Kong. De trouble wit dese Chinese cities is no sooner you've arrived in one, you feel like anudder. But at least Hong Kong is interestin from de point of view dat it's a former British colony, a bit like Nordern Ireland will be when we finally get it sorted out. I was tinkin dis when I met de new governor, Mr Tung Chee Hwa. "Dat's a gas name," says I, "Mr Tongue-in-cheek, wha?". We got on like a house on fire, and in fact I felt quite at home in Hong Kong: de teemin crowds, de high-rise buildins – sure it's very like Ballymun when ye tink about it.

SUNDAY

Up to Fedderbed mountain for de unveilin of a memorial to Captain Noel Lemass, on de spot where he died fightin de Blueshirts in, eh, 1923. It's inspirin to tink of de courage dese fellas showed, on de run and in constant danger from dere former comrades. I know what's it's like meself, because I spent de entire ceremony on de run from feckin Charlie Haughey, who would've enjoyed nuttin more dan gettin his arm around me for de benefit of de cameras. De press lads did get a picture of us togedder, but de main ting is, dere was no touchin.

Off to Croker den for de compromise rules game against de Aussies. Dese Australia-Ireland games are very like Sinn Fein conferences: half de players came down from convicts, and dere's still a lot of support for violence. But, even dough I didn't agree wit de appointment of dat Mead bogman O'Rourke as manager – de job should go to someone who speaks English – it's good to be able to cheer on de lads against foreigners. I didn't agree wit dis new hooter system eider, and it cost us de match: in de old days de ref coulda blown up when we were still ahead.

MONDAY

Good news from Cork by-election trail, where our girl is forgin ahead of sailor-boy Coveney in de private polls. Of course, she's de perfect candidate: young, bright, good-lookin, a woman, young (did I mention dat?), not friendly wit any builders, never met Charlie Haughey in her life, etc, etc.

She also has de benefit of de fact dat her leader is universally loved by de people, wit an approval ratin in de latest polls of 103 per cent. It might be even higher too, but for de complex domestic situation. Of course, we've done a bit of private research on public attitudes to de matter, an de most recent figures were very interestin: turty per cent in favour of divorce and remarriage, twenty-five per cent for de status quo; and de rest eider "don't knows" or "undecideds". I tink I'm a floatin voter meself.

TUESDAY

Today I unveiled me dream plan for a proper national stadium, wit 80,000 seats and state-of-de-art hot dog stands and de whole works. I don't know if it'll ever happen, but de legendary punter JP McManus says he can get £50 million fundin for it, and when JP puts £50 million on a horse, it must have a chance (aldough it could be an each-way bet, of course).

I wish de question of EU funds was as easy, but de cabinet is split on de issue. Personally, I'm in favour of regionisa … regionasil … eh, of splittin de country up, wit special status for Connaught, Ulster and Dublin Central. Some of dem boggy counties in de midlands might get in as well (McCreevy says parts of Kildare are very depressed – I'd say dey are, after de All-Ireland). But de counter argument is dat if de people from de poorer parts get more money, dey'll only spend it shoppin in Dublin, and de traffic is poxy enough already.

WEDNESDAY

Anudder Dail question time, anudder financial scandal. Dis time it's de AIB-DIRT affair, but de good news is dere are no Fianna Fail politicians involved so far (touch wood). De ting is, it's yet anudder investigation and no-one knows how to handle it. Nobody's too keen on givin special powers to de Committee of Public Accounts, which is chaired by one of dose Mitchell boys – I can never remember which – and McCreevy is refusin to ask de Revenue if dey cut a deal wit de bank, for reasons best known to himself. Politicians do have a certain amount of sympathy with bank managers, of course – we bote live in fear of losin our deposits.

THURSDAY

De Nobel Peace Prize is to be announced tomorrow and dere's a rumour dat it's goin to Ireland, so I'm preparin a few words just in case. I tink I'll say dat while I am de one receivin de award, it's doesn't really belong to me, but to de whole people of Ireland and particularly to de many brave politicians in de Nort who helped bring peace about. I'll dedicate in particular to two men, John Hume and David Trimble, who have shown de courage and de vision and de blah, blah, blah. Yeah, dat should do it.

FRIDAY

Feck dat for a game of soldiers. I deserved dat award at least as much as Hume and Trimble did. Well, maybe not Hume – in fairness, he earned it wit his brilliant tactic of borin de unionists into submission by makin de same speech over and over again for years, like Chinese water torture, and maybe now he'll be so busy on de International lecture circuit he'll have no time for visitin Government Buildings and talkin de arse off all of us. But what is Trimble gettin de prize for, when he had to be pushed and pulled every inch of de way, like a tree-legged mule?

SATURDAY

Out and about in Cork, pressin de flesh, spreadin de "Bertie factor". Old Bonzo Bruton is here too, lendin his unique brand of, eh, charisma, to de Coveney camp – makes you feel sorry for dem. Toddy O'Sullivan is fightin a good campaign too, but he's handicapped by his age and by havin a name like "Toddy", which sounds a bit funny, even in Cork. Tings are lookin good for us, provided we don't peak too early. If only we could persuade Bruton to stay here until pollin day, we'd be on de pig's back.

SUNDAY

De by-election turned into a bit of a debacle, after everyting. I know dem bastards in RTE hung us out to dry – and dey'll get deirs in due course – but I woulda still expected our girl to do a bit better in de just-a-minute quiz. Dere's a time for answerin questions an a time for silence. An if she has a career in Fianna Fail, she'll have plenty of opportunity later on for pretendin she knows nuttin. In de circumstances, I was glad to be in Austria yesterday, hobnobbin wit de boys at de EU summit. Had a good chat wit Tony (I sympatised wit him over dat General Ricochet business: tinkin of a certain former leader of mine, I told him it was always hard to know what to do wit an old dictator), and we discussed de chances of meetin de Oct 31ˢᵗ deadline on Nort-Sout bodies. Slim and none we agreed, and slim is outta town, as dey say.

Den it was back on de plane to Dublin to watch thirty women kicking lumps outta each udder in Croker. I missed de start of de match, which I hate because it'll probably cost me a half a point in de opinion polls. But before you could say "wiener schnitzel und chips wit loads of vinegar," I was in me seat in de Hogan, captured by de RTE cameras. Dey're very skillful, dose boys, dey never miss de real action.

TUESDAY

De whole reason we picked October 31st as de deadline for settin up de cross-border bodies was 'cause we taught Halloween might give de Provos an opportunity to get rid of some of de gear. Dey could blow up half of Donegal dis week wit de guards turnin a blind eye, and de Provo hardliners wouldn't know what was happenin (just so long as General de Charolais did). I tried to tell dis to Gerry, but he just stroked his beard and said dat, like many Irish traditions, Halloween was not recognised by de Brits. "No," says I, "but dey get de fireworks out on November 5th, to commemorate Guy Fawkes tryin to blow up de Houses of Parliament". Suddenly, a glint came into Gerry's eye. "Now you're talkin, Bertie!" he says, and he rushes off "to discuss an idea with Martin".

WEDNESDAY

Forty tousand farmers marchin on de Dail is a worrying prospect; so we had de Army on stand-by today, and I carried on my daily business from de underground bunker dat was installed recently under de cover of de buildin work at Leinster House. De marchers massed outside Government Buildins and, if tings hadda gotten rough, we woulda given dem Joe Walsh, an a rope. But fortunately, de protest passed off peacefully. In one of dose tings dat convinces me dere is a God and he's a Dub, it poured rain on de poor f**k*rs from de minute dey arrived in de Park. At least dey had dere wellies on.

THURSDAY

A Cabinet meetin to finalise de estimates. Charlie takin a tough line with his 4 per cent spendin limit, an Biffo Cowen arguin for an exception to be made wit de Department of Health. It was a good, civilised debate and I tink de ting dat swung it for Biffo was when he offered to take Charlie outside and "beat de shite out of him in Kildare Street".

Anyway, I had to rush off for a flight to Scotland to deliver de prestig … presteeg … eh, to deliver de important Lothian lecture on "De Western Isles of Europe at de Millenium". In it, I proposed dat de British-Irish Council could become "a loose confederation along de lines of de Nordic Council". I have no idea what de Nordic Council is, but it was in me script so dat's what I said. I don't tink de Scots understood me accent, anyway, but I'm not goin to worry about de opinion of fellas who wear skirts. I never undertand a word dey say eider (except Billy Connolly and, sure, wit a name like Connolly, he must be one of ours).

FRIDAY

Looks like I'll have to go to Belfast again next week to see if I can sort tings out on de cross-border bodies. Of course, in practice dis means I have to see if I can sort tings out on de cross-border bodies BEFORE I go to Belfast. I'm f***ed if I'm gonna spend a day in dat kip and come out of it wit nuttin, an de papers sayin "stalemate continues as Taoiseach flies home wit tail between his legs". Dat's de sort of ting Jawn Brutal would do, but he doesn't have an 80 per cent popular approval rating to support. No, I'm like Ian Rush when he used to be good: ye put de ball in de box for me, and I'll score every time. But I'm not makin a run anywhere until I see de ball comin.

SATURDAY

Breakfast in bed dis mornin, and herself as sunny as de two perfectly fried eggs she dishes up. I suspect her mood has someting to do wit de extract from de new biology of me bein published in Oireland on Sunday tomorrow, in which I'm quoted as sayin she's "de love of my life" and I'd like to marry her. I know it's a risky business talkin about me private life, but I only cooperated wit de autors up to a point and, eh, I tink I know what I'm doin.

I refused to be drawn on de "D" word, of course. It'll be interestin to see what de public reaction is. After dat, we might tink about makin a run into de box.

SATURDAY

I'm very pissed off wit journalists on account of dat book dat I didn't cooperate wit in any way, so it's not goin to be easy to get me do do an interview ever again. I said dis to de blondie one from de Indo when she came out to interview me durin de week. And today I was shocked to find dat de tree-hour, off-de-record briefin I gave her in me office is all over de paper. I'd be really angry about it only for she made me look so good. She even mentioned me fluffy toy wit "de tree most important words in de English language" written on it. "Jackie Healy Rae," dat must have been. No – wait a minute, maybe it was "I love you." Yeah, dat was it. De ardfheis went off well. I didn't make a balls of de speech – not even de bits Mansergh wrote, which are always de hardest. In fact, de worst part of de day was when de whole parliamentary party squeezed in around me at de end for de television pictures. Donie Cassidy was nearly down me trousers at one point – it was scary. Dat Elaine Moore one turned up at de party, by de way – eat yer heart out Jawn Brutal. And dere's only one word for her: Phoarrrgh!

SUNDAY

De feckin media – dey're bastards, so dey are. I went out to RTE today for anudder off-de-record briefin and, unknown to me, dey broadcast de whole ting live on de "Dis Week" programme. I'd never have said dat ting about a united Ireland in 15 years if I'd known anyone was listening. Meanwhile, de Oireland on Sunday rag printed a facsilim … faximel … eh, a copy of one of de pages from de book wit my corrections on it. F**kers! De corrections were off-de-record too, needless to say.

MONDAY

Mildred is actin huffy again, on account of de man wit de cap gettin Kerry's nose in de EU trough. I told Brennan to have a chat wit her, see what's on her shoppin list – maybe giver her a few loyalty bonus points as well. And speakin of shoppin, Celia's away on a major expedition to buy gear for de Blair visit – she turns into Imelda Marcos on occasions like dese. Still, as long as she steers clear of de jewellers's shops, I don't mind. Meanwhile, it looks like dere's nuttin we can do to stop de rail strike tomorrow; but, eh, de day de DART runs trough Drumcondra is de day I'll start worryin about dat.

TUESDAY

In keepin wit me total ban on de media, today I did an interview for London Times in which I said inter al … inter ali … in which I said among udder tings dat I have no objection to a debate on Ireland rejoinin de Commonwelt. Personally,

I'd join de Manchester City supporters club before I'd join de Commonwelt, but de idea is to galvanise Fianna Fail activists for de local elections next June. I reckon before de end of de week, every county council in Ireland will be plannin a fact-findin trip to Bananaland, to study de implications of commonwelt membership on sewage disposal. So of course dey'll work dere arses off to get re-elected. It's a cunning plan, wha?

De Traffic ran so smoodly yesterday, by de way, we're tinkin of organisin a bus strike as well.

WEDNESDAY

We had de usual parliamentary party meetin dis mornin. De boys from Wexford were kickin up because of de statistics dat show de area is just above Leitrim and Bangladesh in de world poverty charts. I let McCreevy take de rap from dem, but my taughts on de subject are dis: any county dat organises a feckin annual opera festival is not gettin Objective One status while I'm de boss.

De Blairs arrived safely, meanwhile, and went up to visit Macca and de Vienna Boys Choir in de Aras. It was a major security operation, not because of Blair, but for fear any of de choir got assaulted in de Phoenix Park – dat'd be an international incident, with de Austrians holdin de EU presidency an all. Den it was over to de Kings Inns where dey made me an Tony honorary someting-or-udders, an den back to de Castle for de bit o' grub. Very classy affair – no chicken on de menu – and it was rounded off nicely when Tony raised a toast "to Bertie and Celia". It was such a perfect night, we nearly forgot de leaflet drop in Drumcondra to advertise de walkabout tomorrow. But we did it on de way home.

FRIDAY

Unfortunately, nuttin can keep de Kinsealy fella outta de news for long. De Irish Times has two stories about him dis mornin, and it's only a matter of time before de press connects him wit de disappearance of some child's communion money. Still, it's not all bad news – I see also dat Tony Gregory is runnin for Europe. And de furder he runs, de better, as far as I'm concerned.

SATURDAY

I nearly forgot in de week dat was in it, but dat ting dey're puttin up in O'Connell Street is a bleedin disgrace. It's like someting Vlad de Impaler dreamed up. What is de point of it, at all? I haven't seen anyting dat tall, narrow and useless since ... well, since Alan Dukes was de Opposition leader.

SUNDAY

I'm writin dis in me hotel room in Beirut, at de start of me history-makin visit to de middle east (which is a bit like Limerick East – de constant danger, de sinister-lookin' men wit moustaches, Willie O'Dea-style). Even here, dough, I am weighed down by de considerations of domestic politics. I'm sayin nuttin about de EU Commisioner job for de moment, except dis. Dat whoever is in de position next year will be de person best-qualified to represent Ireland's interests. And dat he won't have big bushy eyebrows and a tick Mayo accent. Dat's all I'm sayin.

But ye know, Pee Flynn is such a long lanky bastard dat you'd tink once in a while, when he's aimin' to shoot himself in de foot, he might just fail to find de range. Unfortunately he's a crack shot. And he's a constant source of annoyance to me, him AND his feckin family. If I may paralyse Oscar Wilde for a moment: to have one Flynn in de party is unfortunate, but to have two seems like a Blueshirt conspiracy against us. It makes me tink dat me plan to replace everybody in Fianna Fail wit members of de Ahern family can't happen quick enough.

MONDAY

Down to Sout Lebanon dis mornin to meet de troops. I have Michael Smith for company troughout dis trip, so you can imagine how much fun dat is. But he has his uses. Dere was trouble in de UNIFIL area yesterday, so today I had to wear de flak jacket and helmet, and stand behind Smith at all times. We spent de mornin tourin army outposts, but it was rainin and freezin cold, and after an hour of dis I says could we not visit a few inposts instead. So den we went to an orphanage in Tibnin, where I got to present dem wit a minibus bought by de soldiers. Which just shows you, as I said to Smith, de generosity of de Department of Defence is infectious.

Indeed, everywhere we went in Sout Lebanon, de locals were loud in deir praises of de Irish Army. Not loud enough for de army to hear dem, of course.

TUESDAY

Dis mornin, one of de handlers said we'd be meetin Bibi in Jerusalem. "Is dat where she went to?" says I, "I miss her on de tele – great pair of legs she had!" But it turned out dat Bibi is what dey call de Israeli leader, Mr Netan-yahoo (dat's de way de Foreign Affairs people wrote it in me briefin notes), who is such a manly kinda guy you'd wonder how he ever got a girly nickname. I wasn't lettin him stand behind me, anyway, just to be on de safe side.

But we had a good hour-and-a-half long meetin, durin which he gave me a message for Yozzer Arafat, who I'm meetin tomorrow. De message was dat as soon as de Palestinian Autority implemented its part of de peace agreement, Israel would do de same. "I know how ye feel, eh, Bibi," says I, "ye can't trust dem towel-heads." He congratulated me on me strong grasp of de situation.

WEDNESDAY

"Ye have me sympathy," I told Yozzer, when I met him "havin to deal wit dose Jewboys." He congratualted me on me quick understanding of de middle east peace process, and I was soon feeling so at home here dat I could look at de gear on his head widdout laughin. I was de first ever European leader to fly into Gaza international airport – Tony Blair had to travel dere by road – and Yozzer said de event touched his heart and de hearts of de Palestinian people.

Nuttin personal, but I wouldn't touch deir food as quick, if I had a choice in de matter. Unfortunately, bein a world leader and all, I had to continue talks over dinner. Still, I managed to swallow everyting, including Yozzer's political analysis, which I promised to trow up – I mean, bring up – at EU Council level.

THURSDAY

Yozzer saw me off at de airport. "You must come back for de millennium celebrations in Bethlehem," says he, embracing me warmly.

"Yes," I agreed, waving goodbye, "dat will be my second comin". Den I ascended de stairs of de plane and, shortly afterwards, disappeared into de clouds. It's funny, but ever since de Good Friday Agreement, I tink I've been developin a bit of a messiah complex.

FRIDAY

Some people are wonderin why I didn't bring Celia along on me middle-eastern tour. Well, we discussed dis wit de experts in Foreign Affairs, and decided dat dis was an entirely different situation from de trip to China. De FA boys warned dat we would be dealin wit religious fundamentalists who still had some old-fashioned ideas about de position of women in society, and bringin Celia along might cause embarrassment. "Right enough," says I, "de Church of Ireland can be very touchy like dat".

SATURDAY

It's good to get back to local issues, all de same. And I'm delighted to see dat in me absence, de FAI have unveiled plans for deir own state-of-de-art stadium. I don't take kindly to bein upstaged by a bunch of suits who wouldn't know a handpass from an underpass. But, to show me support, I rang dem today to promise dat if it comes off, de Government will establish a second city airport nearby. "Dis one'll be for flying pigs only," says I.

SUNDAY

Dat effer De Rossa pulls a fast one by attacking my handling of de Duty Free negotiations in '91, claiming that I went in with me hands up. Of course, he'd know all about surrendering but I leave it alone. I must admit I'll miss it meself dough – it's always very handy for de odd bottle of perfume when your one is in one of her moods. Using de Government jet does cut down de opportunities but with Harney off in it, I'll have a couple of opportunities dis week to stock up.

Me interview in de Sunday Times is quite de topic of conversation. I can't understand it: dose comments on decommissioning were strictly off de record, not dat I've any recollection of making dem in de first place. RTE manages to corner me on de issue of preconditions but I simply use me new line – "I didn't put a foot wrong" – and when dey try to figure dat one out, I make a quick exit to de jacks.

MONDAY

McAleese is on de phone givin me an earful about having to fly steerage class to King Hussein's funeral. I tell her it's Harney's fault dat de jet isn't here and ask if she'll bring back a bottle of Poison for Celia but she just hangs up. I'm beginning to tink we should have stuck with Albert – at least he'd always get ya a bottle of Irish or 200 Major.

Charlie comes into de Cabinet meetin and dere are a few comments about his new six bedroom house, mostly from Biffo who wants to know if McCreevy intends to start taking in refugees. We all laugh except Zero O'Donoghue who always panics when he hears de word "refugees". Den, Charlie gets all serious and threatens to put a new tax on Stringfellows so all de boys shut up immediately. We get down to business – de March 10th deadline – and after four hours we have agreed a phrase for having de executive in place on time. Instead of "two chances" de party line is "some slippage". Personally, it sounds to me like de after effects of a hot curry and a few beers but nobody is listening so I give in.

TUESDAY

Some little f**ker from Dun Laoghaire called Conway is making waves about cleaning up de party so I send Biffo Cowen over to have a chat and we haven't heard a word since. Ettics and all dat are very popular right now but John Brutal has come up with some new slogan altogedder at de Blueshirt agm and I can't quite figure it out. I ask Celia what she tinks of "a new patriotism" and all she wants to know is if it's bigger dan de Corolla. I sensed anudder cooling of relations but luckily my trip to Paris to discuss EU financing went off without a hitch so I had time to buy a bottle of de smelly stuff and de job was oxo in no time.

De tribunals are gettin juicy and I'm gettin nervous because every time somebody farts, de Irish Times starts sniffing my underpants. At least I can't be blamed for Haughey puttin de shits up some poor bank manger in AIB and I tink I'm in de clear regarding Celtic Helicopters but den I'm dragged in because I was Minister for Finance when an eejit called Snowden got a Lotto licence. I taut he was just a photographer with a taste for posh birds but dat shows what I know. Celia says I'm a Philistine so I give her more perfume.

THURSDAY

A score draw leaves Utd five points clear but de chance of some slippage before de end of de season will have me nerves on edge again. De MEPs are looking for a hike which is exactly what they should take, de lot of 'em. I've had young Brian Crowley on de blower suggesting de new millennium might be de right time for a crippled commissioner so I asked him if he's had a look at Flynn lately but he just hung up. Then Luigi gave me a call to congratulate me for making Crowley cry and reminding me of de need for an experienced politician to take over as commissioner so I asked if he knew any and he hung up. Babies de lot of 'em.

Speaking of which, Garret gets five lines in de Irish Times over his 200 grand nod and a wink from fatso Suds in AIB and guess who's front page again, dis time over effin passports to some Yank who gave us a poxy ten grand back when young Crowley was in short pants? I don't even know why I read dat rag any more – de sport's all rugby and golf and Speedbump is just shite.

FRIDAY

Relations with de PDs are pretty good dese days despite Dessie's Oscar speech about Charlie. I tink he just needed to get it off his chest so he could feel good about himself again. Harney is still in a good mood after her Government jet junket to de far east and she hasn't mention de word "qualified" once. To keep her sweet I even slipped her a bottle of Obsession I picked up on de way back from de Agenda 2000 talks in De Hague yesterday. What a poxy trip – de Dutch food left me arse in tatters; no wonder dey all eat McDonalds and drink Belgian beer.

SATURDAY

Celia tells me dat de papers have someting about George Redmond bein lifted at Dublin Airport arrivals lounge by de CAB and I say it always takes me an hour to get one but Celia doesn't even smile. Den she says she's very impressed dat Bono wants to write off turd world debt and I say dat it sounds like a crap name for a song but whatever de kids want is all right by me. Which reminds me, I must pick up some more Cadburys for young Cecilia – she's been in de horrors since de *Indo* called her Cecilia Larkin and I've had to keep telling her on de phone dat she's far too good looking to be taken for a Larkin. Needless to say dis has her nibs stomping around talkin about separate beds again. Still, a one-nil away to Coventry puts a smile on me face before bed time.

SUNDAY

Tra la la la la America, tra la la la la America. I've been singing dat one all week driving Mickey Martin mad because him and Joe Walsh are stuck in dis godforsaken country for de holliers, er, de St Patrick's Day festivities. I explain to bote of dem dat I'm only going over to sort out de peace process once and for all but smart arse Martin wants to know why I'm going to California. I play for time and don't mention Celia's tan at all, instead explaining dat California is where dey make de movies. "So what?" says Martin. "So, f**k off back to Cork and stop annoying me" I want to say but I play de cards close to me chest: "So, maybe dere's a movie in dis peace process and maybe Tom Cruise wants to play you". "Really," he says, de big shiny head on him throbbing before me very eyes, "that's great news". And off he goes whistling de theme to Mission Impossible. I know de little git's after me job but I wish he wouldn't make it so bleeding obvious. I tink I'll put him down for Iran for next Paddy's Day.

MONDAY

Bad news from Europe where Niall Andrews has voted for abortion. We kept de udder six onside but Lord Muck likes to do his own ting, just like de brudder. I tink we need some control over dat lot in Brussels but dey're not much better in Ireland where some culchie called Noel O'Flynn has been throwing his weight around. I'm too far away to do anything about it and Biffo's swanning around Paris so dere's just de Cork lads minding de shop. Maybe, it's no surprise dat one of dere own is acting de bo**ix.

TUESDAY

Our chances of a seat on de UN Security Council have taken a knock with news dat de Italians are lobbying but I'm too far away to do anyting about it. I wish tings didn't keep happening dat reminded de public dat I'm on de lig, er, negotiating in America – dey might not understand de pressures on me. Hopefully tings will quieten down now.

Sh**e – de EU commissioners have gone and resigned and here I am in California wearing me shorts. It was a cert anyway – can you believe Santer Claus telling de MEPs to "back me or sack me". If I said dat to de party I'd have more knives in me back dan Darina Allen's kitchen drawer. I send instructions to Dublin to spin some yarn about in depth discussions on de matter and to make sure nuttin else happens until I get back.

WEDNESDAY

I'm not looking forward to Celia meetin Bill. She's gone right off him and refers to Hilary as "that poor poor woman" although I still refer to her as iron knickers (behind her back of course).

Dere are some many Irish Americans crawling out of de woodwork as well as every Paddy from across de water here dat de Yanks have had to put up a marquee for tonight's bash. Celia is fuming because she tinks her dress is more suitable to indoor event but I know she just tinks marquees are common; sometimes she's very Fine Gael. Liz O'Donnell looks de business for de night and I see Bill givin here de eye so I tell him dat Hilary wants a word. "Probably 'sorry'," he says and mopes off – poor beggar, I nearly feel sorry for him. At least he liked me poem from de Whoseday collection which isn't bad if I say so meself. It's quite different from de original version I showed to Mansergh to "tidy up" but essentially it's de same give or take a few rhyming bits.

THURSDAY

Adams is on to me first ting in de mornin – and me with a fierce Budweiser head – asking what I taught about his performance. I agree with him dat de bit about "stretching de republican constituency" was a stroke of pure genius. Our backroom boys – who earn nearly as much as de Shinners dese days – had spent a month trying to tink of a phrase dat meant more or less nuttin or everyting depending on what side you're on but we never came close to "stretch". Dat's a marvellous word I say and make a mental note to use it when it comes to de Eurostat negotiations.

I start to read George Mitchell's book but it's like watching paint dry and when I come to de bit about Spring bein "handsome intelligent and effective" I dump it in de bin. Spring knew exactly what he was doing licking Mitchell's hole – if I'd known about de book I might have tried a bit more of de plámasing meself.

FRIDAY

It's Friday so dis must be Dublin. After a quick Cabinet meetin in which we discuss Jackie Healy-Rae, de North, Eurostat, Pee Flynn and de Berlin summit – in dat order – de news is out dat Clare and Kerry are off de A list. I explain to de waiting hacks dat we had "stretched" de Euro constituency as far as we could which appears to keep most of dem happy.

Den it's off to O'Donoghue's for a few decent pints with Gerhard Shroder who's all right for a Kraut. He shows me a photo of de new wife – his fourth – and she's pretty impressive. I tell him about de pain in de nuts I've been gettin just for having two birds and he says maybe we should up de Irish quota at de Agenda 2000 talks in Berlin next week. What a man!

MONDAY

First ting dis mornin I've Zero O'Donoghue blabbing in me ear about refugees. De oppostion are making de most of dis Kosovo situation with Bruton demanding we take 2,000. Zero's been up all night doing de sums and says dat de most we can handle is 25, 50 if de bunk-beds arrive in time. Of course, he's always been conservative on de refugee issue so I tell him to write to Bonzo Bruton seeking a few acres from his Meath ranch for a refugee hostel. No reply yet.

De lolly keeps rolling in and de latest estimates are for a £1 billion surplus dis year. Needless to say, dis put six-bedrooms McCreevy in a bad mood as he prepares for pay rise claims from every fecker in de country. He's worried about de teachers already but I tell him to go easy because de educational system is de life blood of de country. "Oh, you've been offered anudder honorary doctorate then?" says Charlie. He's only jealous of course.

TUESDAY

I opened de new extension to de zoo yesterday which was great bleedin crack and a few more votes in de bag for yours truly – all for just £15 million. Cunning and devious or what? Tinking of all dem animals caged up reminds me dat I have some party business to attend to so I leg it to Mount Street to set up me very own Star Chamber which will scare every gurrier in Fianna Fail. Now no one runs in de locals unless dey're clean as a nun's knickers, which should do me a few favours when Rambo's s**t hits de fan next week.

Dis Sheedy business is starting to get tricky and I remember what happend to Albert over a legal matter – you can't trust dose wigs an inch. Zero swears on a stack of Bibles dat he knows absolutely nuttin at all – no surprise dere – but just in case, I ship Harney off to Poland for a couple of days so I get a chance to tink. When I'm told dat young Brian Lenihan wrote a reference for Sheedy I demand his resignation – just to be sure like – when Tiny Brennan reminds me dat I never gave him a job. Just shows I was right on dat one.

WEDNESDAY

Good news and bad news from Belfast. De bad news is dat de Shinners have told me where to stick de Hillsborough Declaration but de good news is dat Andrews made an arse of himself. I get on de phone to Tony in London but I'm told he's busy with de Balkans so I call Bill but he's busy with de Balkans too. Just in case dey're blanking me because of our neutrality I release a quick statement supporting Nato and before yu can say PfP Tony calls and invites me to Downing Street. Celia is delighted and says she'll wear her new knee-length boots which I taught were Georgina's but I keep me gob shut.

THURSDAY

I have me new doctorate up on de wall already and it's a beauty. Dat's tree now which is even more dan Mansergh has and him with de huge brain. I drag Mickey Martin in to make him jealous but he doesn't seem too impressed by me DIT certificate. He say I'll be gettin one from DID Electric next but I know he's only jealous. Apparently, some of de Cabinet have started calling me "Doctor Ahern" behind me back but I'm bein kept informed by all de ones I hinted might be in de running for Flynn's job. Cunning and devious, dat's me.

De meetin with Blair is a waste of time but it gives me a chance to show him and Cherie me new doctorate. Tony wants to know if de DIT is like MIT whatever dat is.

FRIDAY

Andrews is off to Indonesia to top up de tan and to call in on Habibi Baskin. He gets de duty free list from de Cabinet and I remind him not to forget de bottle of "Contradiction" for Celia and he says dat's just what de doctor ordered but I can't tell if he's taking de piss.

When he's gone, we open de Sheedy report which makes great reading but Hammo has left it up to us to do de real dirty work. Biffo suggests punishment beatings which is only narrowly defeated and de mood around de table is great because we've just realised dat we can't be blamed for dis one and dere'll be no election. Even Zero is smiling, which I don't tink I've ever seen before.

SATURDAY

I've got me list of possible EU Commissioners in front of me. Dey're all decent skins, good Fianna Fail blood, de cream of de crop. Den I get a fax from Prodi sayin dat de nominees must be chosen for den "personal integrity". Once I've taken all de FF names of de list, I'm left with a blank sheet of paper again. Dis is provin harder dan I taut. On de udder hand, St Pat's beat de culchies last night so some tings are workin out all right.

SUNDAY

Tree more points in de bag yesterday for de Reds is more good news, even if beating Sheffield Wednesday is as expected as Labour Party fighting over foreign policy. Still, dat treble is still on de cards, a bit like me own: most popular taoiseach ever; keep Harney sweet; and keep Celia sweet. So far so good and de news dat de PDs have less points in de bank dan Nottingham Forest means dat Facc-ache's going nowhere for a while. Here we go, here we go, here we go ...

SUNDAY

Arbour Hill. Always a solemn occasion – a bit like a PD party conference. De team of my speech dis year is de peace process: Government still explorin every avenue ... need to build consensus ... important role for General de Charolais and his independent commission ("comission impossible" as de Shinners call it) ... extreme urgency of de situation, given de approach of de marching season. Etc, etc.

Dis is all bollix, of course – a bit like Harney's speech last night. De troot of de matter is we're trying to park de process for de summer, but we just can't find a feckin parkin space. Dere's double yella lines everywhere you go in de Nort – most of dem runnin up de middle of Trimble's back! De latest setback is dat de unionists have rejected Hume's "natural contraception" idea – de Shinners pullin out of de executive voluntarily – which is a pity, cos it's de first new line he's come up wit for five years.

MONDAY

Tings are not all bad, dough. De PD conference was de best ting on television since Fadder Ted. Harney's speech was so witty and so passionately delivered dat I nearly woke up at one point. I'm not sayin she's a wooden performer but, eh, I believe her make-up people use Cuprinol. Mind you, in all fairness, she has her work cut out wit dat crowd: it must be like havin an audience of Terracotta warriors. In fact, de only good ting about givin de leadership address at a PD conference is dat you get a kiss from Liz O'Donnell afterwards – Phoarrrgh! I usually get Donie Cassidy.

TUESDAY

"Joe Burke on line one," says me secretary. "Shite," says I, checkin under de desk for Charlie Bird. "Jayzus, Joe, I told ye not to ring me at de office," I whisper into de phone. He says sorry but he's a bit fed with de media attention himself – if journalists were refugees, dere'd be a humanitarian disaster in his front garden. But when he tells me he wants to make a clear-de-air statement, de alarm bells start ringin. "Jayzus, Joe, get a grip of yourself!" says I, grabbin de desk for support. "I mean about de Sheedy case," says Joe: "you know, like – professional acquaintance, gave him a character reference, no udder involvement in de case, nothing whatsoever to do with my friend de Taoiseach, dat sort of thing."

I relaxed a bit: "Oh, right. Yeah, I like de sound of dat. Game ball." But to be honest dis whole Sheedy business has me on edge: it's like de last days of de Haughey regime – all dese resignations. De press is still lookin for de big Fianna Fail connection, but I can't tink why. Just because young Sheedy knows more party members dan me shouldn't be held against him… or me. Of course, Bonzo Bruton is barkin his head off as usual; I wish dey'd all go away and let dis one die in peace – please God.

WEDNESDAY

De weekly parliamentary party was dominated by an, eh, lively debate on me idea for a code of ettics for de party. Dere was a lot of muttering from de rank and vile over de way we bounced it on dem, and over de alleged severity of de demands on members: all tax affairs to be in order, no more dodgy hairpieces (Cassidy'll be de first up on dat charge) etc, etc.

As I've said before, dey're a sweaty bunch, de parliamentary party, and de only udder time dey're all squeezed togedder in such a tight space is when dey try to get in de camera shot at de end of me ardfheis speech. So de room gets fairly ripe on a Wednesday mornin. We had asked for submissions from de members, but I was near submission meself by de end of de meetin. Anyway, it was decided dat Doc O'Hanlon an de Macken lad would go away and "redraft" it for two weeks' time, but I told Rory afterwards not to change a word – we'll just let de buggers get used to de idea before we bring it back.

THURSDAY

I learn dat Labour are lookin for a referendum on Partnership for Peace. But as I'm sick sayin, de European elections will be a referendum on it, an if dat's not a fair and honest way of dealin wit de issue, den Jaap Stam is a Dutchman. Dese people who say I'm guilty of a massive u-turn on de party's manifesto pledge are missin de point: sure dat was before de election! Anyway, de udder point wort rememberin is dat Switzerland is a member of PfP, and if a country like Switzerland is prepared to join, de massage is clear: dere must be money in it.

FRIDAY

Harney ask me if I've given any taught to Europe. "Who's going to replace you know who?" she says. I tell her dat in my opinion Roy Keane is simply irreplaceable, and de only chance United have is to go on all-out attack and try and win it 5-4 or someting. But I can only stall her for so long. Of course, she means de commissioner job, and to tell de troot I'm no nearer a decision on dis, except who it's not goin to be – dat lanky Labour f**ker from Tralee for one. Unfortunately, de PDs have deir heads in de trough for a job too – eider de commissioner's or de court of auditors nixer. Dis'd be for Dessie, probably, aldough Harney says to me she might like "a change of career" herself.
"Did ye ever consider de priesthood?" says I.

SUNDAY

Wit friends like mine, who needs de Opposition. No sooner have I extric ... extrad ... eh, excavated meself from de mess dat Joe got me into over de Sheedy business, dan me chief speechwriter, Baldy Paddy Duffy, lands me in de shite again over dis NTL crack. De worst ting about it was I had to put up wit Schoolmistress O'Rourke marchin into me office yesterday, hittin me wit her ruler, and sayin over and over: "I told you tho, I thed back in April thith would happen." And all right, I did assure her den dat Baldy was not a director of any company anywhere of any kind whatsoever. But, eh, sure de f***er wrote dat for me as well. I only deliver de lines.

I shoulda listened to Mara when he told me to pay him off tree months ago. De year's notice of his departure was a bad idea: dere's too many people out dere willin to pay big money for access to me – an I'm not just talkin about de women. De trubble is, if ye sit down wit dem PR fellas, ye get up wit fleas every time. Still, I feel a bit sorry for Paddy – we've been togedder so long he was like one of me old anoraks (aldough, come to tink of it, I got rid of dem too when dey treatened me poll ratins).

I used to look up to him because he was a teacher – he helped me wit de old lingo and so on. He had a bit of de French and de Eyetalian as well, not dat dere was much call for dat around Drumcondra. But maybe de best tribute I can pay him now is to say dat I wouldn't speak English as well as what I do today widdout him. An dat's de trute.

MONDAY

On de plus side, de Dubs won yesterday, which put me in a better mood for de launch of de Fianna Fail "Charter for Dublin" today. Dis is a bit of a wheeze de boys in headquarters taught up on Friday (we put de charter on de back of a lorry, so we could drive it away afterwards and no-one'd remember de promises), but it's mainly an excuse for some of our election candidates to get photographed wit de most popular Taoiseach in de history of de State, etc, etc. And sure enough, dese boys stay so close to ye when de cameras are around dat, at times, ye'd be nervous about bendin down to tie yer shoelaces. If ye know what I mean.

TUESDAY

Dis Michelle de Bruin ting is a national tragedy, but we must look on de positive side, which is dat it's pushed de Duffy affair off de front pages ... eh, and also of course dat future generations of Irish atletes will have a better chance of competin in a drug-free environment. We've all seen de horrors dat drug abuse causes: like de East German women dat underwent sex changes, or de current Liverpool football team, just to name two examples. Which is why we're all so anxiously awaitin Dr McDaid's final blueprint for an Irish drug-testin programme (I'm tinkin about intruducin random out-of-election tests for some of our back-benchers, but I'll come back to dat anudder day). Apparently, de tenderin process still has to be completed. Jayzus! I better check dat none of our people are mixed up wit any of de PR companies in dis one – just imagine de headlines: "Government adviser implicated in drug deal". It's a good ting I taught of it in time.

WEDNESDAY

At last, a breaktrew over de Balkans. I know beatin Macedonia 1-0 isn't dat big a deal, but comin on top of de skillful way in which we avoided havin to play de Serbs widdout Roy Keane, I tink de last few days have been a watershed in de development of dis country's foreign policy. Dev woulda been proud, I'm sure. An despite de criticisms, it was de aerial threat dat did de trick, as I predicted. Big Niall, what a header! (Quinn, I mean, not Andrews)

THURSDAY

As soon as de polls closed in de Nort tonight, I announced a new round of talks on de peace process. We have to get someting sorted well before de Twelth, which is de start of de Nort's official Taig-shootin season. De point is: de debacle over de return of de bodies (Mansergh says de term IRA intelligence is an "oxymormon". Or someting like dat, it sounded witty anyway) has pointed de way to a compromise on decommissionin dat can satisfy all parties. All de Shinners have to do is tell us where dey tink de arms dumps are; den we'll dig from now until next Christmas and we won't find anyting. It's a cunning plan, wit someting in it for everyone, I tink.

FRIDAY

So now de Gaiety Teatre has been dragged into de Duffy affair, which ensures dat next week's Dail debate will be a proper pantomime. Still, me main concern is dat de controversy doesn't disturb de air of apatty and complacency about de economy's success dat I predict will keep de Blueshirt and Labour voters at home in deir droves today. It's just a pity de wedder stayed good. Aldough, den again, we don't want to do TOO well in de elections. After all, if de Fine Gaelers get wiped out at de polls, dey might finally get a new leader. An dat would be a disaster.

SUNDAY

Dere was a lotta potential for violence today, what wit de Drumcree march AND de Mead-Offaly game, but in de event, dey bote passed off peacefully. I was particularly impressed by de dignity and restraint on display in Portadown: dat big crowd of journalists in de field coulda got very ugly when dey realised dey were bein denied deir traditional rights to scenes of petrol bombin and sporadic shootin at de barrier. Instead, dey just dispersed peacefully, carryin deir traditional mileage claims wit dem. It was all very moving.

De game in Croker, meanwhile, was a bit of a rerun of Drumcree. A group of 15 selected Offalymen tried to march trew de Mead defence (which is ticker dan any British army roadblock). But dey knew dey wouldn't be allowed, and after a mild protest dey gave up and went home. I only hope deir fellow county man, Biffo, takes it as well when I break it to him dat he's not gettin de Brussels job. It could be like de day I told him I was makin him Minister for Healt. I'm just afraid he might trigger his d'Hondt mechanism, or someting – and beat de shite out of me..

MONDAY

Met de Harney one at de openin of de new Digital Park (whatever dat is) in Tallaght, an she says McDowell will be game-ball if de AG job were to suddenly become available. Personally, I want him at de Cabinet table about as much as I want an invitation to dinner at de Brutons', but it'd be wort it just to see how far de Opposition's jaws would drop. Also, appointing him would be a way of lettin everybody know dat I have no fears about de Flood Tribunal (which may or may or may not be true – I'm sayin nuttin for de moment). An de bottom line is dat if McDowell does get too entusiastic and starts tryin to put Fianna Fail people in jail, or someting, I have a cunning plan. I'll get Biffo to beat de shite out of him.

TUESDAY

Had a bunch of Yanks in wit me today, from de US Congress. I briefed dem on de latest developments in de nort (situation still delicate) and dey briefed me on de latest developments in de White House (female staff still nervous). Afterwards, I peeped in on de meetin to decide de Telecom share price, but it was too technical for me (I heard McCreevy sayin: "I'll see your £3 and raise you 20p," whatever dat meant). De important ting is dat de punters make a quick killing, so dat dey're all as happy as pigs in shite, and not worryin demselves about silly tings like de Flood Tribunal. Dat's my tinkin anyway.

WEDNESDAY

Had de usual pre-Cabinet meetin wit Harney, and we finalised de deal on de commissionership. She was like de cat dat got de cream, between stitchin up Go-Go AND gettin McDowell back in Cabinet, but I figured it was a small price to pay for keepin Liz O'Donnell in de Government. Phoarrggh! Den I rang Prodi and we agreed on de consumer affairs job for de boy Dave. It's not de most important position, but of de tree we were offered (de udders were "janitor" and "refuse collector" I tink we made de right choice). Den it only remained for me to announce de decision at Cabinet, and aldough Cowen asked "Who de f**k is David Byrne?" de choice went down well. No doubt some people, like Biffo himself and Mickey Woods were disappointed, but dere was also a strong sense dat what really mattered was dat Go-Go would feel even worse. (Dat and de national interest, of course).

THURSDAY

Down to Killarney for de ICTU conference, and on de way I did a phone interview for de BBC in Belfast. I taught I was bein very careful, sayin "Ulster" instead of "de Nort" and tings like dat, but all everyone wanted to talk about afterwards was how I also said dat Sinn Fein and de IRA were two different organisations. Now, we all know dere's an overlap, and dat whenever dere's a vacancy on de army council, Sinn Fein always have someone on de interview panel and dat sort of ting. I was just makin de point dat dey have separate corporate identities (different stationery, and so on). But still, de unionists went ballistic about it − even dough I was only sayin what dey're sayin demselves, which is dat dere needs to be a statement on decommissioning from de Provos, and not from Sinn Fein on behalf of de Provos. Effin' unionists − sometimes dey'd annoy you.

FRIDAY

Rambo told de Flood Tribunal about de political trust. I'd heard it before − he told me last year − so it wasn't as funny dis time. But still! He seems to be holdin up well in de dock, and I liked de fact dat he asked de chairman to include in his report a mention of how badly politicians are paid. Dat's typical of Ray − always tinkin about udder people. Meanwhile, de Haughey fella (dat I was never very close to despite what people tink) was up in court today, and is to face trial later dis month on charges of obstructin de McCracken Tribunal. I feel a bit sorry for de man (even dough I never really knew him dat well − hardly at all, in fact) but at least he got bail. Probably because McDowell hasn't taken over de AG job yet.

SATURDAY

De Green Paper on abortion went down well, tanks be to God. I know we had our doubters but, as we promised right from de start, de paper was completely, eh, green. On de udder hand, eh, I'm not. And anyone who tinks I'm gonna act on any of de proposals contained in it dis side of a general election must be eider a tick eejit, or John Bruton, or probably bote. We need a national debate before we go any furder, an I believe everybody in de country should contribute to it – on de Late Late Show, if possible. Whatever happens, we have de right man in charge of de process, anyway. At de cabinet meetin de udder day, we told Cowen he could now invite submissions. "OK," he said, wrestlin Mickey Martin onto de floor: "Submit, ye Cork bastard!"

SUNDAY

Speakin of which, dose Leeside f**kers won de hurlin final today, which woulda been bad enough in itself widdout de game bein as high in entertainment as de collected speeches of Noel Demsey. Which didn't bother Mickey, of course. "We're cleaning up," says he to me afterwards. "Dat'd be a good idea," says I, "de last time I was in Cork de place was filty."

MONDAY

Last-minute preparations for de trip to Moscow. Celia agonisin over what to wear, as usual, and me tryin to prepare de cupla focal in Russian wit me voice-coach and memorisin de names of people we're meetin, like de prime minister. De trubble is, Russia changes prime ministers more often dan I change me jocks. De latest one is called Mr Putin. "Think of rugby – de thing they do in de scrum," says de voice coach. "What?" says I, "ye mean, grab each udder by de goolies?". "Er ... ," says de voice coach, "we better try something else."

TUESDAY

On de flight over, Celia was worried about all de bombs goin off. "Yeah," says I, cunningly, "I believe dey're targetin de main shoppin areas." Dat should ease de pressure on me credit card, I taught to meself. As it happens, one of de places on our itinerary is a big shopping centre called GUM, which is a funny name for a shopping centre, I'm tinkin. I wonder if dat's how de Workers Party became known as de Stickies – dey were always shoppin in Moscow ... eh, allegedly, anyway. When we finally touched down, I had to inspect a guard of honour, which I hate, because it's hard to keep a straight face; especially here, because de Russian soldiers have dis custom of tiltin deir heads as you pass dem an I was afraid one of dose big caps would fall off and I'd break me shite laughin. But dey all stayed on, luckily. Probably de gum.

WEDNESDAY

Met Mr Putin and tried out a bit of me Russian. "Da nyet sputnik one lev yashin," says I, wit a wink, and ye could tell he was impressed. Eider dat or he was just happy to wake up dis mornin and find he was still de prime minister. I made a speech promisin Ireland's help in de fight against de bombers, who are apparently from d'Aga Khan's Liberation Army. "Dagestan," said Mr Putin, correctin me. "Eider way," says I, "I'm not lettin de bastards sponsor de main event at de Dublin Horse Show any more unless dey stop de bombin." Mr Putin thanked me and said that, in return, he could put me in de way of some cheap cigarettes.

THURSDAY

More meetins, includin one from a rude little man claimin to be de mayor of Moscow. "Yuri Luzhkov," says he. "So are you, you little sh**e," says I, not knowin what a Luzhkov was, but just to be on de safe side. He wears a cap, like Jackie Healy Rae, and de udder ting dey have in common is dat I have no idea what eider of dem are sayin. We also met one of de former prime ministers, Mr Primakov, who de Foreign Affairs boys say is still important politically (unlike any of Ireland's former prime ministers, especially Albert) and we have to keep in with him. Den it was off to St Petersburg, which of course used to be called, eh, someting else. And finally, de flight home.

FRIDAY

Back to reality wit a bang, to learn dat Sheriff Mitchell and de boys are goin to step aside for de cross-examination of all de former finance ministers. Dis is a setback. I was hopin Sean Doherty would lead de questionin and I had a prepared me answer along de lines of : "When you're de Minister for Finance, and who knows, Sean, you might just be after de next reshuffle … "Or if Rabbitte tried to get fresh wit me, I coulda given him a dig about Moscow: "Dat's a very sticky question, deputy; you must have put a lot of, eh, GUM on it". Sheriff Mitchell woulda huffed and puffed, to be sure, but his gang can't afford to dig de, eh, dirt eider. Now instead it's all goin to be done be lawyers, which means we'll be dere until Christmas and God knows what'll come up. At least with cheap party-political points-scoring, ye know where ye stand.

SUNDAY

So Mo finally got de chop. I'm sorry to see her go, because she got up de unionists' noses, which is never a bad ting in a nordern secretary. Mandelson might get up dem in anudder way, if de rumours are true, but he doesn't have de common touch. (Hopefully for Blair, he doesn't have de, eh, Clapham common touch eider). It's hard to see him in a Belfast pub talkin sense into de two drunks, as Clinton called dem, aldough of course dat was an inapropriate meta ... eh, meta ... metabolics, I tink is de word. On de udder hand, Mandy is a young man in a hurry (a bit like Mickey Martin, in fact; not dat he's goin anywhere in de near future, except maybe Cork) an he needs to sort out de Nort for his own sake. So dere's hope yet.

MONDAY

Dis coup in Pakistan is a big worry, dem havin de bomb, an all. I was never dat big into de foreign affairs before we signed up to de Partnership for Joining NATO by de Back Door. But now dat we're goin to be military players on de world scene, I have to watch developments and, frankly, I'm very concerned dat de unrest in Pakistan could spread to udder countries in de Balkans (or wherever bleedin Pakistan is). De udder worry is dat our own army could start gettin ideas. I know it's a bit far-fetched, but dey're struttin deir stuff a bit more since de PfP ting. An de generals (come to tink of it, do we HAVE generals?) might start tinkin dat de endless series of revelations from de tribunals is destabilisin de country and dey need to take a hand. Luckily de army is under de control of Michael Smith, an wit his charisma and strength of personality ... f**k me, I better keep de helicopter ready.

TUESDAY

Anudder fun day in de Dail, arguin about de nurses; de Blueshirts and Labour bendin over backwards tryin to suggest dey'd pay dem, widdout actually sayin so. We made dat mistake in Opposition, when Zero got behind de Guards and let dem tink dey'd have whatever dey wanted if we got back in: pay increases, early retirement, a police state, whatever; an we suffered for it since. So de Opposition now are bein a bit more careful, which is fine by us. Biffo is not for turnin on de issue, an his attitude to de nurses is we'll fight dem on de beaches, we'll fight dem in de air, we'll wrestle dem naked in a bathtub full of whipped cream if we have to, but we're not given in. I told de Dail dat dey'd already "driven a coach and horses trew de pay agreement". Dis is anudder example of de use of metabolics, but it's an appropriate one, I tink.

WEDNESDAY

Out to Barretstown Castle to meet Paul Newman, de famous star of such classic films as Butch Cassidy an de Sundance Kid. I can't remember which one of dem he was (an I was afraid to ask him), but I know dey robbed banks back in de Wild West. An by an amazin coincidence, de latest scandal to hit de government involves de writin off by de banks of a £¼ million debt for John "Butch" Ellis, in which his old pal, Albert "Sundance" Reynolds may or may not have had a role. Dis is not a bank robbery exactly, it just sounds like one. Naturally, as de current Fianna Fail leader, my main concern is dat Albert is left swingin in de wind as long as poss … eh, I mean, dat de trute is quickly established. So I rang Albert dis evenin wit a couple of questions, includin whedder he knew which of de two characters Paul Newman played. But he said he had no specific recollection of de film at all.

THURSDAY

More ugly exchanges in de Dail, wit Baldy Noonan (exchanges don't get more ugly dan dat) and udder blueshirts claimin dey knew de identity of de so-called "turd man" in de Ellis affair. I told dem to put up or shut up an, of course, when it came to de crunch, dey had nuttin. Typical Fine Gael. Dey huff and dey puff, but dey just can't sustain a performance (aldough, in fairness, dis is not a criticism you could level at Alan "Three Hours" Dukes. I hear Volkswagon have made him an offer – dey like to test deir cars in extreme conditions).

FRIDAY

Off to Finland for a two-day conference on crime and udder EU harmonisation measures. I was lookin forward to dis, because Oireland has a great record over de last couple of years crackin down all de major criminal operators (de ones wit workin-class accents, anyway). But not even in Finland can I get away from de bleedin Moriarty Tribunal and, sure enough, de hacks were after me de about de latest revelations.

De shirt scandal was bad enough, but dis Coq Hardi crack is if anyting more embarrassing. When I counter signed dose cheques, I was under de impression dat de Coq Hardi was a French charity providin retirement homes for roosters injured in de cock-fighting. Dat's what CJ told me, anyway. I taut he was a secret fan of de so-called "sport" himself (he was always talkin about a "game old bird" he had – Terry, he called it) from de days before he could afford racehorses. He said some of dese roosters were mistreated in deir old age an it wasn't right when you considered all de entertainment dey'd provided. I taut he sort-of identified wit dem himself. It seemed plausible at de time, but how am I goin to explain dis to de tribunal?

SUNDAY

Tings have come to a very sorry pass when dey can bury a former Fianna Fail Taoiseach widdout de current Fianna Fail Taoiseach givin de oration. I had one ready an all: *De fools, de fools, dey have left us our Fianna Fail dead/An while she holds dese graves, Oireland will not only be free but gaelic as well, not only gaelic but, eh, a bit of hurlin too/An when de Moriarty tribunal report takes its place among all de udders gadderin dust on de shelves of de Dail library, den an only den let my epitaph be written* ... before I realised dat dat little feckin turncoat O'Malley had got de Lynch gig.

I even got advice for de occasion from a certain, eh, professional image consultant. She said I was a predominantly summer person wit autumn tones, but dat it'd be winter in hell before she'd work for me again. She's a bit miffed because de, eh, as it were, Partnership 2000 negotiations broke down again. But, eh, she'll get over it given time, and a few more spreads in de Tribune, I'm tinkin.

MONDAY

I was sorry to see de end of Jack, oration or no oration. He was from Cork, of course, but he was all right.

A great sportsman too, who'll be remembered – as I said on de radio – whenever anyone hears de sound of ash on ledder. An even dough I didn't get to deliver de oration, on de plus side at least I didn't have to sit beside Charlie eider. I believe Dessie looked like he'd swallowed a brick when he saw who was next to him. I couldn't look around me durin de mass, of course, but you could feel de tension, especially comin up to de sign-of-peace bit. It was just one of dose unfortunate accidents dat dey ended up togedder, but dere was great relief when dey shook hands (except for dose of us who took de "no handshake" odds from de lads in de protocol department).

TUESDAY

Biffo arrived for de cabinet meetin a bit shook. His car got stuck in a traffic jam outside a hospital in Dun Laoighaire and apparently some of de nurses on de picket line offered him a rectal examination wit, eh, one of de pickets. I tink he's now in favour of a settlement – lucky for us de matter is in de hands of de Labour Court. De meetin also discussed de case of "Butch" Ellis and we agreed he's toast, as far as de agriculture committee job is concerned anyway. We delegated Rory, as party chairman, to meet him next week. Rory is a doctor, of course, an he'll present him with a basic choice: resignation from de committee chairmanship, or a rectal exam wit a rolled up copy of de ettix guidelines. I'm sure he'll make de right decision.

WEDNESDAY

De guards have made yet anudder arms find in Mead. I don't know what's goin on dere: eider dis is covert decommissionin by de Provos, or de Royal County has turned into a hotbed of dissident republicanism. Intelligence reports say dere's very little of it (intelligence, dat is) in de area. But eider way, I've let George Mitchell know, trew de secret channels, dat if it would help de review process I'm prepared to autorise carpet bombing of Mead. I'd also be happy to consider introducin internment in de county – selective of course: lads of football-playing age, an maybe de odd herbalist in his '50s as well. Dis is not a course I'd take lightly. But, eh, if it was in de interests of peace …

THURSDAY

Labour held deir seat in Dublin Sout Central, predictably enough, aldough dey couldn't crow too much because dere's been bigger turn-outs at de PDs' parliamentary party meetins. Anudder woman in de Dail, dough, Mary O'Rourke, says to me dis evenin: "We'll be running thith plaith before long." So I said: "Why don't you start now – run out dere an get me a cup of tea." She hit me wit her handbag instead. Speakin of women, de nurses deal is de sort of devious, cunning plan I'da taut of meself when I was Minister for Strike-breakin. Crucially, dough, I believe it preserves de partnership structure, and won't lead to a spate of udder sectoral pay-claims. I also believe in de toot fairy and I tink de Dubs can win de All-Ireland hurlin championship next year. Maybe I'm an optimist. (Memo: Write letter to Santy Claus soon).

FRIDAY

Mitchell told us tanks for de offer, but he doesn't tink bombing Mead is necessary (we might do it anyway, just to be on de safe side). It seems de review is comin along nicely: de Shinners and de UUP are talkin to each udder like adults, even. An dey bote seem to agree dat an executive should be formed. De only difference is timescale: de Shinners want it now, whereas de UUP tink dat de end of de next century is a more realistic target. De main ting is dat dey're still talkin.

SATURDAY

Mandy has arrived in Stormont, possibly to hold Trimble's hand durin de delicate closin stages of de talks. Dere's nuttin much we can do, unfortunately (I wouldn't know which of Gerry's hands to hold – de one wit de armalite or de one wit de ballot box). But I've cancelled all appointments and told de NIO dat I'm ready to fly in at short notice should a major photo opportunity be necessary.

SUNDAY

Ye have to hand it to McCreevy. He had enough money to end world hunger, buy Roy Keane, and still have enough over to treat de whole country to dinner in de Coq Hardi, and instead he comes up wit de most unpopular budget since de Blueshirts took a shillin off de pension in 1929. "It's a great achievement, Charlie," I told him on de phone, "De odds were stacked against you makin a balls of it, but you pulled it off." He had de bad taste to remind me dat I'd seen all de figures beforehand and I didn't have a problem wit dem. But as I explained to him, I'm a strong believer in de principle of individualisation; and dat's why I tink de Minister for Finance should now be left to take as much of de blame, eh, individually, as possible.

MONDAY

Down to Avondale for de launch of de Millennium Tree Project, a visionary concept which will involve planting a new tree for every family in de country next year, wit identifaction certificates for each one so dat people can visit dem and check on deir progress and – I don't know – cut de f**kin tings down for firewood, or whatever. I'm not dat keen on trees meself since a couple of year ago when I was up every one in Nort Dublin lookin for de dirt on Ray Burke. Still, I taut dis was a cute idea when Mini Brennan told me about it ("Family trees – geddit?" he said). But now I tink it's gonna cause even more trouble when stay-at-home spouses realise dey can't get out of de house long enough to be visitin forests. Luckily, if a row blows up, we have a contingency plan to issue dem wit bonsai trees instead.

TUESDAY

I knew dere was a popular revolt over de budget, but I was shocked at de extent of de hostility on "Questions and Answers" last night an – for once – I nearly felt sorry for Mata Harney. I told her beforehand dat I was right behind her (she's dat big, it's always a safe place to stand) and to go out swingin. But if it hadda been a boxin match, de ref woulda stopped it in round two to prevent furder punishment.

De whole fracas is puttin de wind up de independents, needless to say, an Mini is offerin extra trees to try an keep dem sweet. Our own backbenchers are openly revoltin too, an I'm not just talkin about deir personal hygiene. Speakin of which, you could smell de fear at de Cabinet meetin today; an de consensus was for some sort of carefully disguised climb-down from our budget position, like leakin a statement to de effect that McCreevy was on drugs when he

I'm so used to bein an international statesman now dat, widdout such a role, I'll feel naked.

Kofi asked me if Oireland remained committed to reachin de UN aid target of 0.7 per cent of GDP and I told him dat it was one of our two main national priorities, alongside de drainin of de Shannon. He seemed happy enough wit dat.

I told Clinton everythin was game ball. He didn't seem to understand me – Yanks can be a bit tick like dat – but eventually he got de drift. Den I said dere was something I'd been meanin to ask him as de leader of the world's most powerful nation. He says: What's that? I says: Dat Paula Jones. Did ye really drop de trousers ye dirty fecker, ye?

I expressed de hope dat de Iraq matter could be dealt with by purely diplomatic means, or by bombin de shite out of dem. Whatever works, I said. And I added in de event of a ground invasion, I'd be happy to commit de entire Irish Army to de effort. President Clinton said tanks very much but he'd be happier if I gave dem to Iraq instead. Dat would destroy Saddam's morale in a week, he reckoned.

If Europe felt it needed someone wit proven negotiational skills, from a country dat represented de outstandin success story of de EU, well, maybe I'd have to consider de big EU job. At dis point Jacques Chirac smiled and touched me arm de way he does. He said dat while he was a great admirer of mine, France would have to insist dat any EU president spoke at least basic French. I nodded in agreement. "Naturellement," I said.

McCreevy is in a bad mood as he prepares for pay rise claims from every fecker in de country. He's worried about de teachers already but I tell him to go easy because de educational system is de life blood of de country. "Oh, you've been offered another honorary doctorate then?" says Charlie. He's only jealous of course.

Labour and DL are setting up a tink-tank before dey complete de merger. What a waste of time. Eider dey're mergin or dey're not – just like me and Celia. I don't need a tink-tank to tell me dat a marriage is out of de question, er, at dis particular point in time dat is.

Still, dere was a hopeful sign for de peace process, when Martin McGuinness said de riotin in Derry was "wrong". It's not so long ago when, if he said it was wrong, he'd a meant deir petrol-bomb trowing technique.

delivered it. De only bright spot on de horizon at de moment is de Udaras elections. I don't know what it is about dem Irish speakers and Fianna Fail, but if de results were projected nationally we'd have about 125 seats in de Dail an no worries about pesky independents. Tiochfaidh ar la, wha?

WEDNESDAY

Despite our announcement of a £660 tax allowance to one-income families, de parliamentary party meetin was an ugly affair (an I'm not just talkin about de sartorial standards). Charlie started it by tanking everybody for deir support over de last week – dat got a good laugh – and den told us about a placard in his constituency dat compared him to Henry VIII. He said dis was unfair because he was still only on his second wife, and dat got a good laugh too – partly because it was funny, and partly because everybody was tinkin dat if Charlie was in trouble now, wait till de missus read de next day's papers. Den every feckin party member had to make a speech about how bad de budget was. And den finally, I tried to pour oil on troubled waters by sayin dat, based on personal experience, dere was a "landmine" in every budget, and dat dere was nuttin to worry about except us all gettin de shite blown out of us. I tink dis calmed everyone down a bit.

THURSDAY

De announcement of our £125 million social welfare package has at least got de bolshies in SIPTU back on board – even dough, in terms of dog's dinners, de budget now looks like someting dat Albert's factory would be proud of. Bad an all as tings are, dough, at least Roy Keane has signed a new contract for de Reds. Which, as well as bein a good ting in itself, is reassuring in anudder way. Because, like us, Man Utd had a multi-million pound budget. And, eh, dey've just made a balls of it as well.

FRIDAY

I see de Christmas "RTE Guide" has anudder glowing article about Celia's image consultancy business. Whedder it's in politics or fashion, de headline says, Celia Larkin is in de business of "creating confidence and credibility". Hmm, it might be time to consider givin her de contract for de cabinet: it has predominantly winter tones, I'm tinkin, but it could do wit a bit of a spring-clean. Incidentally, I see de bird who wrote de article also says dat Celia greeted her "in full maquillage". I tink I know what she means. I've seen Celia in one of dose moods as well, an it's not for de faint-hearted.

SUNDAY

Bit of a head on me dis mornin. As somebody said, a millennium only comes around once in a lifetime and ye have to do something special to mark it, so, eh – call me reckless – I had de extra pint of Bass last night on top of me normal. But I tink de celebrations generally went well. I didn't see much of de telly coverage meself but I believe de bit of me on stage in Merrion Square was one of DE international images, alongside de Eiffel Tower and de women wit de big diddies out in de Pacific.

And as I told Mini Brennan afterwards, I believe de approach he took to de occasion was fully justified. Wit everybody else in de world goin for de fireworks treatment, I said, it was very brave of him to organise something dat looked like a mass funeral. De "Mexican wave" of light under de Liffey bridges was a special highlight, aldough it took me a while to cop dat it was de wave of a drowning Mexican. All in all, I taut de whole night was a triumph. Just like de budget.

MONDAY

A great omen for de new century: today I won de office pool for predictin de first John Bruton-calls-for-an-inquiry of de new millennium. It didn't look on dis mornin, but den de word went round dat some of de State papers on de Arms Crisis were missin and, sure enough, Big-Arse took de bait and I was £100 richer. Some of de lads are suspicious about how de rumour about de files started but, eh, I'd say it was de millennium bug meself.

Speakin of which, I'm not surprised dis turned out to be an even bigger damp squib dan any of de ones Mini let off. De big relief for us was dat de weekend passed off widdout a major fire. No sooner had we sent out all dose poxy candles dan we realised what a mistake we'd made, what wit de whole country drunk, and Friday night was de biggest single national insurance risk since Robbo started puttin lights out for de emigrants. I've told Mini dat next millenium, we're issuin light bulbs instead.

TUESDAY

Not much danger of a fire in de midlands where, tanks to global warming, whole counties are disappearing under water. Livelihoods are under threat, homes are bein washed away, and cows are bein eaten alive by shoals of piranhas washed in on de Gulf Stream. On de plus side, de expanded River Shannon should be more dan adequate to deal wit de increased number of German tourists projected by Bord Failte dis year. So I tink dat evens out.

WEDNESDAY

De udder good point about de flooding is dat it will fasilit...fascilitat... it will help our plan for electoral reform – which has now been forwarded to a Dail committee for urgent consideration – and particularly de idea of cutting de number of TDs to 100. Dis is necessary not only for de more efficient workin of democracy but it should also cut down on de smell at de weekly parliamentary party meetins, which would be no bad ting eider.

Anyway, de way de wedder's goin, we can soon phase out most of dose midland constituencies like Laois-Offaly and, eh, Carlow-Leitrim, and I forget de rest of dem. On de udder hand, with de resettlement of de evacuees, Dublin Nort-Central will have to become a nine-seater, which should mean jobs for all me brudders and cousins (as soon as I get a new constituency organiser, dat is). Den de Ahern family will be ready to rule for anudder tousand years, at least.

THURSDAY

Dis extradition case is a bit of an embarrassment for all concerned. I must admit when I heard de name Angelo Fusco on de news, me first taut was "Jayz, I'd murder a bag of chips". But me second reaction was: why did he have to be arrested at dis particular time, just when de Provos are ready to decommission some of de gear. It just shows ye: if de guards spent more time workin de new technology an less time out stoppin people at roadblocks, dese misunderstandings wouldn't happen.

In de meantime, we're stuck wit yer man – it's not like fishing, unfortunately, where you could just weigh de bastard and let him go again. But what we need now is for de case to drag on quietly for weeks and possibly months without a decision eider way. And if I know de Irish legal system, I tink it's in good hands.

FRIDAY

Pity about de Beckham lad gettin sent off in Brazil. He gets a lot of unfair attention (it must be a bit like bein a Fianna Fáil Taoiseach) but de way I see it is, a lad starts wearin skirts, he's askin for trouble. I blame his mott. Dese pop bands can be a very bad influence – an needless to say, dis is a matter of personal concern for me. I've told Georgina dat de moment de Nicky lad starts messin wit women's clothes, she's outta dere. Dat said, he's a good lad, really, an I was delighted to see de boys occupyin de Number 1 spot in two different millennia.

Just like me, come to tink of it.

SUNDAY

Spent de afternoon workin on me article for tomorrow's *Irish Times*. Actually, I spent de afternoon watchin de football on Sky while Mansergh worked on de article, but I did have to listen to him read it over de phone before he sent it in, which wasn't easy. De basic argument he was makin is dat General de Charolais has swallowed de IRA's latest verbal formula, an if it's good enough for him, what are Trimble and de Brits whingin about? He also makes de very good point dat de suspension of de institutions is unconstitutional down here and dat de Government could find itself in de invidi ... eh, in de indiginous position of having to defend a court challenge from de Shinners, when we wouldn't even believe what we were sayin. Ok, I do dat in me ardfheis speech from time to time, but dat's different.

MONDAY

Me head's been so boddered wit dis decommissionin crack, I completely forgot Valentine's Day. Dis is very remiss of me because de two issues are somewhat interlinked. Last autumn, Celia set a deadline of around now by which she wanted to see clear and verifiable evidence dat de marriage process had begun. I offered her a new form of words over Christmas, at which point she offered me a form of words dat I couldn't print in a family diary like dis one.

After dat it was a complete impasse, aldough de confidence-buildin measure of gettin her on de junket to Sout Africa did improve de situation. Anyway, I remembered late dis evenin de day dat was in it, and managed to get a bunch of flowers and a box of chocolates down at de fillin station. But when I delivered dem to her, she said it was too little too late. Dere'd been a six o clock deadline, and she'd already collapsed de institutions, as it were. Looks like anudder spell in de doghouse.

TUESDAY

I was in de middle of me speech in de Dail, telling everybody dat de IRA's latest offer to de general was a dramatic breaktrew and dat I had absolute trust in de integrity of de republicans on dis issue, when someone handed me a note to say "de Fenian b****rds have pulled out of de deal".

Dis would have been bad enough at de best of times, but de way it happened meant I had to put up wit Brutal cryin crocodile tears about dis "deliberate humilation" of "our" Taoiseach. He even praised de "calm and dignified" way I took de news. And when he started on about how dis was de tanks I got for workin "all de hours dat God sends to bring peace," I nearly trew up on de Ceann Comhairle. I'll never forgive de Shinners for exposin me to dat. Never.

WEDNESDAY

Went to Downing Street to try and persuade de treacherous Brits to restore de institutions before de weekend, but it was a waste of time. Mandelson is in Trimble's pocket because of de resignation threat and, short of sendin a ferret in after him, dere's no way to get him out,. I tried to reassure Blair dat de Provos pullin out of talks wit de decommissionin body meant nuttin, but all he said was "I know. I tried de withdrawal method myself and look where it got me."

THURSDAY

Back to domestic matters; an while de peace process may be stuck in traffic, dis week's one-day Dublin Bus strike seems to have been a great success in gettin de city movin again. Once de bus lanes were open to cars, dere were no problems. It's just a pity de work stoppage was such a short one. But, eh, wit CIE's industrial relations record, we're confident dat we'll have a proper, long drawn-out strike soon.

FRIDAY

Grizzly has complained about de "dangerous vacuum" opening up in de peace process. Everybody needs to "stay cawm," as he says. So to give de Shinners a morale boost at dis difficult time, we got him a slot on tonight's *Late Late Show*. Dere's a dangerous vacuum opening up in Pat Kenny's viewership figures, so I knew dey'd get on well; not like Grizzly's last appearance, when Gaybo stood at de udder end of de studio like he was afraid he'd catch someting off him. Anyway, I tink de whole ting worked: I was so cawm half way trew de interview, I fell asleep.

SATURDAY

Of course dere was a deeper significance in de show, which de ordinary public will have missed, in de appearance of Shane McGowan. Basically, dis is de first of a series of carefully choreographed moves designed to restart de whole peace process. Sometime next week, Shane is going to announce he's givin up drugs and drink; an actually hand over some of his "gear" to an independent observer in London. Den de Provos will say, ok, if Shane can do it, so can we; and dey'll make a gesture (not a rude one, we hope) on decommissionin. Den we'll release de White Paper confirming dat we're slashing de size of de Irish Army, as our contribution to takin de gun out of Irish politics. Den de unionists will return to de executive. Den dere'll be an interdenominational service for reconcialiation, concelebrated by Ian Paisley and Sinead O'Connor, wit de Pope on a satellite link-up from Rome. Den dere'll be lasting peace. It's not a great plan, but it's de best we can tink of at de moment.

MONDAY

I was relaxin on de couch wit Celia one night a few weeks ago, enjoyin a supper of toasted crumpet, when I popped de question. "How would ye like to go down under?" says I. She gave me a dirty look. "I've told ye before, Bertie Ahern, I'm not doing that until we're married."

So I explained I meant a trip to Australia in March, en route to de White House for Paddy's Day. But it turned out she already had her bags packed, havin heard about de junket even before I did – probably from doin make-overs on some of dose dolly-bird wives of de lads in foreign affairs. She'd already bagged de aisle seat, for jayz sake, in case she had to do any networkin on de plane. "These trips ARE about promoting Irish business, after all," she says.

TUESDAY

De Minister for Arts, Heritage, de Gaeltacht and whatever yer havin yerself caused a spat at de cabinet meetin today wit her plans for de RTE transmission network. Originally we were goin to set up a separate company to run dis and RTE would have a stake, but somehow, Michelin Woman den decided to flog de whole ting off to de highest bidder, wit no RTE involvement, an circulated a "discussion" paper last week to allow people to discuss what a good idea it was.

De cabinet also approved de final version of de White Paper decommissionin de Army. It's been a hard battle to get it trew; de military outflanked us a couple of times and General McCreevy's rear was a bit exposed in Kildare on account of de Curragh bein in his constituency. But we had an advantage over de Army boys in dat dey're mostly deaf, and I tink we have dem beaten now.

WEDNESDAY

Wit de ardfheis approachin, I granted special access to Charlie Bird for a profile piece on me to go out on de six o'clock news; wit no conditions attached except dat he adopt a servile attitude at all times and not ask me any hard questions. Even so, he cunningly trapped me into a gaffe on de Spencer Dock scheme, which I was caught on camera calling a "monstrosity". Dis is true, of course: if it went ahead as planned, it would overwhelm de surroundin area – including Dermot Desmond's eco-erection. Even worse, it'd mean dat from much of de soutside of Dublin, you wouldn't be able to see de tops of de gleamin new stands at Croke Park dat I've put so much money into.

It's just not a runner, as far as I'm concerned. But, eh, I probably shouldn't have said dat, since An Bord Pleanala is supposed to be independent, an so on, blah, blah, blah. I can tell already dat Brutal will be chewin me ear about dis tomorrow. Oh joy.

THURSDAY

Sure enough, de Mead Mugger was on his feet in de Dail as soon as he got his chance, accusin me of improper behaviour and demandin I apologise to de plannin board. He suggested me comments could leave de Government open to litigation. I told him to f**k off and stop annoyin me. No I didn't, of course, I just taut dat. I also taut about anudder of his ideas lately, dat de Buke of Kells an some udder Mead-related stuff should be repatriated to de museum dere, at least for part of de year. I'm all in favour of dis, if de museum would take Brutal as well. I know I'd pay in to see his big arse in a glass case, whatever about anyone else.

FRIDAY

De first night of de ardfheis went well. Dere was a good turn-out for me openin address, and me call for de closure of Sellafield went down well. I was goin to call for de closure of de Fine Gael party too, which is anudder major source of poisonous emissions; but, eh, I decided dat while dis would certainly get a cheer, it might be misunderstood by de media. So instead I just had a swipe at deir "gung-ho militarism" for wantin to join NATO. I couldn't overdo dis line, dough, because we'd join NATO as well if we taut de public would swallow it. Also, I have to be careful in de current circumstances not to hand de army over to de Blueshirts. Dere's a tin enough line between dem, God knows.

SATURDAY

Of course, de big ting at de ardfheis was de unveiling of de new code of conduct, which basically states dat members of Fianna Fail should not engage in any activity whatever which would leave dem open to gettin caught. It was passed unanimously, provin as I said in my speech dat all de revelations of wrongdoing have left de party disappointed and angry. And as I mingled wit de adorin crowd after me address, de new mood of rectitude among members was obvious: everywhere I went people were winkin at me an sayin tings like "a code of conduct – dat's a good one!" I love de ardfheis, so I do. It's always good to see our old familiar friends from all over de country. Some of dem might smell a bit, it's true; but at least dey're ours.

SATURDAY

When I first heard about de www.bertieahern.com porno website, me big fear was dat dey'd got hold of de pictures from de holidays in Kerry last year, de day I was sunbathing in me jocks in de back garden. Dere's perverts out dere'd pay big money to see dat, right enough, I taut. An it woulda been even worse for me when Celia found out, cause she's always at me to quit wearin de oul Y-fronts an get into silk boxer shorts, tailor-made for de fuller figure.

But of course it turned out dat I wasn't on de site at all. De feckers are only usin me name to embarrass me an de Government in de hope dat we'll pay dem de million dollars dey're demandin. I got anudder reminder today; "One million dollars," it said, "or alternatively, for only 99 cents a day, you can continue to enjoy some of de hottest action on de net right here on your very own website". De bastards. I was in favour of just payin dem off, like we did wit de guards and de nurses and de bus drivers, but McCreevy says we'd need to tie it into some sort of productivity deal. "Like what?," I asked him. "Did ye ever think of sellin those holiday photographs?" he says.

SUNDAY

Willie O'Dea is de latest to have a site in his name created by dirtbirds. Personally, wit a name like "Willie," I tink he was askin for it; aldough, by dat reckoning, I don't know how Micheal "Slick Mickey" Martin has escaped so far. Anyway, we're pursuin de matter trew de official channels to see if dere's any way, legally, we can close de buggers down. But if all else fails I might have to ask Grizzly Adams, as a favour, to get some of his pals on de job. I see he skillfully managed to prevent de Shinners ard fheis from shuttin de door on a future coalition wit us; so it might be a good time to ask him if his, eh, organisation could track down dese cyber-squatters and make dem an offer dey can't refuse. Maybe dey'd settle for an attractive alternative website; like www.baseballbat.com.

MONDAY

Bad an all as de internet is, dere's even more dirt in de Flood Tribunal. Rambo was in de firin line again today, wit news dat a couple of Mayo builders paid him £150,000 over de years from money raised at horse meetins. Apparently, one of de same builders used to put bets on horses for George "effectively destitute" Redmond, an den gave him de winnings. Horses have played a very central role in Irish public life over de past couple of decades, obviously. Dat's probably why Shergar had to die: de f**ker knew too much.

I've put a lot of distance between meself an Rambo, fortunately – de terms "forty-foot" and "pole" come to mind in describing de closeness of our relationship dese days. But I was still hopin de jury in de Nevin case would come in wit a verdict today and keep us off tomorrow's front pages. Instead dey've gone out for anudder night. I told Zero O'Donoghue we shouldn't be puttin dem up in de Berkley Court; it only encourages dem.

TUESDAY

Just our luck. It was Frank Dunlop's turn in de dock today; and dough he was battin on a bit of a sticky wicket himself, his best piece of evidence was dat a Dublin city councillor demanded a bribe – God between us and all harm! – in return for his support on Quarryvale. We happen to know dat de councillor at de centre of de allegation is (a) dead and (b) a Blueshirt. Doubly unfortunate for him, to be sure, but de makins of a good week for us as soon as de press get hold of it.

Den of course de pesky Nevin jury chose today to come in wit de verdict. I don't know why it took dem so long. As I said to Celia, any woman as obsessed as she is wit clothes an make-up, an her husband barely cold in de grave, is obviously guilty. "I don't know," said Celia, fingering a dagger-shaped letter opener she bought recently, "if I'm ever in that position, I'd like to think I'd still look after my appearance." Anyway, in de circumstances, we may have to delay leakin de Fine Gael councillor's name to de press until tomorrow.

THURSDAY

De legendary journalist Sam Smyth has exposed de councillor at de centre of de bribery allegations, which has come as a great shock to us all – especially de suggestion dat de Fine Gael leader was told of de matter at de time. I sent a message of sympathy to Bonzo Bruton, saying how distressing it must be for him; how, while I was frankly relieved dat de councillor was not one of ours, I understood how unpleasant it can to have allegations of dis nature made, and if dere was any advice I could give him – about makin a clear-de-air statement to de Dail, for example – he shouldn't hesitate to call. He sent me back a short note later, acknowledging my letter and tellin me to f**k off.

FRIDAY

A quiet day, and time to enjoy de idea of Mickey Martin addressin de IMO conference, an gettin grief over de plight on junior doctors. A strike seems inevitable dere. An de more I tink of it, de better an idea it was to make him Minister for Health. Any leadership ambitions he has will have to be put on de back burner while he deals with hospital waitin lists, and hepatitis tribunals and de many udder problems of de job. An I tink I can also depend on de junior doctors and nurses to keep him tied down for a while … Hmmm … doctors and nurses … hospital beds … Micheal Martin strapped to a trolley. I tink I have an idea for a website.

MONDAY

Up to Arbour Hill for de Easter Monday commemoration. An sure enough Charlie Bird and de rest of de gang are all dere wit deir notebooks and deir microphones, lickin deir lips like a bunch of feckin piranhas in a swimmin pool.

I was a bit dubious about de backroom boys' advice to leave it 24 hours before replyin to de lies an fabrications in de Sunday papers yesterday: dey reckoned if we lured de Monday papers into it, we could give dem ALL a bloody nose, de bastards. But I enjoyed meself anyway, tellin de hacks dat I never got no money in de Burlington carpark, or de Leinster House carpark, or de multistorey carpark in de Ilac Centre, or de carpark behind de flats up on Mercer Street, or any udder carpark. I didn't get it in 1979, 1989, 1999 or 2009, I said. An in case anyone taut I was still bein anatomical wit de trute, I told dem I didn't get money from ANY unnamed person on behalf of Owen O'Callaghan, ever, or from any named person on behalf of an unnamed Owen O'Callaghan eider.

I could see de hacks weren't expectin such a fully apprehensive statement, an by de time I was finished dey had deir tails between deir legs. By contrast, I left Arbour Hill feelin all fired up, a bit like de 1916 revolutionaries must have felt. (Except of course, dey got caught).

TUESDAY

I nearly forgot, but after dat yesterday it was on to Fairyhouse for de Grand National. Dis would normally involve de risk of runnin into Jawn Brutal, because de racecourse is in de middle of his constituency. But after me tour-de-france performance dis mornin, he was nowhere to be seen. I had to present de prizes in de big race, which was won by de same team dat won de English national. If it hadda been politics, dere'da been a stewards' inquiry, I said to meself; an when I realised de winnin owner was Dermot Desmond, I taut, Jayz, de papers will have a field day wit dis. I was gonna put on dark glasses for de photographs, until me protocol adviser Denise told me dat'd only look worse. So I made de best of it. But when dey gave Dermot de £80,000 cheque an he whispered over to me "I want to make a donation to de party," I was crappin meself. He was only jokin, of course, but it was a worryin moment.

WEDNESDAY

I see Michael Woods got heckled during his speech to de ASTI in Killarney. De ASTI are always de most bolshie of de teachers unions, but even so, it was some achievement for dem to stay awake long enough to heckle durin one of

Michael's speeches. De feckers are lookin for a turty per cent increase now, radder dan wait for de "bench-marking" review in 2002, which was a wheeze we taut up durin de PPF talks to keep de party goin for anudder while. Dey're treatenin to target next year's leavin cert exams, holdin de nation's children to ransom for deir grubby demands. De two udder unions are makin similar noises, an de whole education sector is treatenin to get so ugly, I'm nearly sorry I didn't leave Mickey Martin where he was. On de udder hand, he still has de doctors' strike to look forward to, wit ninety-eight per cent of de IMO voting in favour of industrial action. "Look on de bright side," I told him, "at least it wasn't unanimous."

THURSDAY

De Government's policy of dispersin asylum seekers is proving a huge success, bringin large crowds onto de streets of de towns and villages to welcome de newcomers. Kenmare is a shining example, wit one local councillor predictin "anudder Harlem," which I presume means de town will soon have a good basketball team (some of us tink basketball is what de allegedly great Kerry football team of de 1970s was playin, but dat's anudder matter).

I know Jackie Healy Rae has been givin grief to Zero about de policy. But as I told O'Donoghue meself, if we in Dublin weren't so tolerant about people who look and speak differently to de rest of us, where would him an Jackie be?

FRIDAY

Liam Lawlor has finally stepped down from de Oireachtas committee on members interests. He says it's because of "time commitments". I'd say more about dat here, but I can't. It's because of "space commitments".

SATURDAY

Good to see de boy Roy finally gettin de recognition he deserves. Aldough dis season was a bit of an anti-climax, wit United as far ahead of de opposition as I am in de popularity ratins, it's still well deserved. Roy is de Martin McGuinness of de Premiership (widdout de curly hair, obviously). Dey bote allegedly used to be men of violence but, eh, dey've got it under control now (most of de time), and dey've become leaders on and off de pitch. Dey're bote still a bit scary, too, but dat's part of deir success.

MONDAY

Since de Blueshirts made a dog's mickey outta deir inquiry into donations to councillors, we've been very careful not to fall into de same trap. So de lads on de Star Chamber Committee have assured me dat our report will avoid reaching any conclusion whatsoever about de guilt of any of dose involved, and furdermore will be so long and boring dat only de most hardened journalists will still be conscious after readin de introduction.

Neverdeless, de boys tell me dere'll be enough in it to persuade a certain West Dublin TD to resign, which in turn should be sufficient to ensure dat de excellent workin relationship between de Government partners continues for anudder two years, or to put it anudder way, get de PDs off our backs long enough for us to tink of some way of shafting dem properly down de line.

We figure if a certain person DOES resign, dat'll also take de spotlight of any of de udders dat might come out of de report wit deir flies undone, as it were. Which is important, because we don't want too many of our lads on de independent benches – dey might form a breakaway party.

De udder good news is dat Offaly dumped Mead outta de championship yesterday. When I saw Biffo Cowen dis mornin I felt like kissin him. But I pulled meself togedder in time.

TUESDAY

Brutal has launched a savage attack on me integrity, trying to link me wit de fella from Kinsealy who, as everyone knows, I was never very friendly wit at all, even before I made a final emotional break from him on me visit to Poland recently. I reckon Bonzo is gettin desperate, because despite all de grief I'm receivin from me current and former comrades, he's still as popular as cancer. Luckily for him, dere's nobody in Fine Gael who looks like a future leader except dat little Brian Hayes fella, an he won't be a serious threat until he finishes de Leavin Cert.

WEDNESDAY

I can't tell you what a great shock it was to me when my old friend Liam Lawlor tendered his resignation today, only hours after we issued de report which put no pressure on him whatsoever. I got de message headin for de airport, an when I returned his call I found dat dere was nuttin I could do to persuade him to change his mind. But I didn't try, just in case dere was. Later on I rang Macken and Doc O'Hanlon to tank dem for de very professional, eh, job. Den I rang Harney to tell her de news. Liam Lawlor sleeps wit de fishes, I said.

THURSDAY

Of course, some people might tink it's better to have Lawlor inside de tent pissin out dan outside de tent pissin in. Aldough he was at pains to point out last night dat he would support de Government in all tings, I see already dis mornin, sources close to him have told de Indo he was offered £100,000 by a close associate of myself to act as a consultant on de Phoenix Park casino project. Dis is lies, of course. Dere was no £100,000, and de guy who didn't offer it was no close associate of mine, or any udder kind of associate, and besides I have never supported a casino in de Phoenix Park, or de Burlington car park, or any udder park, anywhere. I'm totally opposed to gamblin, in fact, an I'll lay any odds against anyone provin udderwise.

FRIDAY

Down in Cork for de opening of a £1 million indoor hurlin arena (What will dey tink of next – outdoor snooker?), to learn dat Dessie Richardson has issued a statement pissin all over … eh, clarifyin de Lawlor story. Dessie's de lad who came up wit de idea for me annual fundraisin event, de £120-a-plate (we trow in de food for free) dinner. He also wiped out de party debt in de early 1990s, after I appointed him to de £70,000 job. Dere's nuttin he doesn't know about de subject of raisin money, but when he says he never raised it (de subject – of money) wit Lawlor, I believe him implisit … impliscit … eh, fully. De udder good news is dat de Blueshirts have been forced to apologise to Tommy Morris for de balls-up wit de report on councillors donations. So, amazingly enough, we've come outta de whole councillor donation ting lookin better dan dem. No wonder I tank God daily for de gift dat is Jawn Brutal.

SATURDAY

On de subject of dat udder f**ker, de hoor dat's tryin to overturn Hughie O'Flaherty's job in de courts, and who referred to Celia as me "mistress," I told de media yesterday dat dis was not wordy of comment. And now I'm in trouble wit herself. "What do you mean it's not worthy of comment? You comment on everything else!" she says, in a big huff. When I suggested that head mistress would be a more appropriate description for herself, she gave me one of dose looks. You can never win with wimmin.

SUNDAY

We won de confidence motion as expected but, Jayzus, it's been a gruellin Dail session. When I listened to Baldy Quinn an Brutal yappin on about de Government's incompetence de udder day, I was nearly tempted to get up an announce a general election, just to ruin de f***ers' holidays. Baldy would have been particularly put out, I reckon; spendin a mont knockin on doors in grim housin estates instead of sippin chianti in de sun somewhere foreign.

I prefer a pint of Bass in Kerry meself, of course, an I'll be knockin a few of dem back to celebrate survivin de last few monts. We felt like de Eyetalians against Holland in Euro 2000, except dat we had TWO men sent off, Foley an Lawlor, an our lone striker, "Dead-eye" McCreevy, was too busy shootin his mout off to hit de Opposition goal. I tink come de autumn de team may have to undergo a period of rebuilding, wit new blood in key positions like finance. I need someone young and dynamic dere, and above all someone I can trust to keep his mout shut. Me brudder Noel, maybe.

MONDAY

I tink I better leave Noel on de back benches anudder while yet. Now dat Maurice is in de Lord Mayor of Dublin, de dynasty's grip on power is secure enough – I don't want de press comparin me to Saddam Hussein, or one of dose tin-can dictators. But I'm delighted for Maurice. I tink he has de qualities to do a good job for Dublin, which is de most important ting (well ok, de most important ting is keepin Tony Gregory outta de Mansion House, but doin a good a job for Dublin is a close second).

TUESDAY

De Orangemen have been refused permission to march on de Garvaghy Road next Sunday. Dey shoulda taken Dawson Street while dey had de chance, because if I know me big brudder, dere'll be no second invitation. But now Trimble's in a huff because I praised de Parades Commission for de ban. I heard him on de radio bein asked what he taut about de sight of de UFF turnin up at Drumcree in funny teeshirts, like a bleedin stag party in Temple Bar, an he blamed me! De feckin cheek! An him responsible for de whole mess in de first place for his hand-holding antics wit Paisley de last time de marchers got trew: de pair of dem prancing around like a gay couple after gettin married. I may have made mistakes, from time to time; but nobody can accuse me of ever holdin hands wit a bloke, dat's for sure.

WEDNESDAY

All good news today. Anudder record set of exchequer figures; de FAI votin to cap spendin on deir No-Income Park; an Tony Blair's young fella found drunk and incapable in a street in London. I tink Blair should be grateful: if de lad had been drunk and capable he coulda got into more trouble. An I know we've all overdone it when we were teenagers – I was a hoor for de Bass meself at dat age. But de ting is, de Blairs' family embarrassment will be good for me in de polls, I reckon. Despite me irregular domestic situation, ye never hear of my girls makin fools of demselves. It's all about strong leadership. De best news of all, dough, is de FAI vote. It was a long-shot to start wit, but if dat stadium ever gets built now, dere'll be a blue moon in de sky an Charlie McCreevy will have joined a Trappist monastery. I don't tink we need hold our breaths.

THURSDAY

Fintan McCool was writin in de Irish Times de udder day dat de Government tinks "denial is a river in Egypt". Well, as he'd have found out if he wasn't too much of a smartarse to check in an atlas, denial is a river in de Sudan as well as Egypt; but you never get de full story about anyting from dese newspaper fellas. Vinnie Browne was also havin a go at me, for allegedly ignorin blatant evidence dat Fianna Fail money was misappropriated by certain individuals down de years. Dese are matters for de tribunals, as I've said repeatedly, and it would be inappropriate to air dem even in a secret diary.

But I would say dis: me memory is not what it used to be (or at least what I tink it used to be), and 1989 – when many of dese alleged allegations were allegedly taking place – was a long time ago, after all. It was de year of de Cuban missile crisis, if I recall correctly, an de Beatles played de old Carlton cinema, I tink, an Kevin Heffernan was still playin for de Dubs, if I'm not wrong. So while I'm assisting de tribunals to de best of my ability, I'm just sayin I may not be able to give dem all de detail dey'd like. I've explained dis to Mary Harney an, more dan anyone, she understands how long ago de 1980s were. De PDs were a serious force in Irish politics den, as I recall.

SATURDAY

De udder plan is dat we hang on to power as long as possible, an maybe postpone de elections for a few years in de interests of national stability, while an emergency committee comprisin meself, Noel and Maurice runs de country. It depends on how de polls look in de autumn. If tings go well over de summer, we might just cut an run an see if we can't catch de Opposition on de hop. I'm hopin dat when de freeze on drinks prices takes effect, combined wit de late openin hours, people will be too sloshed to care come October. Especially if we held de election on a Friday: a lot of Labour's support get deir wages Thursday an dey might be too hungover next day to vote. An who knows, maybe if de Dubs win Sam in September and I got Maurice to decree free drink in all city bars for a month.

MONDAY

De game is up wit O'Flaherty. De European Investment Bank lads were on to us trew de back channels over de weekend to say dat dere was more chance of Shergar and Lord Lucan gettin de vice-presidency on a job-share dan dere was of Hughie securing de necessary votes. Come to tink of it, dey said, Shergar and Lord Lucan had excellent credentials for de job since dey'd bote disappeared widdout trace, which was one of de qualities expected of successful nominees to de EIB. Dey were very annoyed dat de affair had attracted publicity to de bank, which until dis had been a better-kept secret dan de turd secret of Fatima, dey added. And dey didn't care who we gave de nomination to now so long as it was someone about as well-known as a nun's knickers. I explained all dis to McCreevy, but he's as tick as two extra-tick planks and he's still refusing to back down. He tink's dey're bluffing.

TUESDAY

Tanks be to Jayzus, O'Flaherty has fallen on his sword. I was on de point of sending someone around to give him a push when I heard de news. Celia's distraught, of course, and is planning anudder high-profile visit to offer Mrs O'Flaherty her condolences. I told her if she does, to let her know dat we'll fix Hughie up furder down de line if a suitable position, like assistant gate-keeper in Herbert Park, arises. But personally I haven't felt as relieved about anyting since de last time Jawn Brutal survived a leadership challenge. De challenge for my leadership now is to put de maximum distance between me and McCreevy. He was still insisting it wasn't an iceberg even as de ship went down. But, eh, I slipped into one of de lifeboats two days ago and I've been rowing like f**k ever since.

WEDNESDAY

When I heard dat a member of de Irish soccer team had put his foot trew de sun-roof of a Ban Garda's car, me first taught was it must be Roy. Me second taut was: I hope he didn't do his ankle. I was on to de Zero O'Donoghue straightaway to ensure dat all necessary steps would be taken: cover-up, charges dropped, Ban Garda transferred to immediate tour of duty in East Timor – dat sort of ting. Den Zero told me dat de lads involved were Phil Babb and Mark Kennedy, and we bote agreed dat in de circumstances, justice would have to be seen to be done. "Lock dem up and trow away de keys," I said.

THURSDAY

Certain people are urging me to reshuffle de Cabinet, moving you know who to something wit a lower profile. I was tinkin it would be funny to make him Minister for de Gaeltacht, since he can hardly speak feckin English never mind de udder national language. But I've never been a man to act precip ... precipit ... eh, in a hurry, and I'm not starting now. Yes, de Government does look about as fresh as a week-old sandwich at de moment, and even apart from shafting McCreevy it might also be a good idea to promote a few new faces in place of people like Mickey Woods, who's been minister for someting or udder since Dev put him in charge of coal-rationing during de Emergency. And I know dat people sometimes accuse me of inertia. But my feeling is, at least with inertia, you know where you stand.

FRIDAY

I woulda loved to be a fly on de wall when McCreevy had his briefing wit de Pol Corrs. I didn't tink he'd go trew wit it, and I believe Mandy had to push him in de door at de last minute. But he seems to have done de needful: ate a big helping of humble pie and managed to keep it down at least until he got outta de room. He said where HE was from, people didn't resign (right enough, I taut, dey're stubborn f**ckers in Kildare), but he admitted he wouldn't be puttin de O'Flaherty affair "in his CV". Dis is true, as it happens: I was studying his CV today (along wit Biffo's and a few of de young tings who might be in line for promotion) and dere was nuttin about O'Flaherty in it anywhere. I had to write it in meself wit a red marker.

SATURDAY

Fair play to Mick McCarthy. When he picked Jason McAteer for de vacant right-wing position on de Irish football team, I taut it was de worst nomination since a certain person insisted Hugh O'Flaherty was de right man for de EIB job. But he played a blinder wit de rest of dem tonight and aldough dey trew away a two goal lead (de second-half reshuffle was a bit rash, I taut, even if de team was as tired-lookin as de Government by den), de result is an excellent start to de campaign and gives us a good chance of qualifyin for de World Cup – wit all de national euphoria dat brings – come de end of next year. Around which time we'll be preparing for de general election, if tings go to plan. Not dat I would be so cynical as to use sport for political gain. But when I was posing wit de winning dog in de derby in Shelbourne Park tonight, I couldn't help tinkin dat dere was flies on one of us, and it wasn't me.

SUNDAY

Anudder bleedin draw in Croke Park, dis time in de All-Ireland Final. De GAA's bank balance is growin faster dan de budget surplus, and de new stand is risin like de inflation rate as a result. Referees are very quick to blow de whistle (de way de PDs used to be, before we put manners on dem) when de sides are level at de end of de 70. And it's no skin off my nose, but you have to feel sorry for culchies from de wilds of Kerry and Galway who have to make de trip again for de replay. Never mind de replay, you have to feel sorry for dem regardless.

MONDAY

Tankfully dere wasn't a GAA ref involved in de Olympic 5000 metres final, or Sonia and de little Romanian would be meetin again in two weeks time. It was a great race. I haven't been dat much on de edge of me seat since Hughie O'Flaherty hit de wall in de EIB nomination maratton, when he had de finishin line in sight. We made discreet inquiries in Sydney about whedder dey could hold up de medal ceremony for 48 hours so I'd have time to get down dere and share de rostrum, but de Aussies said dat was a "rat-shit" idea, which apparently means bad, so I sent Sonia a congratulatory fax instead. It's a terrible pity she didn't win de gold when she was dat close, but as Zero O'Donogue is always sayin at our meetins on de asylum seekers issue, de Romanians are very hard to catch.

TUESDAY

Today was de first Nort-Sout Ministerial Council meetin to be held in de Republic – a great day for Oireland. We didn't actually do anyting except read de joint communique de foreign affairs and NIO boys had written beforehand, but de optics of de event were everyting. Trimble spoiled de photograph a bit by lookin like he'd had dodgy curry de night before, aldough any internal problems he has are from de result of de Sout Antrim bye-election. Him and Mallon wouldn't speak to each udder all mornin and de lunch, as you can imagine, was a bundle of laughs.

WEDNESDAY

Down to Ballysomewhere for me annual appearance at de Ploughin Championships, which naturally was de signal for de skies to open. But dis is an important opportunity to demonstrate to farmers dat I own wellies and dat I understand de problems dey face: muck and shite, and so on. I also took de opportunity to tell de press dat I once ploughed wit horses meself. I've had a few harrowing experiences too, but dat was mostly while listening to Bonzo Bruton in de Dail. Anyway, de organisers were collectin signatures in support of making ploughing an Olympic sport, believe it or not. And you know, I reckon de only way de Irish team could make a big impression in de track and field is wit a plough. But I didn't sign de petition, just in case it was a disguised expenses claim for CJH. You can't be too careful wit dat hoor.

THURSDAY

Arrived in Kilkenny overnight for de two-day party love-in. But de atmosphere has been spoiled by a couple of disastrous sets of figures: first United's 3-1 defeat last night and now an Irish Times opinion poll which shows de Government is about as popular as de Ebola virus. Den dere was all dat violence at de IMF meetin in Prague dis week and McCreevy making it back widdout a scratch. And as if dis wasn't bad enough, TDs and senators have just been told dey have to cough up £300 a year each to party funds. De mood among de parliamentary party is ugly. And God knows, dey were ugly enough to start wit.

SATURDAY

No luck for Sonia in de Ten Tousand metres. She let herself get outta touch early on (a bit like de Minister for Finance) and dere was never any hope of recovery after dat. Dem Africans run fast, as Zero is always pointing out. Still, she's a great girl. De RTE lads were wonderin what she'd do next: one lad said she could run in de maratton in four years time, but Eamonn Coghlan taut she'd probably retire. I'm wonderin would she consider runnin for us in Sout Tipperary, in de Noel Davern Invitational, second leg. She looks like one of ours: but I better get Mickey Martin to make discreet inquiries around Cobh.

SUNDAY

Anudder bad result for United, tanks to a moment of individual brilliance by dat French lad Terry Onree. Dere's a moral in dis, of course. Alex Ferguson reshuffled his team Wednesday night, promoting some new faces to de front bench. Den he put out his best side today. Neider move worked. Dis proves de need for caution in all tings – which is why I'm sitting tighter dan Roy Keane's haircut for de moment. De good news is dat Zero O'Donoghue's car was caught doin 100 miles and hour in Kerry and he got off. De car has de same powers as a police patrol vehicle, as has been pointed out, so it's allowed to speed when necessary. Dey were probably chasin Romanians.

MONDAY

Me stomach is still a bit dodgy after de trip to Seoul, but dis is part of de price you pay for bein de leader of a world power. De main ting is dat de Asia-Europe summit went well, tank God, even dough I was forced to give de Brits a smack on de wrist for recognisin Nort Korea in advance of EU discussions on de subject. I personally wouldn't recognise Nort Korea, but den I wouldn't recognise China unless someone showed it to me on a map. Luckily, de foreign boys had turrowly briefed me on our "Asia Strategy", which is a plan we hatched up a while back for openin embassies and consulates anywhere dey grow rice and dere's a few bob to be made, like Singapore and Shanghai. Of course, we're also very concerned about de issue of, eh, human rights in de region, as I informed Premier Mattedhair of Malaysia in no uncertain terms after he'd told Europe to butt out on de issue.

TUESDAY

Dere's no end to dis international statesman stuff. No sooner was I back in Dublin dan last night I had to go to a dinner up at de Castle for de President of Uganda: Mr Muselini, or someting. I was stuck beside him at one point and I didn't know what to say, so I made de mistake of askin how Idi Amin was dese days. Dis went down like a lead balloon. Den I dug de hole deeper by tryin to remember a rhyme about de fat fella I heard back in de '70s. It must have been when he fled de country or someting, because it was all: "Where Idi?..Idi here?Or Idi dere?", and so on. De bit I remember was: "Idi in heaven? Or Idi in hell? Or Idi just not feeling well?" Anyway, Mr Muselini didn't remember it eider, apparently. Jayzus, was I relieved when Liz O'Donnell came over to him to discuss de bilateral aid programme.

WEDNESDAY

Just when I was startin to miss domestic politics, dere was uproar in de Dail today on de issue of plastic bags. For f*** sake! John Gormless of de Greens got so worked up about de issue he had to be trown out, and Bonzo Bruton was tryin to make mountain out of me supposedly misleadin de house on which minister was responsible for de legislation. As if I give a sh**e one way or de udder. Nobody wanted to know anyting about me performance at de Asian Summit, needless to say. Feckin plastic bags: de big threat to world peace! But speakin of peace, at least dere was some good news today. Namely dat de Provos have reopened contacts wit General de Charolais and are allowing anudder inspection of de arms dumps by Marti Atasafari and de African lad. Dis should help Trimble, who has finally decided to kick sand in Jeffrey Donaldson's face on Saturday, and not before time.

THURSDAY

De udder good news is dat de PDs are still here to cheer us up. De Rottweiler General's plans for a revamp have been de source of great amusement around de house all week, particularly his proposal to rename dem de Ridicule, eh, I mean de Radical Party, wit him as supreme leader. Apparently, he also wants to reposition dem somewhere to de left of Republican Sinn Fein on de national question, wit Harney and O'Donnell in de roles of Maud Gonne and Countess Markiewiez, presumably, and himself givin de oration at de grave of Dessie O'… I mean, O'Donovan Rossa. Contrary to what people tink, me and de Rottweiler are best buddies and, personally, I'd have him in Fianna Fail at de drop of a hat (aldough he'd have to stop wit dat United Ireland stuff, of course). We could do wit his towering intellect in dis party, if only to keep Mansergh company at Cairde Fail dinners. But, eh, he's right to shake de PDs up a bit, because de way tings are now, dey're headed straight for Bolivia *(Surely "Oblivion"? – Ed).*

FRIDAY

Down to Mayo for what I taut would be a triumphant day-long tour of de country, but instead saw me heckled by protesters everywhere I went over de trettened withdrawal of a local cancer screening service. Mickey Martin mentioned someting about dis at de Cabinet meetin on Tuesday, but he assured me de local opposition was slight. I knew dat f****r needed watchin! I was very tempted to make a snap announcement dat not only would de screening service be retained but dat de Department of Health would be decentralised to Belmullet, starting next week. As it was, I confined meself to saying we'd have a long, hard look at de issue and we wouldn't do anyting rash. Maybe we can transfer resources from somewhere less politically sensitive, like Cork.

SATURDAY

De collapse of de peace process has been averted yet again, tanks to Trimble's win in de UUC vote. But aldough de defeat of de no-camp has to be welcomed, it was not widdout de usual messin. Dis time Trimble wants to trow de Shinners off de cross-border bodies if dey don't do de business wit de General. And ,of course, dere'll be yet anudder UUC meetin in de New Year to review de situation, and Jeffrey will popping up again like a turd in a train toilet. But at least we should be safe until Christmas. And ye never know, maybe a jolly man wit a beard will put something in Trimble's sock. What about it, Gerry?

MONDAY

We knew de Blueshirts were plannin a pre-Christmas advertisin campaign, and dat dey were spendin a lot of money on it. But when we saw deir "Celtic Snail" ting yesterday, well, it was all we could do not to piss ourselves laughin. What were dey tinkin? It even rhymes wit Fine Gael, for Jayz' sake! We've already run off experimental posters featurin Jawn Brutal's head on de slug's body, and de focus groups are reacting very positively, I hear. As for de 68-page manifesto on what dey're going to do when dey're in Government (pinch demselves and wake up, I'd say), you'd find more original tinkin in de collected works of Westlife. Brutal keeps yappin on about me bein indecisive. De cheek of him – I can't make up me mind whedder he's serious or he's just tryin to rise me.

TUESDAY

De Cabinet meetin decided to finally bite de bullet on de taxi issue, and go for complete deregulation. Basically dis means dat anyone who wants can get a taxi-plate, subject to certain basic criteria like mental fitness (dis is a new requirement for de trade) and no criminal convictions in de last week or so. De PDs are gung ho for it anyway. Dey're hopin to become identified wit de issue – an if de taximen kick up as much shite about it as I tink dey will, dey're welcome to it.

WEDNESDAY

What wit de blockade of de airport and de rest, de parliamentary party meetin was dominated by de taxi issue. De grassroots were nervous: me brudder Noel was critical of de move and Ivor Callely, who for some reason feels de same way about taximen as Mary Robinson does about refugees, assured us dat de protests wouldn't blow over in a hurry. I told de party to remain calm, it was all just a devious, cunning plot to discredit de PDs. I had Mary Harney in de back of de cab, I said, an I was taking her on a scenic route to de next general election. Dat sort of ting always goes down well wit de country TDs, and dey trooped out slappin me on de back, sayin: "Good man, Bertie, you're a cure hoor, right enough." I was only out of de meetin when Macken rang me wit news of Austin Deasy's motion of no confidence. "It looks bad, boss," he says, "they could be gettin a new leader." Jayzus! Dis was serious, I taut. It's bad enough dat de social partnership is collapsin around our ears and dat strikers can't even get taxis to deir workplaces to mount pickets. But if we lose Bruton, we're f**ked.

THURSDAY

So we swung into action immediately yesterday, first tellin de printers to hold off puttin Homer's head on de slug posters, and den scourin Leinster House to see who was behind Deasy's stalkin horse. De word was Baldy Noonan was disgruntled, but would not be makin a move at dis point. Dukes had been disgruntled for a long time, but he had his gruntle back now and he was as happy as a long string of misery could be. We got Claffey to make inquiries from de hacks, but dey had zilch too. It was weird – dere was nuttin happening anywhere. Some of Brutal's people even sounded us out to see if we knew what was goin on. Finally we decided it was only Deasy on one of his solo runs. Den we heard dat Brutal's supporters were scarin people into line wit de rumour dat we were plannin an election for de early New Year. So just to be on de safe side we started spreadin de rumour too.

FRIDAY

In de midst of de panic, I had a meetin wit de Austrian Chancer *(er, "Chancellor?"* – *Ed)* Wolfgang Schuttle. He tinks I'm his best buddy because I sat beside him at one de EU summits when no-one else would on account of his coalition wit de Freedom Party, an I ruined de picture for de press boys, who wanted to portray him as a social leopard *("Leper?" – Ed)*. I told him I knew perfectly well how you could end up sharin Government wit a minority party of mad right-wingers. He's also grateful because, even dough de sanctions have been lifted, nobody except us would invite him to visit. So we had a good long lunch, an we talked about life in Vienna ("do dey still have de gondolas?" I asked) and EU enlargement and de European Army... eh ... I mean de Rapid Reaction Force. I hope I'm not keeping you from your work, Teeshock, he said. I said no worries, we had all day. In fact, I'd heard de taximen were marchin on de Dail, and I didn't want to be around if dey dragged Molloy out and tied him to de back of a car.

SATURDAY

In Zagreb for a meetin of EU leaders to discuss de situation in de Baltics. Or de Balkans, maybe, I don't know – I leave dose details to de civil servants. De main ting is I had a long meetin wit Blair about de Nordern Ireland Polis Bill, and I told him we couldn't yet recommend dat catalics join de new force. He said dat was OK, dey didn't want any bloody Fenians in it anyway. So we had a bit of a laugh about dat an den we went back to discussin de Serbs and de Croats. And, ye know, it was good to be somewhere peaceful like de former Yugoslavia and out of de madness of Dublin for a while.

MONDAY

Dere's no pleasin Celia. She's always pesterin me to do photo shoots for de Hello and de OK magazines – "At home wit de Taoiseach and his first lady" – dat sort of shite. But den we get a glamorous spread of our holiday in Lanzarote in de Star and de Mirror an she's not happy eider. "Mortified," was de word she used. All right, if I'da known at de time, I'd a sucked in me belly a bit for de sun-bading picture. But, eh, overall I taut it looked fairly classy, meself. I particularly liked de one of me "enjoyin a quiet moment" on me own. A lot of de Fianna Fail grassroots would prefer to have Celia outta de picture on a more permanent basis, so dat's one dey can cut out and keep.

De luxury hotel we stayed in (croissants for breakfast – very posh) had been recommended by several people we know, and it turned out Liam Lawlor had been dere only a few weeks before. Talk about a narrow escape! De hotel people taut he was a lovely man and kept askin me why he was bein persecuted in Ireland for his religious beliefs. Den it turned out dat not only was Seamus Mallon staying at de same place as us, but bleedin John Hume was on de island as well. Dere was a danger we were all gonna get togedder one evenin – dat woulda been a bundle of laughs! – but luckily it never happened. We met a good few Irish people dough, an I posed for pictures and made relaxed conversation wit dem: "De hard man, howya? Ye won't forget me come de election will ye?" and dat kind of ting. It was a grand holiday, all in all. But de photos in de papers put de icin on de cake, especially if it turns out to be an election year. De lads in headquarters will be trilled – ye can't buy dat sort of publicity.

TUESDAY

Speakin of elections, me brudder Noel was interviewed yesterday by de *Cork Examiner* and told dem he expected a June election. Given me repeated assertions dat de Government is goin full-term, it's a matter of concern to me dat me own brudder doesn't believe me. He also said dat I was "difficult to read" (so is de *Cork Examiner*, I taut) and dat he was "straighter" dan me. But, eh, I was always more of a political animal dan Noel. I remember when we were kids him and Maurice would be playin cowboys and indians, shootin guns an arrows, and I'd always be de one offering arbitration, urgin de two sides to get around a table and work something out widdin de confines of de social partnership. I was about five den, but I knew where I was goin.

WEDNESDAY

I know a lot more about Cyprus, on account of us havin de Army and de guards dere on peace-keepin duties. It's very like Ireland, in fact, because de island is divided in two parts – called Armenia and Azerbaijan – and de task of bringin dese mutually distrustful peoples togedder has been a long and painful one. Anyway, I had a meetin wit a man claimin to be de president. I don't know which of de gangs he was from, but I told him we were right behind him in his application for EU membership and we'd also use our seat on de UN Security Council to help ease de tension on de island, even if dis meant bombin de shite outta de udder side. Den one of de officials suggested we visit de "buffer zone" and I said, no way, Celia won't let me take me clothes off in public ever again. But he meant de area patrolled by de Irish Army, between de Greek and Turkish sectors. "Jayzus," says I. "De Greeks and de Turks are fightin here as well? Dis island's in a worse situation dan I taut."

THURSDAY

I'm gettin confused at dis stage, but I tink we're in Morocco. It's Africa, anyway – dere's lads called Muhammad everywhere and de barmen in de hotel have never even heard of Bass. I met de King – Muhammad VI (I don't know where de udder five were, but I wasn't askin), and I was assurin him dat we fully supported Morocco's application to join de EU, when one of de foreign boys gave me a dig in de ribs and said dey weren't applying, so I changed de subject deftly. De real reason we were dere, it turned out, was to assure dem of our support for attempts to resolve de dispute in de Western Sahara. Morocco claims dis territory, which you would tink wouldn't bodder anyone, but it turns out dere are people livin dere and dey want to be independent. God knows why. I promised de king we'd do everytyng we could and den I took him aside and told him quietly about me plans to build a National Stadium. "If we fix you up in de Western Sahara," says I, "will ye sort us out wit a bit of sand?"

FRIDAY

Bein out foreign is all very well, but de best ting about travellin is de comin home, I always tink. I felt like kissin de ground at de airport when we got in yesterday evening. But, eh, I wouldn't want people comparin me to de Pope (who has nuttin like my approval ratings, for one ting) or dey might start talkin about celibacy, and I have enough trouble over de Celia as it is. Speakin of which, we had a bit of a delay at de airport while dey were tryin to find enough trucks to carry her holiday shoppin off de plane. But finally we got reinforcements from de Army, and den it was straight home. I was lookin forward to a pint in Fagan's but I taut I'd check in wit Government Buildings first. "Welcome back, Taoiseach," dey said, "Don't forget you have a meetin tonight with Gerry Adams to discuss de crisis in de peace process." Jayzus, I said to meself; let's hit de Road to Morocco.

MONDAY

It looks like de Blueshirt leadership contest will be a straight fight between Noonan and Kenny. Ivan Yates was de one we most feared, but in a devious, covert operation last week – as soon as Bruton was shafted – some of our back room boys hit Yates's bookie shops in Wexford and backed him heavily to be de next leader. I don't know de full details (I never ask about de covert "ops") but, eh, a lot of it was in doubles and trebles, wit de udder legs bein greyhound races. Den we pulled de dogs out at de last minute so all de money piled onto Ivan. Before he copped what was happenin, he was facin a pay-out of millions on himself if he won de leadership.

Meanwhile, Noonan looks like a shoo-in, but I tink I can deal wit him. I know some people in Fine Gael are saying dey should elect Enda Kenny because he's de one most like me, but if anybody writes dat in de papers, I'll sue.

TUESDAY

It's been clear to me for some time dat Ned "Babe" O'Keeffe's position at de Department of Agriculture is unintelligible *(er, "untenable"? – Ed)*, so I had him in dis mornin for a man-to-man talk. De Opposition likes to criticise me for my supposed inability to take harsh decisions, but of course dey couldn't be more wrong. I laid it on de line to Ned, straight. I told him he was doin a great job and dat he had my full support, but dat, eh, if he felt like resignin for whatever reason, I wouldn't stand in his way.

Unfortunately, Baldy Quinn started badgerin me about de matter in de Dail later on. De overhead lights were reflectin off his forehead de way dey do, and in a weak moment I failed to change de subject, or get de Ceann Comhairle to have Quinn trown out. And now de Pinkoes tink dey've forced me into shaftin Ned. I'd hate to give dem de satisfaction, naturally, so I rang O'Keeffe afterwards and said dat whatever he was tinkin of doin, he should put it off for a few days. He said he was tinkin of gettin something to eat. But I'd say he was just puttin a brave face on it.

WEDNESDAY

De Abbey Teeater is talkin about a move over de river to de soutside. It'll be over my dead body too, if it does. I told de board dere'd be Government dosh available, so long as dey stayed where dey were. But if dey move outta de constituency, dey can go beggin to McCreevy instead, an see how dey like it. Dere's more culture in yoghurt dan dat fella – he'd like to witdraw de subvention altogedder and encourage de actors "into de labour force," as he puts it. But he can't help it, he's a Mickey Mulchie. It's different when you're a Dub – de teeater is in your blood.

THURSDAY

We were tryin to keep it hush-hush, but one of de Scottish newspapers has blown de whistle on de row over me trip to Scotland. De plan was I would go over on Sunday, watch Celtic beat de Huns at Parkhead, have a couple of bevvies, and den open a famine memorial in Lanarkshire, wherever dat is. But a Labour MP criticised de timin of de visit, suggestin it would seen as "triumphalist" if Celtic won.

Of course, I know only too well dat someting like a famine memorial can be a politically divisive issue. For de Catalics in Scotland, de famine was a great tragedy; whereas for de Prods, it was a bit of a laugh. I fully respect bote dese traditions, an I was hopin dat we could bring dem togedder in de ceremony. After all, I know from previous Old Firm derbies dat de Rangers fans sing 'De Fields of Attenry' too, albeit wit different words. But apparently de Scots fear de visit might heighten sectarian tensions, and maybe put my life at risk. Naturally, I don't wish to heighten sectarian tensions, so I'm not goin.

FRIDAY

We leaked an internal party memo to de Blueshirts yesterday, to de effect dat Bernard "Woody" Allen was de potential Fine Gael leader who struck most fear into de hearts of Fianna Fail, and dat we were all hopin and prayin dey wouldn't have de wisdom and foresight to elect him. Unfortunately, dey didn't fall for it and he pulled out last night. Den Mitchell witdrew dis mornin, as expected. He woulda been a tough opponent, particularly since he's still gettin a lot of public sympaty over de liver transplant. But de Gay Mitchell factor – his inability to get a brudder transplant – told against him.

So dat left Noonan and Kenny, and, not surprisingly, de parliamentary party opted for old Baldy in de end. De only surprise was dat, in his victory speech, Noonan started comin up wit policies, which I taut was against de rules of de leadership contest. He wants to ban all corporate donations, apparently, and he's committed de party to de European social model. He loves America, he says, but if he was "old, or sick, or poor," he'd radder be in Europe. True enough, I taut, Fine Gael would never have survived anywhere else.

SATURDAY

I missed it earlier in de week, but apparently a bloke called "Sharon" is de new prime minister of Israel. Cowen tells me he's a real hard-liner (probably because of de raggin he got in school over his name – like de lad in de Johnny Cash song) and he'll probably bomb de shite out of de Palestinians de first time dey laugh at him. I sent him a telegram of congratulations, anyway. But it's just as well we're gettin our boys outta de Lebanon.

MONDAY

Still a bit tired after de flight back from Washington, aldough at least de jetlag doesn't have a hangover for company dis year. Dat's de only advantage of havin a bible-tumper in de White House. Bush is not as up for a party as Clinton was but, eh, at least ye could leave yer wife in de same room wit him for five minutes. If ye had a wife, dat is: Celia wasn't invited, of course, and I'll be hearin about it until next March. I got on all right wit George W, all de same. He told me not to mind de reports about his lack of interest in foreign policy. He was looking forward to visiting Ireland at de first opportunity, he said: "I've heard a lot of good things about Rejykavik." He even made a joke about his diction, saying how he speaks de same way James Joyce writes (like shite, I tink he meant). I told him not to be apologisin: I had de odd dictionary problem meself and it hadn't stopped me becomin a universally-inspected world leader.

   We got back to Dublin in time for Paddy's Day, such as it was, and I spent a couple of hours freezin me b******s off at Leopardstown, listening to American bands dat had been rerouted from de main parade. It was a turrowly miserable occasion. I'd almost forgotten why we go to such lents to get outta de country on March 17th.

TUESDAY

CJH was rushed into hospital overnight, and it looks like de end. Dis is a very sad time for us all. A time for us to pause and reflect on what a truly great statesman he was. His achievements as a minister have been well-documented: de free toot-brushes for children, de extension of de bus-pass to artists, de draining of de Shannon, de founding of de welfare state, and above all de ending of a situation where child labourers could be forced to work for 14 hours a day down de mines. As everyone knows, he led de country outta de economic depression of de 1980s, but in my opinion, he doesn't get enough credit for leadin us into it in de first place, widdout which we wouldn't know how well off we are today. Of course, his firm leadership on de Nort laid de foundations for de peace process and....Hold on, dere's anudder announcement from de hospital...Mr Haughey has recovered consciousness and is out of intensive care. F**k! What do we have to do to get rid of de bastard?

WEDNESDAY

De pressure is growin on me to become personally involved in de teachers' dispute, an use me legendary negotiatin skills to cut a deal. But as I told de Dail today, in a conciliatory but firm statement, de feckers better start gettin real if dey want to negotiate wit me. If dey won't play ball wit de PPF and de benchmarking, dey're "barkin up de wrong tree," I said. And speakin as someone who was up every tree in Nort Dublin durin de Rambo investigation, I know me forestry. Come to tink of it, I can always tell Michael Woods from de trees, too, aldough deir personalities do have a lot in common.

Meanwhile, it looks like we could be runnin outta luck on de Foot and Mout front. Joe Walsh says dere's a suspected case in Loud, which is de most likely we've had yet. It's not confirmed, he says, but I'm tinkin if it walks like a duck, and quacks like a duck, den it must be a duck, eh, even if it's a sheep. Michael Smith says de Army is on stand-by and he can have a "cordon sanitaire" around de area widdin hours. I told him it'd be better just to seal it off. De test results are due in de mornin. We're all holdin our brets.

THURSDAY

De mood was sombre as I told de Dail dat de case had been confirmed. It's a crisis whatever way ye look at it, but eh, it could be worse. Our boys in Brussels are already on de job, stressin dat Loud is not really an integral part of de State. Dat we won it in a card game during de Treaty negotiations in 1921, and dat really, it's a law unto itself, like Sout Armagh. It's not dat far from de trute, in fact. But if necessary, we'll introduce emergency legislation to make Loud independent (maybe we could have de second U2 concert dere, while we're at it). De Eurocrats have bought de line so far, anyway, wit de result dat de automatic EU ban on food imports applies to Loud only, and not to de 25-county Free State area. I don't know what we'll do if anudder county goes down. But, eh, we'll cross dat mat when we come to it.

FRIDAY

I'd only arrived in Stockholm last night, when I ran into Blair. And what do ye know? Despite havin piles of smoulderin sheep de lent and bret of de country, de f***er is still tinkin of callin a general election on May de Turd. He was tellin as much to meself and Yer-mano Prodi, until he noticed a TV camera sneakin up behind him, and den he pretended he was talkin about de FA Cup Final, or someting. De nerve of de fella! Still, I shook his hand, slapped him on de back, and wished him well. Den I went back to me hotel room for a shower, and burned me clothes.

Later on, de Irish hacks in de press corps collared me wit de news dat Beverly Flynn had lost her libel case. Of course, I declined to comment on de grounds dat dere might be an appeal. Dis was a bit like waiting for de results of de second test on a suspect sheep but, eh, it bought me time. De important ting is I have had absolutely no contact wit Beverly during de incubation period, so I'm confident dat, whatever happens, nuttin's going to stick to me.

MONDAY

Tony Blair's embarrassment over de way he was forced to pull de plug on his May election emphasises yet again what a turrowly ingenious politician I am. For de last year I've been listenin to media pundits and udder so-called experts predictin dat I would call an election early dis year, despite me repeated assurances dat we as a Government were goin all de way to de terminus. But no, de smarty-pants political correspondents taut dey knew better – not to mention me own brudder Noel. Dey were anonymous in agreement dat Bertie would go to de country in June. Well, it's a good job dey were wrong, because as smelly as it is at de best of times, I couldn't go to de country now widdout gettin drowned in disinfectant. Maybe it was only me alleged tendency to procreate on all de major decisions dat put me off an early poll. Dat and de fact dat I'm determined to be de first Fianna Fail leader not to collapse a coalition, so I can ram dis fact down de Blueshirts' trotes every time dey mention deir poxy Rainbow government love-in to me again. But dere ye are. Whatever de reasons, I look like a statesman, and Blair looks like a feckin eejit.

TUESDAY

De domestic scene was quiet today: everyting under control, except de teachers' strike, and de Aer Lingus strike, and de Foot and Mout crisis, and de collapse of de tourism industry. So I taut I'd turn me attention to de world scene, and offer to use me legendary negotiatin skills to resolve de stand-off between de US and China. Dis is de sort of ting yer expected to do when you're on de UN security council. I know some of de Chinese lads since de time me an Celia were out dere inspecting deir wall. So I rang de Jiang Zemin fella and marked his card about de Republican administration. Between meself and himself, says I, "dey're lunatics!" I told him about Paddy's Day in de White House, and about how we were tryin to explain Nordern Ireland to dem, but dey just couldn't get deir heads around de concept of decommissioning because it involved people handin in deir guns, and who in deir right mind would do dat? Dey're all right-wing bible tumpers, I said, and dey'd tink nuttin of bombin Beijing in de mornin and speedin up Armageddon. Surely we can find a compromise, I said. Jiang said he'd settle for a grovelling apology adding: "And don't call me Shirley." Well, I tink nuttin of makin grovellin apologies meself – I'm always at it – so I taut Bush would play ball. But when I rang de White House, de secretary refused to put me trew to de "war cabinet" and told me if I stuck my nose in US business again, dey'd bomb us all in "Goddamn Iceland" too.

WEDNESDAY

Alarming news from de Four Courts, where Beverley Flynn has just been saddled for de full bill in de case she took against de Birdman from Montrose and de udder lad. Aldough one's initial reaction must be sympatty for de girl, one's more considered view is dat she is a social and political leper and one will now have to be careful not to be seen in de same room as her. I never trusted her oul fella, eider: he had more hair in his eye-brows dan I have on me back! But before dis happened, I was tinkin of promotin Bev to a junior ministry – maybe in tourism and sport. We could have got her to promote de Bertie Bowl: according to de evidence in de case, she could sell anyting, no matter how dodgy. So much for dat idea. Of course, her experience is also a cautionary tale for, eh, udder politicians taking proceedings to protect deir, eh, good names from bein dragged trew de, eh, Burlington carpark. I'd say more about dis here, but de lawyers for de udder side are demanding access to me diaries, so I won't.

THURSDAY

De papers have been askin questions about de Government's purchase of de Battle of de Boyne site in 1999. But if dey're lookin for a story in dat, dey're barkin up de wrong river. Me and David Andrews had de idea of buyin it durin de negotiations for de Good Friday Agreement. We taut it'd be a nice gesture to de unionists to develop it as a teem park or someting (if dey didn't play ball in de negotiations we could always have used it for landfill). It would be a gesture of reconciliation, we taut. Maybe we could have a massive re-enactments of de Battle of de Boyne dere, and wreck a bit of Mead into de bargain, just for de crack. But – it was just one of dose tings – it turns out dat a mate of mine had an interest in a company dat bought de site before de State did, an he subsequently made a few bob from de deal. Dere's nuttin in it, of course, and we've handed everyting over to de Flood Tribunal so dey can satisfy demselves dat we're all 100 per cent innocent of any impiety *("impropriety"? – Ed)* whatsoever. It just saddens me dat de media should always be so suspicious.

FRIDAY

De word in GAA circles is dere's a major risk of dis weekend's congress votin to allow foreign games in Croke Park. Dis would be a disaster for de Bertie Bowl, in which we've all invested so much personal vanity – er, I mean energy. So it was important we cut a deal wit dem before de congress opened. Dis left us at a disadvantage in de negotiations, but we took a tough line even so. Dey began by askin for £50 million, which was ridiculous. So we offered dem £60 million and dey reluctantly agreed. It was like taking sweets off children. In return – and dis is de important ting – dey have promised to play an unspecified number of high-profile GAA games at de Bowl. We didn't ask for anyting in writing (on de grounds dat journalists could get copies of it under de Freedom of Information Act) but, eh, we have reason to believe dat dese fixtures will include quarter finals AND semis of de Special "B" Under-16 Hurling Championships. Dere's also talk dat de Artane Boys Band will use de stadium for practice. Dey make a lot of noise, as ye can imagine, and de fact dat de Bowl will be out in de middle of nowhere and dat it'll be empty a lot of de time makes it perfect for deir needs.

MONDAY

Church-State relations may be strained, Celia told me in bed tonight, but dey're de only relations I'll be havin for a while. She's fumin over de way she was sidelined at de Dessie Connell gig. When I tried to give her a squeeeze on de way home, she hit me a belt of de crozier, as it were. But, eh, what could I have done? Every priest in Dublin was tellin de media how embarrassed de Cardinal was about her bein de co-host. Even de Protestants were on me case: and deir Church was founded by Henry de Bleedin Eighth, a man who couldn't keep his tights on when dere was a woman near.

Dere was no question of Celia greetin guests at de door, in de circumstances. It was bad enough me havin to do it wit Harney. A lotta old-fashioned Fianna Fail people still tink de coalition wit de PDs is a scandalous relationship, and dat we're living in sin. But, eh, it had to be done. Apart from dat, de night passed off well. Dessie said someting about "marriage" in his speech, but I had me eyes fixed on de ceiling at de time and, trew dis and udder anti-interrogation techniques I picked up from de Shinners during de Good Friday negotiations, I've learned to blot de M-word out. Dere were a few hacks among de invited guests, and ye could see dem takin notes when dey taut I wasn't watchin. But I tink we've averted any public controversy.

TUESDAY

Jayzus! So much for dat teeory. It's just as well we arranged to have today's Cabinet meetin in Loud, as an expression of solidarity wit Dermot Ahern in his attempts to recover from de foot-and-mout crisis. I was certainly glad to get outta Dublin for a few hours. Celia has drawn up a six-mile exclusion zone around her, and dere was a ban on all animal movements in and out of her side of de bed last night. But at least we're gettin some support on de invitation issue. Mansergh was on *Morning Ireland* havin a go at de Dean of St Patrick's, and even Baldy Quinn was critical of de churches' attitude, poiting out dat some day we could have a Gay or Lebanese *(er "Lesbian"? —)* Taoiseach and what would we do den.

WEDNESDAY

It's a great honour bein de leader of Fianna Fail in dis, our 75th year. Wit any luck, I'll still be in charge for de 100th. Who knows? Maybe de country will be richer dan Switzerland den, and de Dublin Metro will run to Kinnegad, and we'll be lookin forward to de imminent publication of de report of de Flood Tribunal. But in de meantime, it was a proud moment for me today to lead de 100-plus members of de parliamentary party on a march to de Mansion House for a lunchtime speech to mark de occasion. We didn't have a lotta time, unfortunately, because de Opposition were actin de b****x in de Dail. Which is why, while I dwelt in de

Dey say dat Bono wants to write off turd world debt and I say dat it sounds like a crap name for a song but whatever de kids want is all right by me.

Bush is not as up for a party as Clinton was but, eh, at least ye could leave yer wife in de same room wit him for five minutes. If ye had a wife, dat is: Celia wasn't invited, of course, and I'll be hearin about it until next March.

Georgina's fella's band are number one in de charts. "Sure dat's nutting," I said, teasin her, "yer oul lad's been number one for years." But, eh, to tell de trute, I'm proud of young Nicky meself. He's a good lad – from de nortsoide an all (OK, Baldoyle, which is a bit near Howt for my likin, but still) – an if tings work out in de long term, he'd be a very welcome addition to de family

De Roy Keane affair is an absolute tragedy for Oireland. Brokerin a deal between him and McCarty woulda been me crownin moment, and now it looks I won't even be asked. It's not fair. I've spent me whole life buildin towards a moment like dis, negotiatin Mickey-Mouse social partnership deals an puttin togedder coalitions and de like. And here I am instead, at home, waitin in vain for de bleedin phone to ring.

Pee Flynn is such a long lanky bastard dat you'd tink once in a while, when he's aimin to shoot himself in de foot, he might just fail to find de range. Unfortunately he's a crack shot.

Today was de official launch of de second campaign on Nice, which as I explained, is de most important question facin de people since de Good Friday Agreement (when, luckily, dey got de right answer).

De discussion covered everyting from de tret posed by de build-up of toxins under de skin, to de dangers of colonic irritation *("irrigation" – Ed)*, which is someting dat Lady Di had, apparently. I can imagine dat livin wit Prince Charles could be a pain in de hole, right enough.

De next six munts will define not only me own personal legacy to histry, but also perhaps de fate of de European project itself. Tanks to Silvio Maccaroni and his pals, it won't be easy. I don't know what we ever did to deserve comin after de Eyetalians in de EU presidency relay race, but de bastards always seem to drop de baton on us.

speech at some lent on de achievements of Dev and Lemass and de udder former leaders, I had to pass over Haughey quickly in order to get back to de Dail in time for Taoiseach's questions. I heard dat, after I left, de backdrop to de podium collapsed on top of Des "Holy Joe" Hanafin. Luckily he's all right. De Church is on me case enough as it is.

THURSDAY

Speakin of which, Liz O'Donnell has leapt to me and Celia's defence over de invitation controversy. She gave de clergy such a hand-bagging dat Fine Gael had to pull her off dem. I'm not sure I like dis turn of affairs. It's one ting having Liz O'Donnell in yer corner – and, eh, de tighter de corner de better, in dat case – but I can't afford to have de Blueshirts posin as defenders of de faith and sneakin off wit de Catalic vote. It's all right for de PDs – de anti-religious ting might be a vote winner for dem. But I need to keep de religious constituency happy. I am a pratisin Catalic, after all. And just because de PDs are all goin to hell doesn't mean I have to go wit dem. De coalition arrangement only extends to de next general election.

FRIDAY

De latest poll shows de Government is still furder out in front dan Dolly Parton. Dis is despite de fact dat de soundings were taken earlier in de week, when de row was raging. Me personal approval rating is down two per cent, but dat was probably Celia ringin de pollsters on Tuesday. De interesting ting is dat Baldy Noonan has exactly de same patetically low approval rating as Brutal had. Nobody knows dere's been a change of leadership, obviously! Dere has been a slight pick-me-up in deir party support, admittedly, but hopefully dis won't be enough to persuade Baldy to move de writ for de Tipp by-election dis side of de holidays. I've spent one day in de sticks already dis week, and ye can get tired of it very quick.

SATURDAY

Nice spread on me in de 'Irish Times' magazine. We let one of deir photographers hang around here for a couple of days, but only on condition dere'd be no pictures of me belly. I taut de interviewer was makin a veiled reference to dis when she quoted a Fianna Fail politician sayin dat "very few people see all of Bertie." But apparently de politician was referring to me legendary cunning. Only "ten per cent" of me is visible to any one person, he said. It makes me sound like a feckin ice-berg. At least Celia was happy wit de photographs: she had all me trouser legs shortened last year after a picture in de papers showed dem bunched up around me ankles, like Charlie Chaplin's. But she's still not lettin me out of de dog-house. She says she'll be seeing "fifty per cent" of me soon if I don't shape up. I tink she means de back half.

MONDAY

De people have spoken on de Nice Treaty, and dey must be respected, gobshites dat dey are. Unfortunately, Eamon O'Cuiv has spoken too, and he's not de people, so I had to give him a bit of a bollicking over de phone dis mornin. In fairness, he did de interview on TG4, so he couldn't have known anyone would ever hear about it. But still. He told me he had a constitutional right to vote any way he wanted. I said dis was true, technically, and I had a constitutional right to move his boney arse to de back benches for de next 10 years. I tink he got me point. Anyway, as I say, de people have spoken. We'll be askin dem to speak again, obviously, as soon as we can be sure de f***ers know de right answer. But de popular will (or, in dis case, de popular won't) must be accepted, for de moment. Allowing de people to have deir say is essential in a modern hypocrisy *(er, "democracy"? – Ed)*.

TUESDAY

O'Cuiv also brought up de bigger dan average Yes vote in his area, incidentally. Dis was a sneaky way of remindin me dat Dublin Central recorded de fourt-highest No vote in de country. Of course, dere were many complex reasons for dis, including de fact dat we forgot to put up any posters, or organise a canvass. But by de time we realised we could lose, it was too late, and even de smear campaign about de money behind de Yes people never got off de ground. Still, ye live and learn, as I told de Cabinet meetin today. "Anyone else here vote no?" I asked, lookin at McCreevy, Harney and Sile Dev in particular. McCreevy just smiled and says: "You know we're all in favour of enlarging de union, Taoiseach." Yeah, I taut to meself: yer in favour of de US bein enlarged to 51 states! Anyway, I laid out me tree-part plan for de way forward: (1) No renegotiation of de treaty; (2) A second referendum sometime after de next election, so dat in case we were outta Government by den, we can at least have de pleasure of landing Baldy Noonan in de shite; and (3) a year-long European forum to allay de public's fears, and bore de bastards into submission. Everybody said it was a good plan.

WEDNESDAY

We're not mentioning de second referendum by name yet, because de public might tink we were arrogant. But de task of reassuring our European allies cannot be delayed. So today, Biffo had de ambassadors of de accession states in for lunch at Iveagh House. Dey were all dere: Poland, Hungary, Bulgaria, Slovakia or Slovenia or whatever it's called, Estonia-Herzegovina, Transylvania, Evaherzegova, de whole lot of dem. Biffo's clear message was dat we were not trying to deny dem de prosperity of EU membership, and pending deir accession, did any of dem want a sandwich? I tink dey were suitably impressed.

THURSDAY

Off to Gothenburg for de EU summit, wit our tails between our legs. It was because of de summit dat we rushed de Nice referendum, so we could act de big fellas and say: here's anudder overwhelming endorsement of de European project, now what have you got for us? Instead, we look like eejits. No wonder Blair was so glad to see me – tanks to de referendum, we've temporarily replaced de Brits as de lepers of Europe. I congratulated him on his election win, which I said was welcome proof dat opposition parties led by men wit no hair would never be trusted by de public. I offered him any advice and help he needed wit de referendum on de Euro and he said tanks very much, he'd get back to me if he was really desperate. We had a good laugh.

FRIDAY

Jayzus! I didn't know Sweden was in a war zone! It's like de West Bank out dere. Dere's shootin in de streets, and riotin, and shops bein looted. De Irish delegation had to be evacuated from de hotel because protesters broke in and started smashin de place up. First we taut it was de European Commission, angry at de no vote and de tret to deir expense accounts. But apparently, it's only anarchists. De police are usin live ammunition on dem, because dey've never had any crime here before, except de odd case reindeer teft, or makin blue movies widout a licence. Until now, dey taut de Molotov cocktail was a vodka-based aperitif popular in Russia. I don't know which are more dangerous – de rioters or de autorities — but eider way I tink I'll be staying in tonight. McCreevy was trapped in his room at one point, which is never a bad ting. Unfortunately he escaped and gave an interview to de press in which he said de Nice vote was great altogedder. Ordinarily, dis would have added to our problems. But wit all de trouble, de Swedes are even more embarrassed dan us. Tank God for anarchists!

SATURDAY

Back home again, in one piece. Before we left, I had a meetin wit de Polish prime minister, Jerzy Bullock, and we issued a joint statement reaffirming Oireland's commitment to de cause of de accession countries. Overall, I tink we've done a reasonably good job in assuring dem of our support; which is important because, if de buggers ever do get in, we don't want dem f***ing us out of spite. De only one we couldn't convince was de Czech fella, who said de Oirish loved comin to Prague and drinking de beer, but dat's as far as deir commitment to de Czech republic went. I told him dis was untrue. For one ting, I was in Prague meself once, and ye couldn't get a pint of bass anywhere. But I also pointed to de extensive commercial links between Oireland and de Czech republic. "Like, eh, Liam Lawlor," I said. "I rest my case," says he.

TUESDAY

Since Starry O'Brien finally witdrew his allegations a couple of weeks ago, me day in court was always gonna be a bit of an anti-climax. In fact, some of de backroom boys taut I shouldn't even show up for de today's hearing, on de grounds dat it might look petty and vindictive, and dat a big public display might contrast wit me appearance at de Moriarty Tribunal, where I was smuggled in and out of de Castle trew an underground pipe. But my feelin is dat dis was an important opportunity to send out a message to de public dat I'm cleaner dan a nun's knickers, and to give de media a good kick in de mickey into de bargain.

It was a great day out anyway. De courtroom was packed, mainly because our side had more witnesses dan Jehovah. Me own contribution from de stand is already bein compared wit Robert Emmet's famous speech from de docks (I don't remember from me history what Emmet was doin down dere, but I must get de Docklands Autority to put up a statue for de bicentenary) and de result was a foregone conclusion. Apparently, de defendant hasn't got two bob to rub togedder, so de chances of me gettin de turty grand are slim. But den, it was never about de money, which I always intended to donate to a favourite charity, like de Dublin GAA training fund.

WEDNESDAY

If it's not one ting, it's anudder. De court victory shoulda been de second part of a one-two, de udder part bein de opinion polls ban, which between dem woulda had de media sittin on de canvass between now and next year's general election. But me day on de front pages was ruined by de collapse of de polls legislation, which as Shane Smarty-Pants Ross announced last night in de Senate, has a loophole big enough you could fit Brian Cowen trew it. Apart from anyting else, de affair raises questions about de role of de Seanad: personally, I was not aware dat dey were allowed to make telling contributions to Oireachtas debates, and if dis trend continues, we'll have to start imposing standards on who we let in dere. I'll discuss wit Donie when I get de chance. But de opinion poll ting itself was a complete fiesta *("fiasco"? – Ed)* from day one, and it gives me no pleasure to say it was all Fine Gael's idea. Dis mornin's Cabinet meetin agreed anonymously *("unanimously"? – Ed)* to drop de measure. But obviously, dis is something I need to distance meself from quicker dan you can say "de Hugh O'Flaherty affair". Tank God for de crisis in de peace process.

THURSDAY

De talks may be stalled, but de Twelft of July passed off peacefully enough, and Belfast nationalists even joined in de celebrations by organising deir own bonfires in Ardoyne. Dey couldn't find any firewood, obviously – I suppose de Prods had it all already – so dey used cars and buses and even a fillin station instead. But it's good to see de two communities united in celebration. All right, I'm bein sarcastic here. De Ardoyne situation was a riot, I know, and what's more de Brits are sayin de Provos organised it. Dey're probably right, too. Wit de talks resumin in England tomorrow, a bit of a street violence illustrates de Shinners arguments better dan a slide show. But de way I see it, it's as well to have someone in charge of dese tings.

FRIDAY/SATURDAY

A late night at de talks here in Shropshire, which is a picturesque area of England where dey used to have a lot of sheep. De Unionists arrived back yesterday in a huff over de riots, but wit de Twelft behind dem, dey seemed more relaxed. Even Jeffrey, who looks so much like Daniel O'Donnell dat when I close me eyes I can see him singin "Mary from Dungloe" to a roomful of grannies. Den I wake up screamin, and realise I just nodded off while reading de latest position papers. De party leaders chewed our ears as usual for most of last night and to tell de trute, me and Blair are sick listenin to dem. But we know where dey stand now better dan dey know demselves, which is why we've decided dere'll be no furder talks before de August 12th deadline. We're puttin everytng into a package and we're gonna to present de parties wit a "fait accompli," as dey say in Spanish.

SUNDAY

Still no sign of a breaktrew for de Dubs in de Leinster Championship process. Mead were shite today, but de Dublin forwards couldn't organise a riot, even in Ardoyne. I've been meaning to get de Department of Helt to organise an inquiry into Sean Boylan's herbal remedies, but I tink I'll postpone dat for anudder year. Our lads can still qualify trew de back-door system, of course. On de basis of today's performance, dough, I don't fancy deir chances of findin de doorway.

MONDAY

Last minute preparations for de trip to Latin America. I spent last night leafin trew me old Latin school books – am I glad I kept dem! "Pacem bello antepono..." might be a good one to impress de Brasilian president wit, but I'll try and learn a few more phrases on de plane. Celia's in a ladder of excitement, needless to say – especially about visitin Argentina. Ever since Evita was at de cinema a couple of years back, wit Madonna in de lead role, Celia's seen herself as an Eva Peron-type figure. I didn't know what she was on about until I read de sleeve notes from de soundtrack: "blonde, glamorous, loved by de people, married to a great, populist statesman" – and it's a scary coincidence, all right, give or take de married bit. Come to tink of it, I hope de generals behave demselves during me temporary exile. Maybe I should get Smith to give de Army two weeks holidays.

MONDAY

I'da been as happy to spend de whole holidays in Kerry, but not even de tret of ETA's bombing campaign could persuade Celia against de now-annual visit to Spain. So here we are on de Costa Balaclava, lashin on de sun-cream an tryin to ignore de undercover Spanish policemen who are all over de gaff disguised as ice-cream sellers and lifeguards. Dis is part of de drill when yer an international statesman. Celia couldn't get used to de presence of armed police, at first. But now she's well into it, and she's told dem if dey see any photographers from de Star of de Mirror, dey're to shoot on sight and seize de cameras.

I don't mind de snappers meself, especially since I got rid of de belly. Wit de sun tan I got in Kerry and de bronzed hair on me chest, I look like a Greek god – like Apollo 13, or someting. But Spain is deadly. Ye have to try something different, Celia is always tellin me. And right enough, Spain is very different from Kerry because, in August, it's full of Irish people.

TUESDAY

De language can be a bit of a problem here, of course. Dey speak English in most places, but deir annunciation is not de Mae West, to say de least. We went into a sandwich bar de udder day, for example, and asked de lad what dey had, and he said "bocadillos". And I said: de same to you little bollix ye. But it turned out he only meant sandwiches, so I had to apologise for de misunderstanding. Anyway, he brought us a couple of his best Peccadillos, wit stuffed olives on de side. And even dough I never touch de olives – dey'd have ye in de jacks all day – de Spanish undercover policeman who was sittin at de next table disguised as a customer insisted on searching dem for explosives.

WEDNESDAY

I'm readin up on de history of ETA. Basically, it's a geurilla organisation dat wants independence for de Basque Country, which is an anonymous (*"autonomous"? – Ed)* region in de nort-east of Spain. I don't know what it is about de nort-east, but dat's exactly where we have de same trubble – I must ask Mansergh about dis when I get back. Anyway, de Basques have traditionally enjoyed a degree of self-government, but dey were brutally suppressed by General Franco during de Civil War, when de bombing of a town called Guernica was brilliantly captured by de famous artist Pablo Pissarro. Pissarro himself was a member of de so-called "Cubists," who I presume were seeking independence for Cuba, but dat's beside de point.

Since 1968, de Basque separatists (I'm nearly sure Celia has one of dem in her lingerie collection) have been fightin for complete independence. Dere was a peace process a couple of years ago, modelled on de Irish one. In fact, de political wing of ETA, Herri Batasuna, were gettin regular advice from Herri Adams and his pals. But eh, somebody trew a Spaniard in de works and dat was dat.

THURSDAY

All de news from home is bad. United only drew with Blackburn, and Jaap Stam is on de way out. Also, de economy is going down de spout. Celia doesn't let me read about Ireland on de holidays, but I was flickin trew El Pais lookin for de football results and I accidentally hit on a story in de finance pages headlined "Adios, el Tigre Celtico!". So I rang Harney, who's just back from her own holidays in de Balkans, to find out what was goin on. She sounded scared. Tings were bad, she said. De high tech companies were sheddin jobs left right and centre, and everybody was just hopin for de best. Whatever happens, I told meself after I put de phone down, we must remember dat it's individuals who will be hurtin if dere's a new recession. I'm tinkin in particular of de advisors who talked me out of an early election.

FRIDAY

We got back into Dublin last night, after a very pleasant flight. I suppose we'll all have to fly feckin Ryanair next year now dat Tony Blair has started de trend. Him and his big-family economies – if he'd keep his zipper fastened, he could still be flying business class like de rest of us. Of course, Ryanair doesn't fly to Spain, which is a bit of a lucky break. But even if dey did, dey have dis "no-frills" rule, and Celia buys a LOT of clothes when we're on holiday, so dat would never work for us.

SATURDAY

De serious business of rescuin de economy begins next week. But dis evenin it was off to Slane for de U2 gig. Henry invited me and Celia up to meet de lads, on account of how I swung de second gig for dem, and we got a tour of de whole site and everyting. Him and de missus have done a lovely job wit de house, aldough as I told him, de aluminium double-glaze windows would have finished it off nicely. Maybe dey'll get dem in now – with de dosh dey're makin from de two concerts dey have no excuse. Of course, I wouldn't have missed de gig for anyting, even widdout de invite. I'm a big fan of de U2. We're fellow nortsoiders, after all, and when dey sing about "where de streets have no name," well, I tink I know dat part of Finglas too. We tried canvassin dere once but dey ran us out of it wit spears. Me favourite album would have to be "Unforgettably Dire," I tink. But me favourite song has to be "One". It's me favourite number anyway. And hopefully, I'll get a few of dem as a result of hanging round bleedin Slane on a Saturday night, gettin me ears hurt, when I could be at home watchin de Premiership on de telly.

MONDAY

De pressure is on to show solidarity wit de Yanks in de wake of de attack on de free world by Hosannah Bin Liner and his pals. I taut de day of mourning would do de trick, but Bush was on de blower again dis mornin askin what we could do for dem in terms of military or legalistical *("logistical"? – Ed)* support. De use of de airports would be handy, he suggested. Jayzus, says I, you wouldn't want to land at Dublin airport dese days – It's a bleedin mess out dere. But he said he'd be expectin to hear from us soon if we wanted to remain friends of America, and now if I'd excuse him, he had anudder 57 world leaders to call.

TUESDAY

Had a phonecall from Ground Zero (O'Donoghue's office in de Department of Justice) dis mornin, assuring me dere's no evidence, despite reports, dat any of Bin Lederhosen's people are operatin in Ireland. Dis was a big relief as I prepared to address de special Dail debate on de crisis. Lookin around de chamber, I could see dat politicians were still in shock at events: de early recall of de Dail is difficult at de best of times, but during de summer recess it's particularly traumatic. Basically, me message was dat de American response should be measured. And de most important ting for dem to measure was de fuel in any B52s leavin de States, so dere'd be enough of it to get dem to Asia widdout a stopover. I also warned against people here takin revenge against innocent people. Just because somebody has a beard and looks sinister, I said, glancing at Ruairi Quinn, is no reason to abuse dem.

WEDNESDAY

Over to London for talks wit Blair about bleedin Nordern Ireland. De Nort would give you a pain in de hole at de best of times, but at a moment when de future of de free world is in doubt, you'd like to tell Adams and Trimble and de rest of dem to go and shite. Dere's not a lot we can do anyway, except for yet anudder tactical suspension to give everybody more time for squirmin. De Shinners in particular have a lot of squirming to do. Ever since deir involvement in de Colombian student-exchange project came to light, de Yanks have been turnin up de heat on dem. De udder good news is dat John Hume is steppin down as SDLP leader. I know he's a livin saint and all dat and we'd never have had de peace process widdout his Hume/Adams diatribe *("dialogue" – Ed)*. But if I had to listen to dat speech again, about de need for us to start spilling our sweat and not our blood, I tink I'd have shot meself. I don't know if I want to live in his agreed Ireland, anyway, if it's gonna be dat sweaty.

THURSDAY

De Provos have promised to "intensify" deir contacts wit de decommissioning body. Deir statement also says de army council never ordered dose lads to go to Colombia. Presumably dey just asked dem nicely. But at least tings are movin in de right direction and maybe Christmas will see de executive up and running again, and de whole ting will be wrapped up neatly in time for de elections here. God knows, we're gonna need someting, what wit de world economy goin down de spout and factories closin every udder day. Maybe if tings get bad we could declare a state of emergency and postpone de elections, in de national interest, until 2010 or dereabouts. But we'll see. Dere's always de World Cup.

FRIDAY

We've decided to offer de Yanks de use of de airports, provided dat dey tidy up afterwards. In fact we're bein cunning and devious, because we only offered dem for activity connected wit UN resolution 1368, which de Yanks are going to bypass anyway. But de important ting is we're bein publicly supportive while at de same time emphasisin de role of de security council, which of course we'll be chairing next mont. It was Biffo, I have to admit. De udder ting is dat it will annoy de Greens and Joe Higgins, which is always a bonus. Here in Brussels for a meetin of EU leaders, de mood is one of caution. Blair is toadying up to de US as usual, acting as Bush's campaign organiser in Europe. But de udder leaders, like Jacques "de Jacques are back" Chirac and Gerhard Shredder are closer to our way of tinkin. At least, dey've all forgotten about de referendum on Nice.

SATURDAY

Spent a quiet day at home, studying de atlas. It's important, wit us in de security council chair an all, dat I know me Tadzhikistan from me elbow, as it were. But dis is easier said dan done. Dere was a major outbreak of countries in central Asia after de Soviet Union collapsed. And it's hard enough tryin to sort de Uzbeks from de Kazaks and so on, widdout havin to consider all de ethnic divisions widdin de state borders. Dere's more tribal strife in dat region dan anywhere outside of de Fianna Fail organisation in Kerry, I reckon.

SUNDAY

All-Ireland day in Croke Park is always a time for reflection. And today I was tinkin what a force for good de GAA is. While de fundamentalist zealots of udder countries are tryin to blow up de world, in Ireland dey're only trying to run a sports organisation. And a great job dey do too. It was a perfect day in Croker. Autumn sunshine, a last-minute equalisin goal for de Dubs in de minor match and, eh, de right result in de senior. Global crisis or not, nuttin seems as bad, somehow, after you've seen Mead get de shite beaten outta dem.

MONDAY

Now dat we're part of de international war on tourism *("terrorism" – Ed)*, it's important to reassure Ireland's ethical *("ethnic" ? – Ed)* minorities dat we're not targeting dem. So today I paid a visit to de Icelandic *("Islamic" – Ed)* Cultural Centre in Clonskeagh to assure de Muslims dat dey were a valued part of Irish society, despite Zero's attempts to stop any more of dem gettin in. Dis sort of event can be a diplomatic minefield, so I was carefully briefed beforehand by de protocol boys in Iveagh House, who gave me some useful tips – like when dey pass de food around, don't ask for a ham sandwich, and so on.

TUESDAY

De resumption of de Dáil after de summer recess is always a time for mixed feelings, all de moreso dis year. What wit global recession and de turd world war and all dat, de pat to de general election is looking a lot more tricky dan it was at de start of de summer. But dere ARE reasons for optimism – in particular de Opposition, which luckily hasn't changed since June. Seein dose ugly faces again across de floor calmed me nerves a bit. Wit de glare from all de baldy foreheads – Noonan, Quinn, O Caoláin, and de rest – you'd need sunglasses for sittin in my seat. But de view reminded me dat when it comes down to a hard choice, de electorate won't want any of dose lads kissin deir babies. Speakin of babies, I enlivened proceedings on de first day back by announcing anudder abortion referendum for de spring. As Des Hanafin said to me: "Is that a rabbit in your hat or are you just pleased to see me?"

WEDNESDAY

News dat Sellafield is goin ahead wit its plans for processin oxides – de so-called POX facility – is a major setback to Joe Jacob's master plan for closing de plant down. Joe is still lying low since de Marian Finucane interview; de last I heard he was wearin white protective overalls and testing radiation levels outside his office to see if it was safe to come out yet.

THURSDAY

De collapse of Swissair lent added urgency to de Dáil debate on Aer Lingus. It's sobering to tink dat even Switzerland, up dere in de Pyrenees, can feel de chill winds blowin trew de world's economy. De Swiss banks could be de next ting to go. Jayzus! I just remembered, JP McManus lives in Geneva: I hope he has de £50 million for me Bowl stashed somewhere safe! Anyway, Aer Lingus's transatlantic traffic has collapsed, apparently, and dey're goin to run out of cash reserves if dey don't put in for refuelling soon. And ok, it wouldn't be de end of de world if de company went under – we'd still have de Government jet, after all – but a lotta nortsoiders work in de airport, an I wouldn't want to face dat flak on de doorsteps durin an election campaign. We got a sneak preview in de grief Mary O'Rourke was gettin from de Opposition today. She looked like a chief stewardess dealin wit a combination of drunken passangers and severe air turbulence. I was glad I was in de cockpit.

FRIDAY

Hosannah Bin Liner may be still at large, but de world is a safer place followin de jailing today of Denis Riordan. Dis man has terrorised de Government for de last four years wit his bleedin constitutional challenges. We never knew where he was goin to strike next. So it was a big relief to hear dat he'd been done for contempt of court, and especially dat he was prepared to stay in prison for "as long as it takes". As I understand de contempt law, unless he apologises to de beaks he can be kept in dere indefinitely or for de rest of his life (Whichever is longer). Before I leave Government – after de 2017 election, please God – I must consider givin him a pardon.

SATURDAY

Today's World Cup matches have cleared de way for Ireland's qualification for de World Cup, a crucial part of me election strategy. OK dere's de small matter of de play-off against de Asian turd-place team: it looks like bein eider Saudi or Nordi Arabia – I can't remember which. But dis is where our membership of de Security Council can pay off. Obviously in de current circumstances it would be unreasonable to expect our lads to travel to de Middle East for de away leg. But with a bit of help from our allies, I'm sure we could get de Arabs to accept a deal whereby dey play deir "home" game in a neutral venue, such as Cork. Roy and de Irish wedder will look after de rest. Den we can unveil de election posters of me In de green jersey, and it'll be a case of Bob's yer uncle, Mick's yer opposition leader, and five more years in Government.

SUNDAY

Spent Sunday evenin watchin de war on telly. It's better dan de *Week in Politics*, God knows, but I'm a bit miffed dat I didn't get a call from Bush about it, even dough I was in all day. I rang de White House for a briefin but I was put onto an answerin machine dat said de president was busy at de moment and if I was a world leader callin to ingratiate meself I should leave a message after de beep. I had a good mind to take de airport offer back. But den again, with Aer Lingus goin down de spout, we might as well use dem for something.

MONDAY

Black clouds are continuing to gadder over de economy and all over de economy and all de wedder forecasters agree dat rain is now likely. Up to dis, de Government always took de view dat dare'd be no need for umbrellas. But as politicians, our main area of expertise is forecastin which way de wind will blow next, so de current consensus among economists is worryin. IBEC is de latest group to issue a pessimistic forecast for next year, in which de say grote will be no more dan tree per cent. Meanwhile, McCreevy tells his physical *("Fiscal"? – Ed)* returns have slowed dramatically. Government spending is way ahead of tax take and if dis trend continues, Charlie says, we'll be in breach of de Maastricht Stability and Grote Pact guidelines. We wouldn't want dat, apparently. It's not like McCreevy to worry about de European Commission, but I tink what's really stickin in his trote is de taut of all de money he might to give Mickey Martin for his helt strategy.

TUESDAY

Accordin to de Irish Times, de Flood Tribunal is investigatin possible links between Ray Burke and de 1980s development of de Plantation site, "a tree-filled oasis" in Georgian Dublin. Dis must be anudder ting dat escaped me attention when I was givin Rambo de turd-degree back in 1997. As everybody knows, I was up every tree in Nort Dublin at de time lookin for information, and dat's a lot of climbin. Talk about a tree-filled oasis – it's a feckin jungle up dere! I was busy enough widdout havin to search plantations in bleedin Baggot Street as well.

WEDNESDAY

Ah, Halloween. De season of ghoulies and ghosties and long-legged beauties *("beasties"? – Ed)* and tings dat go bump in de night. A great time for de kids. A few of dem called around to de house dis evening in deir Bin Laden costumes, demandin money and telling us to pay up or else dey'd break all our windows. De innocence of it. Dey wanted more dan I was willin to give, of course, considerin de current spending constraints. Den I went back to carvin a face in de pumpkin – an extra-scary one dis year, I taut, "Look at dat," I says to Celia when it was finished, 'it's like some of de women who come to you for beauty treatments." I didn't say it was like some of de women who leave after de beauty treatments, but she still gave me a dirty look.

THURSDAY

A black day on de jobs front, as dey say on RTE. De shut-down of Tara Mines is a hard blow for de people of Mead, and God knows, after de All-Ireland Final, dey've suffered enough. Maybe dey can use Seán Boylan's herbal remedies to cheer demselves up for a while. Harney rang me on a bad mobile phone line to say de collapse in drink prices had left de mines wit no choice but to close. I didn't understand de logic of dat, unless de problem was dat management couldn't get workers out of de pub. But anyway, we were just about to issue a statement lookin forward to de mines reopenin whenever drink prices recovered, when Harney rang back on a better line to say "ZINC prices, ye big eejit".

FRIDAY

Unemployment is up, year on year, for de first time since 1996, when de Raincloud shower was still in power. De seasonally maladjusted figures show anudder 5,200 people signin de live register in October, and dat was before yesterday's setbacks. It's beginning to look bad, but we have to keep tings in Perspex.

SATURDAY

Speakin of de unemployed, David Trimble no longer has de votes in his party to elect him first minister, tanks to de decision of Peter Weird and Pauline Hermitage to vote against him. We warned him dis would happen, but de tick f*****r wouldn't listen to us. It was a lucky break for him dat he even got decommissionin in de first place. It would never have happened only de Yanks had de Provos by de financial short and curlies after Colombia and de 11th of September. Grizzly is goin round talkin about de "pain" republicans are goin trew as a result of puttin a few weapons beyond use, but it's nuttin to de pain dey would have felt if dey hadn't.

SUNDAY

Down to Bodenstown for de annual commemoration of de fadder of Irish Republicanism, Wolfe Tone. It's a special occasion dis year, followin our success wit de Kevin Barry funeral, an event which has established me as de fadder and mudder of modern Republicanism, whatever de Shinners like to tink. When it comes to unitin Protestant, Catalic, and de centre *("dissenter" ? – Ed)*, I'm yer man. (Memo to meself: I wonder if dere'd be a case for transferring Wolfe Tone to de Republican plot in Glasnevin? Must get Mansergh to look into it.) Anyway, after Bodenstown, it was back to Dublin for anudder important event: de unveilin of de first Luas tram on Merrion Square. I know some people say dis is a cheap political stunt. But in fairness, it wasn't dat cheap – £50,000, I believe. De main ting is dat it's an opportunity for Dubliners to get a glimpse of de future. A future of fast, efficient public transport, and no traffic jams, and everybody as happy as pigs in shite. And, eh – did I forget mention? – a future wit me still de Taoiseach. Yes, dat's what de tram display is about. All aboard now, ladies and gentlemen: next stop de general election.

MONDAY

De launch of de new currency has been smood as a baby's bum, tank God, and already de people are completely familiar wit deir euros and centimes. De chaos dat some pessimists predicted, and dat might have destabilised de Goverment in de run-in to de general election, has been avoided. We had de Army on stand-by to protect Brown Thomas's in case of an Argentina-style lootin situation. But dere were no real problems, and profiteerin by inscrutable *("unscrupulous"? – Ed)* traders has also been rare. I must admit I was a bit nervous on January 1st when I went down to me local shop with a Belgian start-up kit I won in de card game at de Brussels summit, and a posse of journalists and TV cameras up me arse. But it was a PR triumph all de way. And in general, de success of de launch would nearly tempt me to go for an early rerun of de Nice referendum. Now dat de people have got deir hands on a bit of European money again, I tink we could swing it.

TUESDAY

De official start of de election campaign is still four munts way, but already de parties are jockeyin for position. Me pre-emptive attack on de Shinners – to de effect dat we couldn't consider a coalition wit dem while de Wolfe Tones were still making records – obviously touched a nerve, because Martin Ferrit has now hit back, accusin us of hypocrisy. Meanwhile, in de battle of de baldies, Quinn is still tryin to insist dat Labour will run on its own platform while Noonan is makin overdrafts *("overtures"? – Ed)* to de Greens on de Nice Treaty. De part of it dey don't like (i.e. de text) can be dropped, he says. Personally, I tink dat when it all pans out, I'll be doin business wit Mr Angry, despite what de likes of Roisin Short-haul have to say. Dat's why, in me New Year interview wit de Business Post, I also set out me socialist credentials: emphasisin dat I was a life-long trade unionist and dat I saw meself in a line of great left-wing leaders includin Connolly and Larkin and, in de international sphere, Lenin and McCartney. In dese uncertain economic times, I said, my message is a simple one: "Workers of de world, good night."

WEDNESDAY

Lawlor has given de media de slip again. Havin made history as de only man ever to escape into jail, twice, he was smuggled out again today, and dere's still no photograph of him in de vicinity of de prison Of course, he also recently managed to enter de State unnoticed, which nobody else can do – apart from tousands of asylum seekers, dat is. Apparently, after his New York holiday he arrived back into Dublin Airport, and he was in de baggage reclaim area (in more ways dan one), wit de press hoverin outside de exit to de arrivals hall. But den Dermot O'Leary arranged for him to be smuggled trew a side-door, and now de opposition is askin questions about why proper photo-call *(surely "protocol"? – Ed)* procedures were not observed. Among udder tings, it seems Lawlor didn't go trew customs. He says he had nuttin to declare anyway. But, eh, dat's what he tells de Flood tribunal too.

THURSDAY

De good news is dat de Abbey Teeater is not movin to de soutside, whatever happens. As a regular attender – I was dere only last October to see de Tom Murphy classic "A Whistle in de Park" *("Dark" – Ed)* – I appreciate de urgency of a solution to de teeater's space problems. We're still considering a number of locations in de nort inner city, an area dat could loosely be described as my constituency. Dey already have de Dáil, for example, which is a year-round pantomime.

FRIDAY

More pre-election manoeuvring. De Wolfe Tones have announced a total cessation of activities from midnight, pavin de way for a deal whereby de Shinners support a minority Fianna Fail administration. It's hard to believe, after turty years of violence and so many ears permanently damaged, and dere's still some scepticism about it. It could be just a tactical move: de band could reform again in a year's time and record an album worse dan anyting dey've done before. But I welcome it as a positive development. De instruments are silent for now – dat's de main ting. And at least bleedin Albert Reynolds can't take de credit for dis one. Anyway, as part of de deal wit SF, we've agreed to appoint David Andrews as a special envoy to Colombia to investigate de situation of de tree republican lads held on suspicion of training gorillas *("guerrillas"? – Ed)* for de FARCE movement. I had him in dis evening for a briefin. Officially, he's travellin in a private capacity at de behest of campaigners for de tree lads. I've explained to him dat if he falls into de hands of de local press, he's to swallow de cyanide pill immediately. He says he's cool wit dat – he'd do anyting for a foreign trip, dat lad.

SATURDAY

I meant to watch Baldy Noonan on de Late Late, but I fell asleep before he came on. It's amazin – I've stayed awake trew entire Michael Woods speeches, and I can watch De Week in Politics no bodder. But de Late Late knocks me out every bleedin time. Anyway, Joe says he recorded it for me. De bad news is dat Pat Kenny didn't ask Baldy any awkward questions about his role as Minister for Helt durin de Hepatitis C affair. De good news is de crap is hittin de fan over de non-appearance on de show of some actor called Brendan *("Brenda" – Ed)* Fricker, who – if I understand it correctly – is playin de part of Baldy in a new TV series on de subject. Accordin' to de papers, de series is expected to prove "embarrassing" for Mr Noonan, especially comin so close to a general election. Right enough, dat IS unfortunate timing – hee, hee, hee.

MONDAY

De biggest danger to us winnin de general election, I reckon, is de wedder. De storms in Dublin were so bad we nearly lost Ringsend, which has a strong Fianna Fáil vote. It was a frightening glimpse of what could happen wit global warnin, which John Gormless says will leave half de country under sea level – aldough hopefully not before May. Naturally, we'll have to compensate dose who suffered flood damage dis time, even dough I heard Michael McDowell's brudder on de radio dis mornin sayin dat dey shoulda had insurance. It's all right for de McDowells to talk: dey're so far up on de high moral ground dey never get deir designer shoes wet. But ye wouldn't be safe anywhere down around Ringsend, I reckon, except in bleedin Noah's Ark. Dis is anudder reason why I'm opposed to de Abbey Teeatre movin to de docks.

TUESDAY

Speakin of Flood damage, Lawlor is back into de clink, for de turd time. I don't know what kind of regime John Lonergan is running dere, but he must be givin customer-loyalty bonuses or someting. Not dat I'm boddered – I have udder backbenchers to be worryin about, anyway. I had to censor *("censure"? – Ed)* Noel Redneck O'Flynn in de Dail today, for example, over his attack on asylum seekers in Cork. Dere was a certain irony in dis. Many Dubliners have always taut of Cork people who come to de capital as refugees fleein oppression, or at least economic migrants who can't afford de return bus fare; and some of de less enlightened among us resent de fact dat dey come up here takin our jobs and women, and drivin around in cars. It just shows how far de country has come dat de likes of O'Flynn now has someone to to look down on. Of course, I know he's only defendin his seat (and he has one of de biggest seats in de Dail, de fat b*****d). Obviously, dis kind of comment goes down well wit de grassroots. But I have to send out de message dat dis Government will not tolerate racing *("racism"? – Ed)* of any kind.

WEDNESDAY

De massive fraud in de US involvin an AIB subsidiary is a proud moment for us all. I don't pretend to understand de ins and outs of it, udder dan dat de lad at de centre of de controversy was investin in so-called "dirigibles" *("derivatives" – Ed)*. But de impressive ting about it is dat de AIB says it can take de loss no bodder. I remember back in '92, when I took over as Minister for Finance, and de country didn't have an arse in its trousers. We were still recoverin from de Fine Gael-Labour coalition of de 1980s, which as we all remember took a shilling off de old-age pension and banned children from wearin shoes. If one of our banks lost seven grand at de time, de World Bank would have repossessed de country and put everyting up for a garage sale. But dat's all changed, tank God. Now we can light our cigars wit 500-euro notes and we can blow £750 million on lottery tickets. Plenty more where dat came from.

THURSDAY

We were hopin to get de Dáil debate on Lawlor out of de way quick dis mornin, but de bleedin High Court ordered dat we'd be infringin his conjugal *("constitutional"? – Ed)* rights if he didn't attend personally. So we had to stall de ball while a Mountjoy escape committee was organised. And as bad luck would have it, de prime minister of bleedin Eutopia *("Ethiopia" – Ed)* was visitin de Dáil at exactly de time dat Lawlor was driven in in de Hi-Ace. I said me bit in de debate and stayed on for a few minutes to listen to Baldy Noonan frautin at de mout. Den widdout waitin for Lawlor's speech, I high-tailed it over to Government buildings, where we had a lunch laid on for Haile Selassie, or whatever his name was. It was goin well enough, and I was makin de usual small talk, based on de briefin documents de foreign affairs lads gave me: "How are tings in Abu-Dhabi?" *("Addis Ababa"? – Ed)* and so on. And suddenly yer man raises de subject of our human rights record. He wanted to know if de "member of parliament Mister Lawlor" had been imprisoned for his beliefs. I said: "In a manner of speakin, yeah – he believed he was above de law". So Haile said he might have to take de case up wit Amnesty International. He also appealed to me to hold free and fair elections in de near future, and said Eutopia would send observers if we needed dem.

FRIDAY

Today marked de end of de old money in general circulation. So we needed to do someting symbolic wit de last few quid, for de press cameras. Somebody suggested we donate it to a good cause, like Trocaire, or de Mountjoy prisoners' dependants fund. But I said, Jayzus, it was donations dat started all de trouble in de first place. Instead, McCreevy insisted dat, since we were in de run-up to an election, we should do someting to emphasise dat de public finances were in good hands. So in de end, we took de money down to de bookies.

Dere were de usual novelty bets on offer: 1000/1 Liam Lawlor to be next Taoiseach; 5,000/1 Ireland and Scotland to host de 2008 European championships, and so on. But we finally plumped for a £100 bet on de outgoing Government to be returned, at 7/2. Charlie muttered under his bret dat he'd backed a lot of nags in his time, but dis was de first time he'd bet on a pantomime horse. Fianna Fáil were sure to pass de winnin post first, he said, but he wasn't sure when de back end would arrive. I know what ye mean, says I, as we headed back to de office, "but if de worst comes to de worst, we can slip Baldy Quinn into de costume at de last minute". In de meantime, it was all about confidence: we had to send out de message dat dis government had delivered prosperity. "All de boats are rising," I said. "Especially in Ringsend," says Charlie.

TUESDAY

I know dat RTÉ has been castin aspersions on me moral compost *("compass"? – Ed)* lately, but de trute is dat I care deeply about de abortion issue. Okay, maybe "deeply" would be puttin it a bit strong. In fact, me doctor says I have a rare "psychodermatological" condition which means I'm not capable of carin deeply about anyting, udder dan savin me own skin. But when I warned people at de launch of our referendum campaign dat defeat for de amendment would mean de introduction of liberal abortion into Ireland, and dat soon dey'd be givin dem out free wit packets of cornflakes, I was speakin from personal conviction. Unfortunately dat hasn't worked wit de voters, so in me final appeal today, I tried someting else. I hinted dat defeat would make feck-all difference because I "wouldn't be in a hurry" to legislate for de X case anyway.

WEDNESDAY

Down to de Protestant school in Church Avenue first ting to vote. De media gang were all dere, of course. But apart from Charlie Bird, it was anonymously *("ominously"? – Ed)* quiet. De word from around de constituency is dat de turn-out could be de lowest in Dublin, and dis on top of de humiliatin No vote here on de Nice referendum. De bastards don't deserve me, I often tink. In general, it's not lookin good for de Yes campaign. Votin in Donegal is slower dan Tom Gildea, apparently, and de wedder trewout de west is atrocious. Ye'd tink wit Dessie Connell on our side dat any divine intervention would be positive, but den dis happens.

THURSDAY

I had been plannin a triumphant visit to de RDS count, but me brudder Noel was on de blower to warn me to stay away. De early tallies were de worst figures he'd seen since de women's shot put at de Moscow Olympics, he said. Dun Laoghaire was bad, as we expected. But de second biggest No vote in de country was Dublin Sout East, home of de bleedin architect of de amendment, Mickey McDowell. I tore up me victory speech and issued de usual statement: dat de people had spoken and dat deir's was de last word in a democracy (except on de Nice Treaty). Den I watched Baldy Quinn and Dana, and Hopalong Owen smilin for de cameras at de Custom House, and I nearly trew up.

FRIDAY

De referendum defeat is bad enough, but de controversy over de contract for de national acrobatic *("aquatic"? – Ed)* centre is a bit of an embarrassment on de eve of de ardfheis. Normally at times like dese, I like to keep me head down. But dis is not easy to do when you have to make a live televised address to de bleedin nation.

Still, de ardfheis is a great occasion. It's always pleasant to meet our members from de country, especially now dat many of dem wash regularly. And Fianna Fáil on an election footing is an awesome sight. Dere's no doubt dat de party is ready for de mudder of all campaigns. We struck de first blow dis week wit de postal stamp campaign: de blueshirts are only whingin because DEY didn't tink of it.

SATURDAY

I tink me speech went well. After Baldy's Lazarus performance at his party conference, de pressure was on, so nuttin was left to chance. Even me makeup took hours, aldough I insisted on puttin on de Brylcreem meself. De 200-euro pension line went down well wit everyone except McCreevy and I got a standin ovation just for mentionin de national stadium. Fianna Fáil is a party of sports lovers, of course. And to prove de point, as soon as me speech was finished, dey were off and runnin in de annual get-in-de-TV-picture-wit-Bertie handicap hurdle race. It was a close-run ting, but Donie Cassidy won by a hard neck, as usual.

SUNDAY

We're all very excited about David Trimble's comment dat de Sout is a patetic, sectarian, and monocultural state. At first I taut dis was an insult. But Mansergh pointed out dat since de Nort is patetic, sectarian, and monocultural too, dis is obviously a coded invitation from de unionists for talks on reunification.

MONDAY

Off to de States for de Paddy's Day jaunt. Dere was an awkward moment on de plane when an undercover American security guy objected to me carryin de bowl of shamrock as hand luggage. But it was all smooded over. I also have a special clearance certificate from de Department of Agriculture, in case de US customs people – what wit de new post-September 11th attitude – tink it's a cannabis plant. It's good to be headin back to de States, dough. I'm hittin Chicago first, to open an off licence, or someting. "De windy city" – it'll be ardfheis all over again! Den it's on to de White House to present de traditional gift. President Bush has learned a lot about Ireland since last year, when he offered us foreign aid to end de potato famine. He's promised to put out de welcome mat for us at de White House, and says dat if dere's nobody in when we call, we can leave de "bowl of clover" on it. Of course, we'll also be bringin him a message of support from de Irish people for his important work in bombin de shite out of various turd world countries. And we'll be stressin dat, while Ireland sounds a bit like "Iran" and "Iraq", and while we sit beside dese countries in de UN General Assembly, dere's no udder connection whatsoever. We'll be askin him to draw dis to de attention of his airforce.

MONDAY

As we celebrate dis special time of de year for Republicans, it's time to turn our tauts once again to dose brave men who fell for Oireland during Easter week: Pearse and Connolly and MacDiarmada back in 1916; and more recently, poor old Paddy Teahon. Since de tragic events of last week, when Paddy went out bravely to face certain det before de firin squad of de Public Accounts Committee, under de cruel orders of Field-Marshal Rabbitte, dere has been time for all of us to reflect on what he achieved. He went down like a true Gael, clutchin our proposition to his bosom, and udderwise sayin nuttin, as agreed.

TUESDAY

Me Arbour Hill oration was especially movin dis year, on account of de fact dat it could be de last speech Mansergh ever writes for me. If he gets elected in Tipperary Sout, I'll lose him as a Government advisor. God love him, he wanted to run, and at least de idea of him and Noel Davern sharin a platform gave us all a laugh. Macken told me it was a dream ticket. "More like a gas ticket," says I.

WEDNESDAY

Down to Kerry for a few days to clear de head before de campaign. It's always a great place to relax, de Kingdom, aldough Zero insisted on increasin me security detail on de grounds dat I was at risk of gettin de shite beaten out of me by Sinn Féin vigilantes. De big question facin me is when to seek de dissolution of de Dáil. Personally, I tink it's dissolute enough already, and I don't want to add to de problem. Unfortunately de Constitution says I have to do it before June and Macca is now on 24-hour stand-by in de Áras, waitin for me visit. I was plannin to go for a long walk in de hills dis evenin, to let de Kerry air clear me tauts but Zero says he hasn't secured de ground yet.

THURSDAY

Zero said it was now safe for me to go out, so long as I didn't get involved in any criminal activity. So I spent de day wanderin around Dingle, tinkin about me options for de election date. Me own preference is for Tuesday, May de sixteent. Dis would be exactly half-way between de first and de tirty-first, an on any potentially divisive issue, me instinct is to come down firmly in de middle. On de udder hand, dere's a school of taut dat says a lot of Fianna Fáil voters get paid on Tuesday and go on de batter for de night, so dey're liable not to vote. Den again, if we have it on a Saturday, for example, students home for de weekend enter de equation, and it's well known dat a lot of dem vote Labour, especially if dey're on drugs. Also, de Shinners are plannin to bus down tousands of Nordern refugees to vote, and a Saturday would suit dem too. I was still wrestlin wit dis problem when I went down to Dingle pier dis evenin to look in de waters, literally and metaphysically ("*metaphorically*"? – *Ed*). And – Jayzus – what did I see only bleedin Fungi de dolphin. Dis is a message, I taut. A fish means Friday: May de seventeent, in udder words! I need to consider dis idea furder, obviously, but at de moment I tink I like it. Especially if we could close de pollin boods at 7pm, before de students get home from Dublin. I must ask Dempsey if dis would be legal.

FRIDAY

Dere's still nuttin but good news comin in from de constituencies. De word on de ground is dat de Blueshirts are on de run, and dat Labour would be only too happy to get into bed wit us after de general election, provided we wear protection and promise to be gentle. Me devious plan in Government to agree wit everybody and never make a decision has worn de opposition down completely, as I calculated back in 97. No problem has arisen dat couldn't be solved by a tribunal or by somebody udder dan me resignin, and de result is dat de public tink I'm cleaner dan bleached nuns' knickers. I'd give anyting to know what CJH tinks of me performance.

SATURDAY

Tings are goin so well, in fact, I'm seriously worried now dat I might win an overall majority. I'd miss havin de PDs te blame every time we had to get rid of one of our lads for some misdemeanour. And wit all dose extra TDs, I'd have more people lookin for jobs. As it is I'm gonna have to promote de likes of Mini Brennan, who would only agree to dealin wit Jackie Healy-Rae for five years if we gave him free counsellin and a senior ministry at de end. And of course, when people can't be scared into line by de possibility of an election, dey can start plottin against ye, de way we did ... eh, I mean, de way dey did against Jack Lynch. Dey could be plottin against me even now, come to tink of it. De bastards. Maybe I better get back to Dublin. I've been in de bog too long.

SUNDAY

RTÉ has made us anudder proposal for a debate between me and Baldy. I tink I could take him any day, but for some reason de lads in headquarters want to minimise me "exposure", as dey put it. I don't see how dis would be a problem if de debate was indoors, but anyway, I do what I'm told. TV3 suggested one involvin all four leaders of de main parties, and de lads were in favour of dis initially on de grounds dat nobody would see it. But den dey decided dat it would be beneet me dignity to debate wit de smaller parties. Now RTÉ is proposin a head-to-head between me an Baldy. Wit a head as ugly as his, I reckon I couldn't lose. But de lads say dey're only pretendin to consider de RTÉ offer, and de plan is dey're gonna go on pretendin until about two weeks before de election. Den we'll agree to all de terms, but we won't be able to find a suitable date.

MONDAY

De lads in election headquarters have planned de campaign to maximise me exposure to de gen'ral public, so dey have me visitin ev'ry hole in Oireland, spreadin meself around like de winter vomitin bug. De drill is, we arrive into some one-horse town and I'm straight into de local Fianna Fáil-owned pub. I shake de hands, slap de backs, say "howyiz lads", grab de women, pose for a picture wit de horse, and den I'm back in de car and down de road at 90 miles an hour to de next stop. Ev'rywhere I go dere are crowds. Dey can't get enough of me in de country – grabbin at me like I was Padre Pio, or someting. Mara says he's gonna cut up me clothes for relics and send bits to all de constituency organisations, so de candidates can rub dem. I wouldn't mind, eider, if it cut down on de travel.

TUESDAY

De hacks back in Dublin are complainin about bein manipulated by de lads down at de Treasury Building. Apparently dey rang Charlie Bird 27 times to discourage him from doin a story about me dodgin a debate wit Baldie Noonan, and dey told him dey knew where he lived, or someting. I rang dem to say what a good job dey were all doin, but I said we should draw de line at trettenin journalists wit violence, at least until de last week of de campaign. It's not just in Dublin, dough – de hacks followin me round de country are also whingein. For one ting, dey can't keep up wit us, on account of de fact dat DEY have to observe de speed limits. Dey're also annoyed dat we don't tell dem about evry stop. Dis is because PJ has vetted all de grassroots people we're meetin, and if any of dem are ugly, he doesn't want me appearin in photographs wit dem. Speakin of ugly, I had to meet Pee Flynn when I was passin trew Castlebar yesterday, and of course Bev. We debated dis beforehand and decided dat if I snubbed him, it might go down well in Dublin 4, where dey hate us anyway, but it'd only lose us support in Mayo, where dey tink de high moral ground is de top of Croagh Patrick. So de idea was I'd meet Pee in de absence of de media, who'd be told I was in Sligo. But de lanky bastard must have leaked it because de hacks were onto us like flies on a sheep's arse.

WEDNESDAY

When I heard about McDowell describin de national stadium as a "Ceaucescu-era" project, I taut it was a compliment. I taut Ceaucescu was de lad dat missed de penalty for Romania in de 1990 World Cup and I said to meself, right enough, dat was a great era for Oireland. I was nearly gonna ring de Rottweiler to tank him for de support when I arrived in Tipperary dis mornin and Mansergh explained to me dat it was intended as an insult. Apparently Ceaucescu was a communist bollocks dat built big ugly buildins all over Budapest *(Bucharest – Ed)* and impoverished Bulgaria *(Romania – Ed)* before he was overtrown and shot by a firin squad. Feck dat, says I. I know McDowell is desprit for votes, but comparin me wit dictators, especially dead ones, is not on. If we win de election, not only is dat bastard not gettin de AG's job back, but I'm gonna send his file to de secret police. I miss havin Mansergh to write me speeches, dough. He woulda come up wit someting witty, comparin McDowell to Mussolini or some udder hysterical *("historical"? – Ed)* figure. De only consolation is dat he has no chance of bein elected in Tipp Sout. I just hope Davern lets him have enough votes to get his deposit back. I wouldn't want to see his pride hurt.

THURSDAY

Mara has initiated de Fianna Fáil Emergency Plan to deal wit de situation arisin from comments wee Jimmy McDaid is supposed to have made at a yoot forum in Donegal. Apparently he said people who committed suicide were "selfish bastards". Dis is very a controversial opinion, because it implies dat selfish people are in some way bad, whereas Fianna Fáil party policy specifically states dat, in de modern economy, selfish people are de cornerstone of progress and dey deserve tax breaks radder dan criticism. Also, it's a direct insult to our partners in Government who depend heavily on de selfish bastard vote. But bad an all as dis is, apparently de comments have also been interpreted by some people as an insult to suicide victims. So one way or anudder, de country is in uproar. PJ has drawn up a tree-mile exclusion zone around McDaid's home in Donegal and no party traffic is allowed in or out of de area in case de infection spreads to de rest of de herd. In de meantime, everybody's been told to get out on de airwaves and express shock and dismay at de comments, to reassure de public dat we're all clean. He says he'll decide later whedder wee Jimmy has to be put down.

FRIDAY

It had to happen soonci or later, but de *Orrish Times* opinion poll is a cruel setback to us all. It only confirms what we've known for monts, dat de overall majority is a possibility. But it was important de word about dis didn't get out because de electorate gets very nervous. I get nervous about it meself sometimes considerin what we did to Jack Lynch de last time we didn't have a junior partner to stab in de back. But it would have been a fedder in me cap if I'd pulled it off all de same. And now, tanks to de bleedin free press, all our hard work is gone to waste. Of course, we tried bannin opinion polls last year, an dat didn't work, so what can you do? It is a democracy, after all – for now anyway. PJ says we'll just have to adopt a variation on de usual Fine Gael line: sayin de polls are not a true reflection of de picture on de ground, dat de only poll dat matters is de one on May 17th, dat de reception we're gettin on de doorsteps is complete shite, and dat we'll be lucky if we win 50 seats. He doesn't tink de electorate will fall for dis, but it's wort tryin.

TUESDAY

De Roy Keane affair is an absolute tragedy for Oireland. De taut of de country's greatest-ever talent missin out on what could have been de biggest triumph of his career is depressin. All dat ability wasted – it would break your heart tinkin about it. And ok, I know dis is not ALL about me. Dere are udder victims too – like Roy himself, who looks like missin out on a World Cup. It's just dat brokerin a deal between him and McCarty woulda been me crownin moment, and now it looks I won't even be asked. It's not fair. I've spent me whole life buildin towards a moment like dis, negotiatin Mickey-Mouse social partnership deals an puttin togedder coalitions and de like. And here I am instead, at home, waitin in vain for de bleedin phone to ring.

WEDNESDAY

I taut we had it in de bag wit de Tommy Gorman interview last night. I know Roy didn't apologise, as he was supposed to do, but when Gorman asked him if he'd meet McCarty "half-way," he seemed to indicate dat he would. As far as we could work out from de atlas, half-way would be Tehran, give or take a few hundred miles. So we asked de Iranian government to make a safe house available for peace talks, and JP offered us de use of de jet and evryting. It was all fallin into place. We'd get Mick and Roy into a room togedder, and we'd have signed off on a deal before dey knew what hit dem. Den it'd be de old tree-way handshake at Tehran airport, wit de world media lookin on. "A lot done, more to do," I'd have joked to de TV cameras as Roy and Mick headed back to Japan side by side. But now de little Cork bollix has pulled de plug on de whole ting.

THURSDAY

Meanwhile, back in Dublin, dere's a bleedin Government to negotiate. I could do it wit me eyes closed. But when Dempsey rang me from de talks today for advice, me heart just wasn't in it. "Yeah, yeah," I said, "two senior ministries and two juniors – whatever de bastards want, give it to dem. And don't worry about Abbotstown. If dey'd prefer us to do a paint job on Tolka Park and make dat de national stadium, it's ok by me. I can't be boddered any more."

Celia suggested I should get involved in de Aer Lingus dispute, or someting, instead of mopin around de house. But as I told her, dat'd be like Roy Keane playin for a Sunday league side. A better idea hit me while watchin de Sky news. Apparently, de Turd World War is about to break out between India and Pakistan, so I rang de Indian embassy and offered to mediate in de dispute between deir fella and General Omarsharif. "Dey're bote good lads" I said. "If I could get dem into a room togedder, I'm sure we could work someting out on dis cashier problem". De embassy said to leave it wit dem. But dey still haven't haven't rung me back eider.

FRIDAY

If it wasn't for de Fine Gael leadership contest, I'd be depressed. After deir election debacle, I was afraid dey'd do something radical, like give de top job to dat good-lookin young one from Offaly, Olwyn Allright. Or de Coveny lad, who's nearly as good-lookin, when de light hits him a certain way. But in a surprise move, dey seem have decided dat a boring middle-aged man should lead de party for a change. And in yet anudder surprise, dere's actually four-way contest for de position. I don't envy de parliamentary party deir task in makin de choice. Certainly, from a Fianna Fail viewpoint (and I mean dis sincerely) dey're all very, very good candidates. Any one of dem would make an ideal Opposition leader, as far as we're concerned. If I was forced to choose, I tink dat Gay Mitchell has de special edge dat we – eh, I mean – dat Fine Gael needs at dis time. But as I say, dey're all excellent, in deir own way.

SATURDAY

Up at de crack of dawn to watch de game from Japan. And Roy Keane or no Roy Keane, de team proved de old sayin: "You'll never beat de Irish – unless you're a Garda on riot duty." I must admit, after watchin de Senegalwegians beat France in de openin match yesterday, I taut we were in trouble. And when Patrick Mboma (dere must have been an Irish granny dere) put de Cameroonians a goal up, de writin was on de wall dat we had our backs to. But Mick McCarty must have held a clear-de-air meetin in de dressin room, because de team came out fightin after de break. Once de goal went in, we were all over dem. And de draw is a great result, even dough ye can't help tinkin what might have been, if de team had not been deprived of de services of our one, truly world-class negotiator.

SUNDAY

De Government deal is more or less wrapped up, and it'll be big relief when de new Cabinet is made known. I've had about 57 lobbyin phone calls so far – and dat was just Willie O'Dea. Come to tink of it, formin a Government is very like pickin a World Cup squad. Dere'll always be resentment from people who tink dey should be in de final 23, and dere'll always be criticism of some of de Gary Breens dat make it onto de list. But I believe in rewardin players who have done de job for me in de qualifyin rounds. Having said dat, I also need to stamp me autority on de side. Dere could be difficult times ahead, and readin de next set of exchequer figures could be like arrivin at a Pacific island trainin camp and findin dat de pitch is a car-park and de balls haven't turned up. So de bottom line is I need to be wary of Corkmen who tink dey should be runnin de team. Maybe I'll leave Micheal Martin where he is, to keep him busy.

WEDNESDAY

De FAI's deal wit Sky is a betrayal of Oirish football supporters, and de public can rest assured dat de Government is determined to be seen to be doing someting about it. For a start, as a matter of urgency, we're drawin up a list of sports events dat will protected from similar commercial exploitation in de future. De GAA has already indicated a willingness to have de Special B Under-16 Camogie championships included in de preservation order, and we're in advanced negotiations wit de organisers of de annual Christmas swim in Sandycove as well. I know some people will say dis is puttin de cart before de horse after de stable door is bolted; but ye have to start somewhere. De udder part of de Government's initiative is to explore ways dat de FAI/Sky decision could be reversed widdout us: (a) havin to pay compensation, or (b) gettin on de wrong soide of Rupert Maxwell *("Murdoch" – Ed)*, de respected media magnate who owns a lot of newspapers dat are popular wit impressionable voters.

THURSDAY

De Dáil was back today for a special debate on de Ansbacher Report, but not even Baldy Quinn could get excited about dis, which is sayin someting. De report is a model for udder potentially sensitive publications, like de ones due from de Flood and Moriarty Tribunals. In particular, de idea of releasin such a complex document early on a Saturday mornin, when journalists have more dan de usual trouble focussin, was a stroke of genius. Secondly, not even Fianna Fáil's most devious news management experts would have taut of makin a report so big dat you need a wheelbarrow to carry it. But de fact dat Ansbacher had no revelations in it was de best idea of all, and one dat I hope will be copied when de tribunals publish deir findings sometime in de next decade.

FRIDAY

De Government's strategy towards potential No voters in de referendum on Nice has been to scare de shite … eh, I mean, to ensure dey are properly informed about de issues. De start of de campaign has gone well, wit various business leaders explainin calmly dat if voters exercise deir democratic pejorative *("prerogative"? – Ed)* and say No again, dey'll turn de country into a post-industrial wasteland dat'll make de 1980s look like a fun-park. However, it's important dat we don't give de No soide any ammunition, which is why I moved swiftly to defuse de row caused by Mary McAleese in Attens. I'm sure her pro-Nice comments were unintended. But luckily, Biffo was out dere wit her to help clarify de issue, and I followed it up at dis end wit a statement of support. Hopefully de incident didn't damage de Yes campaign. But it's important dat de President should be completely above politics, even when she's one of ours.

SATURDAY

De meetin wit de FAI yesterday went well. We reminded dem of de shit-load of money we recklessly promised last year to buy off de No-Income Park project, and we pointed out dat dere had since been a serious economic downturn and we might have to revise our priorities – hint, hint. We also explained dat, if push came to shove, we could force de broadcastin of games on RTÉ under de EU's "Television without Tears" *("Television without Frontiers" – Ed)* directive. De FAI lads were cool up to dis point, but I was keepin me trump card till last. Lowerin me voice, I told Brendan Menton dat if he didn't play ball, we could arrange for him to face de ultimate sanction: an emotional TV interview with Tommy Gorman.

SUNDAY

De Sunday Indo has a story claimin dat me relationship wit Celia has "changed" and bases dis on a conversation I'm supposed to have had wit some hack in de Burlington. First of all, I'd just like to say dat I never received any cheque from anyone in de Burlington car-park, or any udder car-park. Secondly, de story is rubbish. Sure I might have said someting about how Celia was seein a lot less of me lately. About a stone and a half less of me, to be exact, tanks to de diet she has me on since Christmas. But as for de speculation dat we've split up, dis is part of a misinformation campaign bein put about by certain elements in Drumcondra. Celia's takin a bit of break in France at de moment, and I didn't go wit her partly because I always find dat France is full of French people, and partly because I was needed here for important State occasions like de National Day of Commemoration, and de Dubs playin Kildare.

MONDAY

Bit of a head dis mornin after de match. But it was a great feelin when de final whistle blew yesterday. As I said to McCreevy, pointin at de scoreboard: "dere's anudder serious deficit for ye to wrestle wit". He predicted dat rampant inflation would now set in wit Dublin supporters's expectations, and we'd be in for a hard landin in de next round. But nuttin could spoil de occasion. Dis was de Dubs first Leinster Championship since I became Taoiseach, and I felt like joinin de team on de lap of honour. Certainly, all de money I gave de GAA was wort it, just to see 78,000 Dubs (all right, dere might have been a few hundred of dem from Kildare) in Croker. Imagine: nearly eighty tousand fans, and de game live on terrestrial television! I must mention dat to de FAI boys next time I see dem.

WEDNESDAY

De Special Branch have warned me dat me movements have become too predictable. Dey say dis leaves me at risk from sinister elements. Apparently dey found maps of all me regular routes in de offices of de Sunday Independent, and dey have information dat de gossip columnists dere may be plannin anudder interview attempt, possibly in Kennedy's Pub, in de near future. Dere's a whole range of lunatics out dere waitin for deir chance to take a pop at me, apparently: everyone from de Al Qaida network, to crazed Mead supporters, not to mention all de disinfected *("disaffected" – Ed)* Fianna Fáil back-benchers who tink dey shoulda got jobs. So until I get de all-clear, I have to vary me routes – especially for de mornin jog – and also change me social patterns. In keepin wit de new policy, I went to Fagan's last night, radder dan Kennedy's.

THURSDAY

Speakin of personal danger, Celia was on de radio dis mornin for an interview about helt and beauty. De discussion covered everyting from de tret posed by de build-up of toxins under de skin, to de dangers of colonic irritation *("irrigation" – Ed)*, which is someting dat Lady Di had, apparently. I can imagine dat livin wit Prince Charles could be a pain in de hole, right enough. But anyway, it all reminded me of de row we had after de media coverage last week. Dis started when she told me I must have had a build-up of toxins in me brain before I decided to discuss me personal life wit a hack from de Sunday Indo. I pointed out dat it wasn't very long since she herself gave an interview to Oireland on Sunday and said dat we'd be gettin married "somewhere down de road". She said dat was different, because she always chose her words carefully, unlike me. So I said dat suggestin we'd get married down de road, or up de road, or at de side of de bleedin road, wasn't very careful. At dis point, she trettened to insert a hose in me. But luckily, me bodyguards intervened in time.

FRIDAY

Today was de last Cabinet meetin before de holidays, and McCreevy warned everybody not to turn up widdout deir proposals for spendin cuts. Of course Charlie says dat if anybody asks, we're not to call dem cuts. "They're moderations in de increases," he said, to general laughter. Dat's a good one, says I, memorisin it for de press conference. Of course, public spendin is only one of many serious problems facin de economy, and de public can rest assured dat dis Government will be workin on dem full-time trewout de holiday season. For example, de Cabinet meetin also discussed de collapse of de tourism industry, which is especially serious in de west. So Joe Walsh proposed dat, as an emergency support measure and to express solidarity, we'd all go to de Galway Races next week.

SATURDAY

De opposition have copped dat we covered up de extent of de down-turn durin de election campaign. But as McCreevy explains, dis was in keepin wit Government prudence. We were just bein economical wit de trute, he says. It was in de national interest, because if we'd told people how bad tings really were, dey might have panicked and made Baldy Noonan Taoiseach, and den where would we all be? So de only cuts we mentioned before May 17th were in de crime statistics; and funny enough, dis is de one area where dere are no moderations in de increases. In fact, de latest figures show dat crime is goin trew de roof (as are some of de better-equipped burglars) and de estimates for next year predict continued grote in most areas, especially arson, assault and battery and drug offences.

SUNDAY

One of me last jobs before de holidays was to announce de automatic nominations for de Senate. And Jayzus, am I glad to have dat over. De Senate is de Leinster House version of de Intertoto Cup: career politicians who didn't qualify in de main competition last May have to stay competitive over de summer, when de rest of us are tryin to relax. When de Senate elections are over, it gets even worse. We're all windin down, and suddenly we're gettin de arses lobbied off us for de last 11 seats on de gravy train. Not dat it did de lobbyers much good. Most of de 11 were already spoken for, anyway, what wit de schoolmarm, and de lad Cyprian, and so on. And of course we had to give four to de PDs, aldough after winnin 8 seats in de Dáil, Harney barely had enough party members left to fill dem.

MONDAY

De only udder big decision I had to make before headin west was de deputy leadership of de party. I had considered givin dis to Zero as a compensation for makin him Minister for de Arts. But in de end, I opted for Biffo. He'd be de best man to lead de party if – God forbid – anyting were to happen to me. And besides, on dat very point, I'm plannin to expand de job of deputy, which was hidderto a mainly ceremonial one. In future, I'll be accompanied by de second-in-command on all major public occasions. And if anyone takes a shot at me, like dey did wit Jacques Chirac, it'll be de duty of me deputy to trow himself into de line of fire. Dat's why, on de advice of de security people, I picked de biggest guy we had.

MONDAY

Today was de official launch of de second campaign on Nice, which as I explained, is de most important question facin de people since de Good Friday Agreement (when, luckily, dey got de right answer). Unfortunately, de event and de teem of me speech were overshadowed by yesterday's defeat of de Dubs. Just as de Nice Treaty offers increased opportunity to de downtrodden nations of eastern Europe, so de Good Friday Agreement opened up de Republic for de people of Armagh, who had also long suffered under de jackbute of oppression. Now dat de Dubs' feel-good factor has disappeared, we'll just have to go back to Referendum Plan A, which involves scarin de shite out of everybody about de flight of jobs and capital dat will follow immediately if dey don't vote Yes.

TUESDAY

Sout Africa is an ideal venue for de Ert Summit. It's a country wit enornmous gaps between de rich and de poor, high levels of violence in de townships, and huge infrastuctural problems, includin a helt service overwhelmed by de challenges facin it. But apart from dat, it's not like Ireland at all. It's a lot warmer for one ting. Unfortunately I'm not here for a holiday, dough. Dis is my chance to perform on a world stage, literally and metabolically, and I tink me speech to de pulmonary *("plenary"? – Ed)* session today made a good impression. Certainly, quite a few delegates came up to me afterwards askin for a copy of de script – or de "English translation" as one of dem humorously put it.

WEDNESDAY

Today was a day for relaxation, an for baskin in de glow of de summit agreement, which was arrived at against de odds and at de cost only of droppin most of de original aims. John Gormless, who's here as part of de environmental lobby (it must have been some trip on de bike) says it's a shabby compromise. But den "compromise" was always a dirty word wit de Greens. De fact is dat de summit has made important progress in issues such as sanitation, energy and human rights. We couldn't have done much more widdout de Yanks on board, and from Ireland's point of view, bindin targets might not have been a good idea at dis time, anyway. McCreevy says de economic figures are so bad, we may have to scale back on de sanitation ourselves soon.

THURSDAY

I gadder dat de review of de National Stadium is recommendin de Phoenix Park as a possible venue for a scaled-down project. De way tings are goin, we'll end up playin de Euro 2008 matches in de Fifteen Acres, or in a converted monkey enclosure in de Zoo. I'm determined to press ahead wit it, somewhere or udder. Personally, dough, I'd be against puttin it in de Park. Dere'd be a serious danger dat dis might attract unfavourable comparisons wit Farmleigh, anudder ting we spent millions on, which is hardly ever used.

FRIDAY

Dis stadium stuff is gettin to me, and Harney seems to be enjoying seeing me with me arse out de window. I do have one ace up me sleeve – de National Fundin Development Agency. Dis is exactly de sort of ting that de PDs are always bangin on about and it brings an element of physical attitude *(fiscal rectitude? – Ed)* to de whole project. I'm not sure what it is meself and de advice is dat it's not really here for de long term but if de Agency keeps de heat off me while de UEFA lads are over, den it'll have done its job.

SATURDAY

What a day. Mick McCarty won't be rushin back to Moscow and who could blame him? What an arse kicking dat was and to concede four goals in a single afternoon he must have felt like Ned O'Keeffe. I knew we'd miss Roy and his aggression but dere may be hope now for a reconcil … reconcilli – a bangin togedder of heads between de manager and his only superstar. What better man to broker a historic deal dan yours truly. I've got all de credentials – Reds fan, Green fan, industrial relations guru … and I've read Dunphy's buke.

SUNDAY

Mara says it was a good idea to describe de No side's philosophy as "dingbat stuff" but I should go easy on de Greens – coz dey're only a bunch of girls' blouses. Instead he tinks it's time we really put de boot into de f**kin backbenchers plannin to sit on dere arses when I'm out on de canvas. I may not have Roy Keane on my side but I do have de next best ting – Biffo Cowen – and dere could be some nasty off-de-ball incidents over de next month. Back to Croke Park which was jam-packed with culchies for de All Ireland and to tell ya de trute I didn't pay too much attention to de match. Wit de Dubs gone for anudder year me heart just wasn't in de whole hurlin razamatazz but I had to put on a good face for de GAA boys. Ye never know when I might need a favour, say in 2008. At half-time someone told me dat Enda Kenny had dropped a real clanger by mentioning de "N-word" at some blueshirt bash and he'd had to apologise. I knew Noonan wasn't exactly de most popular ex-leader ever but I didn't tink tings were dat bad. Politics can be a cruel game.

TUESDAY

De referendum campaign is swingin our way at last, tank God. Ever since we did de job on Big Ears Barrett, de No side has been in disarray. De lads in Pembroke Street had been tryin to get deir hands on his buke for weeks – ringin up de No to Nice headquarters pretendin to be research students doin projects on de history of intellectual taut in Longford, and dat sort of ting – but dey couldn't get it for love nor money. So finally we called a meetin of de Army Council and decided we'd have to go wit de stuff we had from de internet – dat Big Ears was friendly wit a lot of short-haired Germans, and so on – and leak dis to de press. De hit went down exactly as planned and now, as dey say in de gangster fillums, Justin Barrett sleeps wit de vicious *("fishes" – Ed)*.

WEDNESDAY

I'm just back from de game at Lansdowne Road tonight and, Jayzus, it was a soberin experience. De parallels between de national soccer team and de economy are strikin. De feelgood factor of de summer has disappeared completely. De midfield is leakier dan McCreevy's end-of-year projections, and de back four is now even slower dan economic grote. De big difference is dat nuttin about de current economic situation is as predictable as Kevin Kilbane, unfortunately. Most worryin of all is de tret of jobs losses – Mick McCarty's in particular. It's a matter of concern to me dat a guy who had sky-high approval ratins only a few munts ago should suddenly become about as popular as Fine Gael.

THURSDAY

Sure enough, de latest opinion poll in de Times shows dat me popularity ratins have collapsed. Me teflon coverin has worn off – probably from all de shite its had to deal wit since I took on dis job – and now tings are stickin to me, big-time. Even so, de public are a fickle bunch, an no mistake. Before de election I had higher personal approval ratins dan Saddam Hussein. Now less dan half de people are happy wit de job I'm doin. De next ting will be a section of Fianna Fáil supporters chantin "Biff-o, Biff-o" from de stands.

FRIDAY

Tankfully de crisis in de peace process is continuin and I'll soon have an opportunity to use me legendary negotiatin skills to save it, dereby distractin de public from de crisis in de economic process. Trimble is a dead duck, we reckon, so we're already makin overtures to de DUP about a new agreement. We tink Peter Robinson is someone we can work wit, and his recent statements have been very carefully nuanced – like when he referred to de need for unionists to reach

Formin a Government is very like pickin a World Cup squad. Dere'll always be resentment from people who tink dey should be in de final 23, and dere'll always be criticism of some of de Gary Breens dat make it onto de list.

I wished Enda well in his attempt to climb Mount Riodejaneiro *(er, Kilimanjaro – Ed)* next week. "Come back safely, Enda – de country needs you," I said. De trute is, wit de way de polls are, I need him a lot more dan de country.

As I said to Páidí Ó Sé, education is vital, and I hope young Kerry people can learn how to play football again as soon as possible. Páidí gave me de sort of look dat he used to give to Dublin corner forwards. I taut for a minute he was goin to bite me leg off, but de moment passed.

On a personal level, I feel a certain sympatty wit Beverly. But on de level of a leader already facin a drubbin in de June elections, I have moved decisively to ensure dat, hencefort, dere will be a forty foot pole between me and her at all times.

Bush's intrest in Oireland grows greater evry year, a point underlined today by his gratitude for de traditional gift of shamrock, aldough he referred to it as a "salad bowl" and said he'd get Laura to rustle up something special wit it later on.

Back to Dublin for de unveilin of de first Luas tram on Merrion Square. I know some people say dis is a cheap political stunt. But in fairness, it wasn't dat cheap – £50,000, I believe.

De e-votin commission has recommended against usin de machines on June 11. Cullen has emerged from dis lookin like a second-hand car salesman. Aldough, ye had to admire his neck. When anyone mentioned resignation, his attitude was no, he wouldn't be acceptin any.

I've got me list of possible EU Commissioners. Dey're all decent skins, good Fianna Fáil blood, de cream of de crop. Den Roman Prodi says dat de nominees must be chosen for deir "personal integrity". Once I've taken all de FF names of de list, I'm left with a blank sheet of paper again.

Anyway, I'm very proud of de girls and what dey've achieved. But den dey were always very much driven. A bit like meself since I got de State car.

out to deir neighbours on de "Fenian scum" side of de community. In de meantime, I still have to win de Nice Referendum.

SATURDAY

It's all over bar de shoutin. De electronic results from Dublin and Mead are overwhelminly Yes, so de rest is a formality. Tanks be to God for dat. We did have a back-up plan: in de event of anudder No vote, I was gonna say: "next poll wins". But I was never dat entusiastic about it, and I'm glad de electorate got de right answer at de second attempt. I rang Dick and Biffo and de rest of de lads tonight to congratulate dem but I also warned evrybody dat dere was to be no gloatin tomorrow. "We have to appear humble," I said, "however difficult dat is".

SUNDAY

Just to reassure de people dat we're not gettin carried away wit all dis European stuff, I spent de mornin at Bodenstown, and de afternoon at Croke Park. Mandy rang me from Dublin Castle at half-time in Croker to say dat everybody was blamin me for de delay in de declaration, and de mood was gettin uglier by de minute. Of course it had nuttin to do wit me – de European Broadcast Union fixed de slot for 5pm and I couldn't change it. But apparently even Garret Fitzgerald was havin a go at me for delayin de show because of a football match. So as ye can imagine, dat made de second half of de game even more enjoyable.

MONDAY

I spent de day baskin in de glory, takin congratulatory calls from de lads in Brussels and also, of course, from de grateful applicant countries. De prime minister of Poland rang to say he drank a pint of Guinness last night in Oireland's honour, followed by six or seven udder pints. He also admitted he was very worried beforehand because of de high numbers of "don't knows" in de opinion polls. So I said we had an old sayin here: dat dere's only one poll dat really matters. Den suddenly he got into a huff. He said he taut de Pope was a great man too, but dat didn't give me de right to insult de rest of his people. I didn't know what de feck he was talkin about, and we ended up havin to get de ambassador in Warsaw to sort de problem out. Den dis afternoon me secretary said: "De Vatican on Line 1, Taoiseach". And sure enough dere was dis frail voice on de line, tankin Oireland for allowin de Polish people into de EU. Don't mention it, Holy Fadder, says I, it's de least we could do for our fellow Cattalics. But he tanked me again and added: "Prime Minister off Irelant, I laff you". Den I heard laughin at de udder end of de line and I realised too late it was only Biffo windin me up. He's a hoor for de funny voices, Biffo.

MONDAY

Tings have settled down now for a bit, tank God. Wit de Nice referendum outta de way, we can get on wit plannin de first of de two or tree savage budgets dat McCreevy says will be needed to get de economy back into de sort of shape where we'll be able to buy de next general election. Nobody likes cut-backs, but it's important dat we control unnecessary expenditure so dat de Government can deliver on de essentials – like de SSIA Free Money Scheme, which in happy coincidence is due to mature in April 2007, tree weeks before pollin day. De revolt on de backbenches has calmed down too, tankfully. De committee jobs have bought most of me critics and de rest can like it or lump it until me mid-term reshuffle. Unless, something happens in de meantime. On dis score, we're all a bit concerned about de precedent set by yer woman in Britain who resigned as education secretary because she taut she wasn't up de job. For feck's sake! If dat caught on here I could lose half de bleedin Cabinet. Dey're funny people, de Brits.

TUESDAY

Speakin of funny people, de Labour Party's decision to replace Mr Angry wit Mr Smartarse as leader trettens to make de Dáil a livelier place dan it's been for a while. Tings have changed, dramatically: I'm suddenly faced wit a situation where de two main opposition leaders have hair. Dey're also bote from Mayo, which is a radder sinister coincidence, I tink. But on de whole, I'm more worried about Rabbitte. Not dat Labour could ever win an election or anyting. But it's only a matter of time before de Stickies take over de Blueshirts. Den de next ting we know, dey'll be proposin a merger wit us and den – bingo – dey'll have de one-party state dey were plannin back at UCD in de 1960s. In de meantime, Smartarse is trettenin to take me on in Dáil debates. I saw him on de Late Late Show criticisin de way I do talk. He also said someting about how dere was no "sin tax" in anyting I said. And whatever about de first point, he's right about de second, anyway. I don't even know what sin tax is, but I can say right now dat McCreevy will not be introducin it in de fortcomin budget. We'll leave dat to Labour.

WEDNESDAY

De Flood Tribunal is back, and so is Frank "Moneybags" Dunlop. De latest globule *("module"? – Ed)* of de inquiry is about land in Carrickmines and all I can say is, at least dat's nowhere near Drumcondra, tank God. I haven't been up any trees in Sout Dublin, so I have no idea what might be in dem. But de Tribunal has obviously been shakin a few, and de councillors who've fallen out so far seem to be mostly ours. What a shock dat is. Still, I'm sure dey all had good reasons for bein up dere. And I wish Mr Justice Flood well in his efforts to unravel de trute, which I hope will be as slow – eh, I mean as successful – as dey have been to date.

THURSDAY

Today is Halloween, and it's also de openin session of talks on anudder social partnership agreement. I'm not sure which is de scarier prospect. De chances of a new deal look grim. If we do somehow manage to revive de partnership process one more time it'll be like de scene at de end of Carrie where ye tink it's all over and den a hand reaches up outta de ground and scares de bejayzus out of everyone. Certainly, de openin positions of de two sides are as far apart as Justin Barrett's ears, and I don't know how we can reconcile dem. De unions want a socialist myopia *("utopia"? – Ed)*, as usual, while IBEC are demandin de reintroduction of widespread, grindin poverty, as a first step to restorin competitiveness to de economy. It's just as well I'm de world's greatest negotiator. But if I can broker a compromise here, I'll be ready to chair de talks between Mick McCarty and Roy Keane.

FRIDAY

Down to Cork tonight to address a meetin of de party fateful on de state of de economy. De usual guff: tings not lookin too good ... need to hold de line ... modest grote possible ... Jack Lynch a great fella altogedder, etc. Den it was back to Dublin as fast as de Government plane could carry me. It's a good ting I can fly on dese occasions, now dat Mini Brennan is lurkin behind every ditch with his feckin speed cameras. I taut it was very ironic how de guards criticised de speed wit which he introduced de scheme. Changin Garda work practices is a turty mile an hour zone, as everyone knows, and Brennan was doin at least 60, apparently. But fast as he was, I'm glad he didn't have de system operatin durin de general election. Udderwise, I'd have had enough points at de end of it to get me next grocery bill free.

SATURDAY

De Yanks are puttin de squeeze on us over de resolution on Iraq. Dey want a flexible wordin dat allows dem to start bombin immediately in de event of Saddam Hussein bein found to have a moustache; whereas we tink dat even if absolute proof of him having a ronnie does emerge, de Yanks should give de UN a second chance to rubber stamp de decision. Ireland's membership of de Security Council means we have to defend certain principles, and as I was sayin to Biffo de udder day, dis is new ground for dose of us reared in de traditions of Fianna Fáil. Maybe de Russians or de Chinese will get us off de hook by usin deir vetos. But personally I tink de UN should delegate Vladimir "Gas man" Putin to go to Baghdad, accompanied by some of his special forces, and negotiate a peaceful solution to de crisis. Dat ought to bring Saddam to his senses, if nuttin else will. Come to tink of it, maybe dere's a role for Putin in de next round of talks on Nordern Ireland.

MONDAY

I'm writin dis on a beach in Montenotte *("Lanzarote"? – Ed)*, where I'm gettin a bit of colour after 12 monts of soakin up de rain. I pre-recorded me New Year interview for RTÉ's Dis Week programme yesterday – it was mostly about de need to tighten belts and batten down de hatches, and all dat shite – and den it was off to de Canaries before you could say: "Hasta la Vista, baby". But I tink I deserve it, for all de aggravation I have to put up wit from de press. De latest controversy before I left was over whedder I had a feckin drivin licence, for Jayzus sake! It's so long since I had to drive anywhere, I couldn't remember. I'm nearly sure I passed de test once, but when you've performed as many tree-point turns as I have over de years, it's hard to recall if any of dem was in a car.

TUESDAY

I believe dere's a bit of flak flyin at home over de fact dat me and Harney are bote abroad. But de public can rest assured dat I still have me hand very much in de till *("on the tiller"? – Ed)*. I'm keepin firmly in touch wit reality even as I stroll among de palm trees on dis island off de coast of Sout America *(er, Africa – Ed)*, and I'm in hourly contact wit udder members of de Cabinet. In fact, Joe Walsh has been on de mobile several times today about de farmers' protest, especially after Ned O'Keeffe climbed on de bandwagon (or maybe it was a tractor). We put de Army on stand-by, just in case.

WEDNESDAY

Whatever about de public finances, de Ahern finances are well and truly secured. First Georgina got de ring from de Westlife lad, and now Cecelia's after securin a megabucks advance for a buke she's writin. I knew she was workin on someting dis last while, but I taut it was for de oul journalism course she was doin. Come to tink of it, she told me last year dat she was movin into fiction, and I said: great, ye'll have no problem gettin a job in de newspapers so – dey'll probably make you political correspondent!

THURSDAY

De money keeps rollin in for de buke, and dere's talk of a Hollywood fillum, wit Julia Roberts or Oliver Barry *(Halle Berry? – Ed)* in de lead role. I'm nearly jealous, at dis stage. At de risk of bein unmodest, Cecelia obviously got de literary talent from her fadder, and in anudder life I tink I could have been an extinguished *("distinguished"? – Ed)* novelist meself. Of course, I'll probably write me autobiography eventually, if I can get over de memory block from de Haughey years – I can't recall much from dat era at all, somehow.

FRIDAY

Sippin beer on de hotel balcony here in Puerto del Carmen, it's hard to imagine dat we live in a troubled world, trettened by de spectre of war. De Middle East was a dangerous enough place even before dose Israelians started tryin to clone babies, God knows. Meanwhile, dere's good and dere's bad news at home. De good news is dat we've finished top of de world globalisation league again. De bad news is dat people are protestin about de numbers of American soldiers passin trew Shannon on de way to de Gulf. Unfortunately, dese events are not unconnected. If we say boo to de Yanks at dis stage, we could find ourselves very quickly slippin down de globalisation league. Before ye know it, we could be in de bottom tree, and facin relegation to de nationalisation league, currently led by Nort Korea. So in dis as in all tings, I have to move carefully, if at all.

SATURDAY

Back in Ireland briefly, I find meself havin to clarify de situation at Shannon vis a vis Irish neutrality. De fact is dat, while we're allowin de US troops to use de airport, we have insisted dey don't carry weapons while passin trew. De way we monitor dis is by gettin dem to fill in cards wit a series of questions, such as "Did you pack your suitcase yourself?" and "Are you carryin any guns, razors, penknives, nuclear arms, etc?" We also ask dem deir reason for visitin de Middle East: (a) business, (b) leisure, (c) bombin de shite out of Iraq at de earliest opportunity. And provided dat dey don't tick (c), our neutrality is safe. If dey do admit to carryin weapons, or to havin aggressive military ambitions of any kind, den of course we will take de necessary action: ie, look de udder way.

SUNDAY

Spent de day packin for Mexico, apart from a trip into Moore Street to get meself photographed for de Monday papers, so people would know I was home. Dey might even tink I had someting to do wit de breaktrew in de national pay talks, which would be no harm eider. Of course, Mexico is an increasingly important tradin partner for Ireland, so de five-day visit dere will be all about cementin dis relationship. But dere'll also be an important symbolic element to de trip. I'll be layin a commemorative reet in honour of de Irishmen who fell in de 1846-8 war between Mexico and de US. Apparently dey fought on bote sides of dat conflict (men after me own heart). And in dese troubled times for our neutrality, I tink it's important dat I send out a clear message about where we stand.

MONDAY

I was watchin de post-match discussion on Saturday's United-Arsenal game when I got a call from Tom Kitt, who was monitorin de peace march in town. "Bad news, Taoiseach," he says. "Yeah, tell me about it" says I. "Did ye ever see a miss like Giggs's – de little Welsh bollix?" Kitt cleared his trote: "Actually Taoiseach, I was talkin about the size of the anti-war march. There must be 100,000 here, and they're not all crusties, eider. A few of them actually look like Fianna Fáil voters." "Jayzus!" I said, as I watched yet anudder replay of de goals. Den Kitt spoke again. "Maybe it's time for a move in the direction of the French," he suggested. I considered dis tautfully. "Ye could be right," says I: "Viera played Keane off de pitch – but do ye tink he'd be available?"

TUESDAY

In de wake of de marches, de meetin of EU leaders in Brussels was as tense as a United dressin room. De French were still arguin for more time, while de Brits wanted to start bombin Baghdad – or failin dat, Paris – by de end of de week. For a while, it looked like we might not agree a joint statement, but tanks to a few suggestions from me and Biffo, we cobbled one togedder in de end. I contributed de last line in de fourt paragraph – stressin de need for a peaceful resolution – and Biffo came up wit de first line of de seven paragraph – trettenin immediate war. Dese were bote in keepin wit de position we've taken since de start of de crisis. But Gerhardt Shredder – de German chancer *(Chancellor – Ed)* was impressed, and asked me if I was familiar wit de work of somebody called "McAvilly" *("Machiavelli"? – Ed)*. Dat must be one of our lads in de Berlin embassy, I taut.

WEDNESDAY

Meetins of de parliamentary party are not normally dominated by global issues. De average Fianna Fáil back-bencher is usually more worried about road-widenin schemes dan de tret of World War Tree. But a number of speakers today made de point dat we are a national movement. And dat, whenever de Oirish people protest in deir tousands, de leader of Fianna Fáil has traditionally placed himself at de head of de march, and led de people in de direction dey want to go. Dis was a fair point. And as luck would have it, Biffo – who's been conductin research at de UN to find out what way de wind is blowin – had already decided de time was ripe for a change in our position. So after de meetin, I rang Charlie Bird and arranged an interview for de six o'clock news. And just as Biffo had briefed me, I told de nation we believed a second UN resolution was now a political aperitif *("imperative"? – Ed)* before any war starts. Charlie asked me did dis mean I was in disagreement wit de Americans, and I said, call me Mister Controversial, but yes it did.

THURSDAY

It doesn't mean any such ting, of course. De Yanks are already workin on anudder resolution, and whenever dey run dat flag up de pole, we're plannin to salute it. But one of de attractions of de new resolution route is dat, hopefully, it'll put de war off until after St Patrick's Day. It'd be a bit embarrassin if I was presentin de traditional bowl of shamrock on de Whitehouse lawn, just as Bush was presentin de traditional B52 cargo on de presidential palace in Baghdad. Accordin to de new timetable, de war should start de week after Paddy's Day, and I'm hopin to watch de openin ceremony on CNN in de safety of me own home.

FRIDAY

Under cover of me dramatic shift in position on de war, I've also changed tack on de State indemnity for de religious institutions. It's obvious we made a balls of dis deal, and Pat Smartarse is gnawin away at it in de Dáil every day, like a dog wit a bone. So far, me line of defence has been dat, when Labour complain about how much it's goin to cost de State, I accuse dem of tryin to deprive de poor abused orphans of deir rightful compensation. But dere's only so long I can fudge de issue about de numbers likely to claim. So I've subtly shifted me position. Instead of relyin on legal advice to limit de numbers, we will now be relyin mainly on prayer.

SATURDAY

Talks on de Nort are reachin de crunch. Barring a late attack of stage-fright, de Provos are ready to take deir bow. Meanwhile, de Brits are preparin to shaft Trimble, who we all tink has as big a future in politics as Saddam Hussein. Of course dere'll be de usual last-minute manoeuvrin, de trettened walk-outs, and all dat shite. But de good ting is dat de parties have to do a deal in de next week or so. After dat, de Paddy's Day season begins.

SUNDAY

Speakin of which, de scramble for de St Patrick's Day junkets is not as intense as usual dis year. Wit de prospect of war, and Icelandic *("Islamic"? – Ed)* reprisals, de US is less attractive dan normal. Even so, neider Biffo nor Harney needed deir arms twisted too hard to go to California. Mary Hanafin bravely volunteered for New York; Mini Brennan got Boston; and Dick Roche is headin for de windy city – everybody agreed he was de natural choice – of Chicago. De big winner in de raffle was Martin Cullen, who won Brazil; while poor Ivor Callely drew de short straw of Birmingham (England radder dan Alabama). But we have people goin nearly everywhere, from Norway to New Zealand. Funny enough, de Muslim countries are an exception. It's just as well dey don't go too big on Paddy's Day in Karachi.

MONDAY

Say what you like about Tony Blair, but his presence in Hillsborough today proves his commitment to peace, especially at a time when he's so busy preparin to bomb Iraq back to de middle ages. Dere's certainly no doubtin de sincerity of his beliefs. Dere was almost a manic look in his eye when he spoke to me of de need "to stop dis evil man before he becomes any more powerful". One of his aides explained later dat he was talkin about Gordon Brown. De good ting about de fortcomin war is dat it gives de talks here a deadline, which is always a handy ting to have. Back in 1998, we wrapped up de deal at Easter. But we're goin for an earlier deadline dis time, because I'm hopin to give Nordern Ireland up for Lent.

TUESDAY

So much for dat idea. Despite our best efforts, de deal has stalled over sanctions. De unionists wanted an automatic red-card system to punish Sinn Féin for any off-de-ball incidents, which we broadly supported. But of course de Shinners have had deir own ideas about discipline over de years, so it was probably too much to expect dem to agree. Me and Blair got our heads togedder tonight to work out a late compromise. But true to form, Trimble fecked off to London on "urgent business" (maybe he had to see his tailor, to be measured for a big girl's blouse).

WEDNESDAY

Every cloud has a silver linin, dough, and because of me late night in Hillsborough I escaped havin to attend de Dáil dis mornin. Leaders questions are a pain in de hole at de best of times, but between Iraq and McCreevy's new Freedom from Information Bill, Pat Smartarse and de rest have been especially hard to listen to lately, so I enjoyed de lie-in. Of course I didn't let de mornin pass widdout droppin into de church to get me ashes done. Me make-up girl can do dem perfectly well: she has special ones for sensitive skin, and long-lastin ones dat ye don't need to touch up durin de day, and all dat. But I prefer to get de job done properly, by a priest. Ashes to ashes, dust to dust: nobody can accuse me of not doin me bit to promote recyclin policies.

THURSDAY

Anudder ting I do promote is openness and conspiracy *("transparency"? – Ed)*. But de Freedom from Information Bill is de result of a review of de original legislation, which has been workin in certain ways dat weren't intended back in 1997. De most obvious example is dat, in 1997, none of us taut Fianna Fáil would still be in Government in 2003. In fact, we didn't tink we'd still be dere in 1998. Wit all de tribunal stuff, de general feelin was dat de party would soon be in opposition, if not in jail. So de FOI seemed like a good idea to annoy de Rainbow Coalition Part II. Wit de collapse of de opposition, however, our priorities have changed. God knows, we could be in Government for decades, so we felt it was time to streamline de whole information area, and achieve certain "economies", as McCreevy calls dem. If dis goes well, we might press ahead wit udder much-needed reforms, such as de suppression of de newspapers.

FRIDAY

De situation wit Iraq has taken a major turn for de worse. Our neutrality was already like a pair of knickers wit de elastic gone, but now Bush and Blair have come up wit a March 17 deadline for Iraqi disarmament. Which means dat de Turd World War will probably now be named after Ireland's national day! Dis is not our fault, but you can be sure we'll be blamed for it anyway. Up to now, de Government's policy has been to keep our heads down, invoke de name of Kofi Annan at every opportunity, and urge consensus at de UN. War must always be de second-last resort, we believe: de last resort is us havin to make a decision about it on our own.

SATURDAY

Today was International Wimmin's Day. So after makin a speech at de Fianna Fáil wimmin's conference about our commitment to equality, I decided to put me words into practice. I rang Harney: "Good news, Mary," says I. "I've decided dat to mark Wimmin's Day, you should go to Washington wit de shamrock instead of me. And sure, while your there, you can go up to Boston for a few days. I know you're always sayin how much you prefer it to Berlin." But Harney just laughed. "Nice try, Taoiseach," she said.

SUNDAY

Half de British cabinet is trettenin to resign over Blair's Iraq policy. At least dis is one problem I don't have. I could declare war on France and nobody in de cabinet would notice, dey're all so busy packin for deir Paddy's Day junkets, or for Cheltenham. I sometimes tink its dangerous leavin such a power vacuum here at dis time, especially wit de St Patrick's Day festival startin at de weekend, and big crowds on de streets. But when I suggested to Biffo dat maybe I should stay at home in case of a coup, and dat he should go to Washington instead, he just laughed. "Nice try, Taoiseach," he said.

TUESDAY

I lost de head a bit in de Dáil today. De Opposition were harassin me about de rise in violent crime, but dey were hecklin me like a bunch of corner boys. So I told dem all to shut up and listen for once, which only made dem worse, of course. In de middle of de din, I could hear Hanafin whisperin behind me: "Deep breaths, Taoiseach." So I pulled meself togedder, and resumed me normal laughable *("affable?" – Ed)* style. I don't tink dere was any real harm done. But as me anger-management terrapist says, de big danger when I lose de rag durin question time is dat I might start givin de Opposition answers dey can understand.

WEDNESDAY

No question time for me today, tank God, due to de summit in Attens. Attens is of course de "cradle of bureaucracy". And today was an historic occasion as, in de shadow of de Apocalypse *("Acropolis" – Ed)*, we welcomed ten new members to de brudderhood of bureaucratic nations dat is de EU. As de Greek PM, Mr Costas Afortune said, it was an event dat marked de end of an era of deep division on de continent of Europe. Of course we were also markin de beginnin of a new era of deep division on de continent, with de French and de Brits not speakin to each udder, but we all put a brave face on it.

THURSDAY

Ye have to be philosophical as a United fan. Luckily dis is easy in Attens, de city of such great tinkers as Aristotle and Pluto. Of course, Greece has had famous football players too, such as Socrates (how did he end up playin for Brazil, anyway?). But not even if we had Socrates and Zico combined could we have beaten Real Madrid last night. As I said sportingly to Jose Maria Aznar dis mornin: "Dat must make up for yer personal approval ratin of minus 15 per cent, eh?" He went away in a huff before I got a chance to say dat if ever needed a body double, Willie O'Dea was wort considerin. Speakin of de war, today we met Kofi Annan to discuss de UN's role in Iraq's reconstruction. I told him Fianna Fáil could give him de names of a few good builders if he was interested.

FRIDAY

Today was a poignant day: de fift anniversary of de Good Friday Agreement. And what have we got to show for it? As I said to Blair in Attens, "we're like de ancient Greeks at dis stage, floggin a wooden horse". He looked puzzled at de reference – probably because he didn't do de Classics in school. But I tink he agreed wit de general sentiment. De situation is dat de Provos are unable to perform deir acts of contrition *("completion" – Ed)*, so it looks like de institutions will have to be put in deep-freeze till after de marchin season. De moderate parties are probably goin to be wiped out in next mont's Assembly elections, which we can't very well cancel because dat would look bad. And all in all, de Nort seems more bogged down in de quagmire of sectarianism dan ever before. OK, dere's more violence now on de streets of Dublin at de weekend. But dat's only a small consolation.

SATURDAY

De SARS virus is a big worry to de Government. Obviously anyting dat keeps Mickey Martin busy at a time when backbenchers are mutterin about me leadership can't be all bad. But we're naturally concerned about de tret posed by de Special Olympics, and we'll have to consider any medical advice we get about curtailin de event. Naturally, also, we'll, look at udder events dat pose a public helt risk, due to deir potential for mass airborne transmission of disease. I'm tinkin of de elections in de Nort, maybe. Or, eh, Dáil question time. Cancellin any of dese events would, of course, be regrettable. But we'll be led in anyting we do by de advice of de spin-doctors.

SUNDAY

Up to Arbour Hill dis mornin for de annual commemoration of de Risin. A more dan usually sombre occasion dis year, what wit de crisis in de peace process and dat. But I used me speech to appeal to de Shinners, in de name of God and of de dead generations – or in de name of feckin Joe Cahill, if dey prefer – to do de necessary and get de show back on de road. I don't know whedder it'll do any good, but Easter Sunday is a time for hope. Maybe even de Good Friday Agreement can rise from de dead

MONDAY

Easter Monday is a time when we reflect on dose who have made de ultimate sacrifice for Oireland. It's also a time when we reflect on de plight of Noel Dempsey who, aldough he hasn't made de ultimate sacrifice for Oireland, has to listen to a week of speeches from whingein teachers, which must be de next worst ting. Unfortunately, I couldn't reflect for long on dese matters dis mornin because as Taoiseach, me onerous duties involved goin to Fairyhouse to present de winner's cheque in de Grand National. Tanks to McCreevy, dis is about de only occasion left where I can be photographed by de newspapers givin away money, and I'd hate to miss it.

MONDAY

De college fees debacle has been a big embarrassment for de Government, and as Taoiseach I take full responsibility for ensurin dat evrybody knows it was Dempsey's idea to reintroduce dem, and nobody else's. Luckily he made dis point well enough himself wit his midnight speech in de Seanad and de attack on Mammy O'Rourke. But I was a bit exposed on de issue too: me arse was so far out de window at one point dat de dogs in de street were queuein up for a bite of it. Den, tankfully, Harney found dat twelve million in a drawer and offered it as an olive branch *(surely "fig leaf" – Ed)*. I hosted de peace talks in St Luke's, and somehow we persuaded Humpty Dempsey dat it would be in his best long-term interests to fall off de wall. I promised we'd put his credibility togedder again – resources permittin – at a later stage.

TUESDAYS

If de fiasco achieved anyting, as I said to de Cabinet today, it was to expose Labour as de party of de middle classes. "Dey call demselves socialists," I said, "but we're de real party of Connolly and Larkin." Dere was sniggerin around de table. "Is that Big Jim or Celia?" asked Biffo. De f***er's gettin even cockier dan he was now dat his main rivals for de succession have turned into de Dempsey and Martin Laugh-in.

WEDNESDAY

De udder big issue before de Cabinet yesterday was de Rottweiler's plan to clamp down on alcohol abuse. We talked him out of some of de more controversial proposals, which would have seen senior Cabinet members limited to a maximum of four pub openins, or tree pubs and two off-licences, per week. But de legislation is still hard-hittin. De main focus will be on preventin young people enjoyin demselves, which McDowell says dey continue to do despite Government policy. Under his plan, detectives disguised as banjo players will monitor pubs for early signs of craic developin. Dey will den radio reinforcements. And if de trouble escalates de ERU can be called in.

THURSDAY

MJ Nolan was on again askin me if I'd line out for de Oireachtas first 11 in Sunday's friendly against de House of Commons at Old Trafford. It's a great opportunity to play at de famous ground, but unfortunately I have a bit of a dodgy back at de moment so I had to cry off. I know United have tree or four dodgy backs and it hasn't stopped dem, but even so. But den again, dis sort of ting is probably beneet de dignity of a world leader. And if I made a mistake, de press would have a field day. So all and all, I've decided against riskin me credibility. Dat and me back. Me front's not in great shape eider.

FRIDAY

We'll need Old Trafford for Georgina's weddin de way de guestlist is growin. She's spent tousands on invitations alone, and her total budget for de event sounds like de annual estimate for de Department of Social Welfare. I don't know how dey're gonna fit evryone in. De embarrassin ting is dat, despite de lent of de guest-list, you-know-who hasn't got an invitation. I told Georgina dis was up to her. De only ting I asked was dat, if Celia wasn't comin, maybe dey'd issue de invites in someone else's name radder dan mine – Cardinal Connell's, for example. Unfortunately, de cards were already printed.

SATURDAY

Off to St Petersburg for a global summit to mark de terminology *("tercentenary"* *– Ed)* of dis great city, founded in 1703 by Ivan de Terrible *("Peter the Great" – Ed)*. Dis is a place dat has witnessed many historic events. It was of course here dat Lenin and Chomsky *("Trotsky" – Ed)* launched de October Revolution, an event directly or indirectly responsible for a lot of de terrible tings dat happened in de Twentieth Century, includin Joe Higgins. But St Petersburg also has some of de most magnificent art treasures in de world, and our Russian hosts are ensurin we visit as many of dem as possible. Dis is a massive pain in de hole, as ye can imagine.

SUNDAY

Dere's no escape from home, dough, and de travellin hacks are on me case about a story in de papers dat we're plannin to phase out de tribunals. Maybe dis is anudder of Dempsey's bright ideas, but as I said when I appeared before de Moriarty inquiry a couple of years ago, I know nuttin. Not dat de inquiries shouldn't be wound up. De whole point of dem was to take de heat off Fianna Fáil by borin de arse off de public, and in dis sense dey've achieved more dan we could ever have asked for. But closin dem down now would hit de vulnerable barrister community hard – it's deir version of de community employment scheme. So I woulda taut it was a non-runner wit de PDs, given deir commitment to improvin de lot of de severely advantaged. And even if de PDs went for it, we'd surely never get it past Labour.

MONDAY

Still on a high after de openin ceremony at Croker on Saturday night. What an occasion! De colour, de noise, de sheer bret-takin spectacle of it all. De famous names: Muhammad Ali, Nelson Mandela, Arnold Shwarz ... Schwartz ... eh, de lad from de Terminator fillums, and of course his lovely wife Minnie Driver *(er, "Maria Shriver" – Ed)*; de list goes on. Everybody had deir own favourite moment. But I tink for me, it was de sight of Team Oireland bein led into de stadium by Zero O'Donoghue, a man who had overcome his own serious physical disability – a progressive hardenin of de neck – to take part. And to tink dat I got booed just for makin a feckin speech! But anyway. De week ahead is all about one group of people, and in dis respect it should be an unparalleled opportunity for hobnobbin wit de Kennedys, eh, I mean, wit de special atleets. So as de man says: let de games commence.

WEDNESDAY

Meanwhile, back in Leinster House, de rejectionist Blueshirts are tryin to renegotiate de historic 2002 pact – de Holy Tursday Agreement – which limits me appearances in de Dáil to two days a week. Dis is still two days too many as far as I'm concerned. But it was a major breaktrew for me to get Tursdays off, a deal I was able to squeeze out of Labour last year in return for lettin dem go ahead of Joe Higgins and de gang of 22 in Dáil debates. Now Fine Gael are tryin to upset de apple tart, and Labour say dey may support a motion renegin on de original agreement. I'd be more worried about dis if de summer recess wasn't so close. By de time we get back in de autumn, de Blueshirts will hopefully be even nearer to extinction, and dey'll probably have forgotten de plan. But eider way, de recess can't come soon enough. Let de holidays commence, I say.

THURSDAY

De Special Olympics continue to inspire us, and today I did anudder tour of de venues to see how tings were goin. De venues demselves have been among de stars of de week. Of course, de Paddy Teahon Memorial Pool has been a great source of pride to us all, and a pregnant *("poignant"? – Ed)* reminder of what might have been at Abbotstown had de visionaries among us had our way. But dere has also been great praise for de equ ... equest ... eh, de horesridin centre at Kill, where I watched part of de massage *("dressage"? – Ed)* event dis afternoon. And yet probably de key ting in de success of de games so far has been de volunteers. Tousands of entoosiastic young people, workin all hours of de day and night for absolutely nuttin, except de satisfaction of a job well done. As McCreevy says, dis could be de basis of de next social partnership agreement.

FRIDAY

De resignation of Mr Justice Flood is a good ting and a bad ting. On de one hand, he's dropped us in de shite as regards costs. On de udder hand, his departure may allow us to pursue alternative mettods for continuin de tribunal. When we launched de inquiry back in de middle ages, de whole point was to put certain tings on de long finger. But de lent of de finger has surprised even us, and wit predictions dat de tribunal could now take anudder two centuries to complete, I tink it may be time to act. McDowell has a number of possibilities in mind. One is dat we could privatise certain areas: eg, put de Quarryvale module out to tender, and give de job to cheap foreign lawyers. Anudder option is dat we could take parts of de inquiry "underground", wit private hearins in de Dublin Port Tunnel. And de final possibility is dat we could have a big fire in Dublin Castle, which would solve evryting. I'm keepin an open mind meself.

SATURDAY

Praise de Lord! De Dubs bandwagon is on de roll again. Today's result at Clones is first and foremost a triumph for Tommy Lyons and de lads in blue and navy, but we must also give enormous credit to de GAA. Having generously given over Croker to de Special Olympics for consecutive weekends, de lads in headquarters were quick to realise dat, after de debacle against Laois, Dublin was a team wit special needs. Namely an extra week off before meetin Derry. Today's victory is a triumphant vindication of dat decision and I bet dat, whoever we get in tomorrow's draw, de organisation will reap de profits next weekend.

SUNDAY

Anudder incredibly emotional evening. A packed Croke Park. A tear-filled closing ceremony. Yes, tonight's draw on De Sunday Game, which saw de Dubs pulled out of de hat wit Armagh – dere-by guaranteein a capacity attendance at Croker next Saturday to see de closin ceremonies of de Orchard county's reign as All-Ireland champions – was a wonderful occasion.

So was de closin ceremony of de Special Olympics which, by coincidence, also happened tonight. Dis too was very emotional, especially wit me future son-in-law on stage; aldough probably me favourite bit was hearin Louis Walsh get booed instead of me. It was wit a special feelin dat I sang de games antem for de last time tonight: "So come we all/To take our chances/For we're prepared to try/To run the race/To face the challenge/And may we never/Have to say/Here are de resources for a proper disability bill/Goodbye."

MONDAY

De calm before de storm. I'm lyin low here in Kerry, enjoyin de long weekend and a few days peace between de Galway races and de weddin. I bailed out of Galway before Ladies Day, because God knows, I'm in enough trouble on dat score already. If I'm seen anywhere in de virginity *(er, "vicinity?" – Ed)* of a blonde dese days, de tabloids turn it into a story. I wouldn't mind only de Fianna Fáil tent does have nearly as many blondes as builders in it durin de races. But after de shite de papers wrote about Deirdre Heney last week, I had to stay well clear of her in particular. Just as well it's a big tent. De fundraiser was a massive success, as usual. Even so, Des is tempted to do a deal wit Hello magazine next year for de exclusive rights.

TUESDAY

Back to Dublin, where de pre-marital tension is risin fast. Needless to say, I didn't go out to Wicklow today for de registry office job. Partly because it was enough of a circus already, and partly because of an aversion to registry offices dat I've had for de past, oh, 15 years. So I just watched de pictures on de telly like everyone else. And Jayzus – de cut of Nicky! He looked like a lad who was arrivin to be charged, radder dan married – all he was missin was de handcuffs. It must have been a hard night. Speakin of hard nights, I celebrated de happy event wit Joe Burke in Fagan's dis evenin. I'm supposed to be off de gargle until de weddin, but I told Georgina I'd stick to de diet Bass, and she said it was ok. I only had de five or six.

WEDNESDAY

Spent de day packin, except for a housecall from Louis Copeland to check dat me waist measurement hadn't changed. Obviously I'll be in Louis's tin of fruit for de big day itself. But Georgina told me to make sure and pack shorts as well. Dere's a heatwave in France, she says. But dere's also de fact dat, after forkin out a million for de rights, de Hello people will probably want a centre-fold of me in me Calvin Kleins at some stage. She said it'd be no harm if I got a bikini wax, just in case. But, eh, dere's only one place I know in Drumcondra dat does dat, and I'm steerin clear of dere at de moment.

THURSDAY

D-Day minus two. Have safely arrived here at Chateau d'Excrement, *("d'Esclimont" – Ed)* where de weddin operation is in full swing, and de situation is growin more tense by de minute. De place is crawlin wit armed guards. Some of dem belong to Hello, while de udders have been assigned by de French government to look after me personal security. I can't tell which is which, but I just hope dey don't get into an argument, because if dey do dere'll be no survivors. Apart from de armed guards, I am now also under de control of de weddin organisers, who have planned de event like de Normandy landins. De rumour is dere'll be a full rehearsal at de church tomorrow, but I haven't been told anyting yet, for me own safety. For de moment, me orders are to stay in de room and await furder instructions.

FRIDAY

As expected, we were ordered to de church today for a dry run. Dry is right. Dey issued us wit bottles of mineral water to avoid dehydration, but I'da murdered a pint of Bass. Tankfully, I was allowed to wear a teeshirt and shorts for de run-trew, and tankfully as well, we only had to run trew it de once. I was smuggled into de church, a bit like when I appeared at de Moriarty Tribunal a couple of years back. And it went widdout a hitch, apart from a fracas in which de Hello bouncers gave a martial arts demonstration usin some of de tabloid snappers as volunteers.

SATURDAY

De big day. Back to de church, only dis time for real. It was a very emotional occasion and when Georgina said "I do" dere were tears rollin down everybody's cheeks. Den again, it coulda been sweat – it's 40 degrees in de shade here! Dere were definitely tears rollin down people's cheeks by de time de Hello photographers were finished. De bastards took six hours and gave everybody a big pain in dc hole. Of course, I couldn't relax completely until I had de speech over me. I was up half de night tryin to tink of someting good, but eventually I decided to speak from de heart. At first I had a bit of trouble findin it – it's been years since de last time I spoke from dere – but when I did, it all came out right. I got a standin ovation at de end. It's amazin what a bit of raw honesty does. I must try it in de Dáil sometime.

SUNDAY

I believe we're gettin roasted in de media at home. Apparently dere were "ugly scenes" involvin locals outside de church yesterday. But Jaywus, I can't be responsible for what French people look like: it was us Hello wanted de pictures of, and at least we were all turned out well. More worryin is dat de papers also claim we were booed and jeered, because de people resented deir village bein hijacked for de day, when dey were prevented from seein anyting. I didn't hear de boos meself, but after all de hassle it's caused, I'll say dis for nuttin: if Hello magazine come lookin for de exclusive rights to Cecelia's weddin, I know what I'll tell dem. A million and a half, minimum.

MONDAY

De summer is well and truly over, and autumn is settin in. De evenins are gettin shorter and de leaves are gradually flutterin to de ground, a bit like de Government's opinion poll ratins. De return of full-time politics is imminent, and wit it de season of mists and yellow truthlessness, as de poet W.B. Keats put it so well. Soon, de trees of Nort Dublin will be completely shorn of deir foliage (aldough ye still won't find anyting on Ray Burke up dere). Soon too, like de birds flyin sout for de winter, I will have to fly to de soutside for de new Dáil session, and de warmer climate dat results every time Pat Rabbitte opens his mout.

De bastard has fired de first shots of de season, claimin dat me and de Government are "gripped by paralysis". Dis is of course not true, aldough unfortunately, we continue to be beset by problems on all fronts. For example, I see dat Mini Brennan has had anudder one of his honesty attacks and admits dat puttin de LUAS trew de Mad Cow Roundabout is a balls-up. Now he wants to put a bridge on stilts across it. For Jayzus sake. He might be better off puttin himself on stilts. Den he could be seen more easily in a crowd, and he mightn't be such a hoor for de publicity.

TUESDAY

Down to Kerry for de Listowel Races, and anudder balls-up at de Great Suddern Hotel. We taut we'd drop in for a quiet lunch. But unbeknownst to us, de Blueshirts were havin a get-togedder of de parliamentary party dere – a retreat, or a counsellin session, or someting. Dere's so few of de f***ers left, you wouldn't notice dem now, except in a very small room. Anyway we only copped it when we were half way up de drive and somebody spotted Charlie Bird on de lawn. Normally, you'd hear him 100 yards away, but Westlife were playin on de car radio and I had it turned up. So we had to perform de quickest U-turn since Dempsey's college fees debacle. If Rabbitte tinks I'm gripped by paralysis, he shoulda seen how fast I got outta dere today.

WEDNESDAY

We couldn't find a new pub anywhere in Kerry, so instead dis mornin I performed de official openin of a school in Listowel. As I said to Páidí Ó Sé, education is vital, and I hope young Kerry people can learn how to play football again as soon as possible. Páidí gave me de sort of look dat he used to give to Dublin corner forwards. I taut for a minute he was goin to bite me leg off, but de moment passed. Den it was off to de races, where I bumped into Enda Kenny, dis time on purpose. Unusually for him, Enda had just backed a winner

THURSDAY

Aldough de Nordern marchin season passed off peacefully, de upcomin All-Ireland final between Tyrone and Armagh is a soberin reminder dat violence is never far away in de Nort. Dat's why we're makin anudder big effort to get de political institutions up and runnin again. And I'm glad to say dere's major progress on dat score. David Trimble has been refreshed by his long break from democracy, and he's been strentened by de fact dat now de UUP have sorted out deir internal difficulties, he has de unanimous support of almost 51 per cent of his party. Grizzly Adams, meanwhile, is also anxious to get on wit tings, because Sinn Féin activists can get twitchy when dey don't have eider a war or an election to work on.

FRIDAY

De imprisonment of Joe Higgins over de refuse charges row is a worryin development. On de plus side, he'll miss de return of de Dáil and I won't have to put up wit de usual guff from him for a couple of weeks. In fact, it's temptin to wonder if we could find an excuse to jail Rabbitte for a munt or twelve: maybe we could introduce a retrospective charge for de use of sarcasm. But de downside wit Higgins is dat a period in de gulag could turn him into a martyr. It's probably part of his master-plan for seizin power, like his pals Lenin and Tolstoy *(Trotsky? – Ed)* in 1917. Wit de local elections comin up next year, I don't want any popular movements breakin out on de nortsoide. But I wouldn't put it past him now to go on a hunger strike, out of pure badness.

SATURDAY

Speakin of martyrs, dis weekend marks de 200th anniversary of Emmet's famous speech from de Docks, and his subsequent execution. Unfortunately, de site where he made de speech is gone – dere's been a huge amount of development in de docklands in recent years – so dey had to have de commemoration today up in Tomas Street instead. Even so, it was a very movin ceremony: dey had de wooden block where Emmet was beheaded and evryting. I had to lay a wreet beside it, and needless to say I was a bit nervous. As a politician, I don't like to be near a choppin block in any circumstances, and especially not wit a bunch of Joe Higgins protesters behind me. For all I knew, dey could have had a hatchet. But de event passed off peacefully, tank God. As one of de speakers said, de atmosphere at de execution was ugly too, but Emmet defused it by not makin inflammatory comments from de gallows. So, like Emmet, I said nuttin. And unlike Emmet, I left wit me head intact. Silence is often de best policy, I tink. As I told me driver on de way home: when Enda Kenny takes his place among de national leaders of de eart, den and only den let me epitaph be written.

MONDAY

Just in time for de return of de Dáil, me backbenchers are fallin over demselves to embarrass me. First GV Wright runs down a pedestrian while drunk, and now Michael Collins runs up an unpaid tax bill while – apparently – sober. Wit a name like Michael Collins, I don't know how he ever got past de Fianna Fáil selection process in de first place: he sounds like a Blueshirt plot to undermine me. I suppose I'm lucky he was only a backbencher. He's already resigned de party whip – before I hit him wit it – which means dat officially he's not one of ours anymore, but dat he'll continue to vote wit de Government anyway. Dis is an ideal situation, when you tink about it: it might be an idea to remove de party whip from all our backbenchers, in advance of dem bein caught doin someting illegal.

TUESDAY

Everybody knows dat de Dáil needs major reform, but some of the experimental changes we've introduced seem to be workin well. In particlar, de jailin of Joe Higgins on a pilot basis has been a great success, and dere's a strong case for extendin his one-munt trial period to, say, five years widdout trial. In most udder respects, however, de resumption of de Dáil today was a case of business as usual. Enda Kenny made it back from Transylvania *("Tanzania" – Ed)* safely, tank God. He seems a bit more aggressive dan usual, but maybe it's de malaria tablets. God love him, even if he pointed an elephant gun at you, you wouldn't be too scared. Not unless you were one of his own feet.

WEDNESDAY

De Composer and Auditor General claims de deal Woods did wit de religious orders could cost de State a billion. When I tink I could have built me Bertie Bowl for dat, it breaks me heart. But what adds to de grief is dat de issue has given Pat Smartarse a stick to beat me wit. Somebody must have tipped him off dat McDowell was excluded from de negotiations as AG, because he's bein goin on for munts about de election lamppost stunt, tryin to tease de Rottweiler out of his kennel. In fairness to McDowell, he didn't take de bait – we were puttin sedatives in his Pedigree Chum, just in case – until Woods started blabbin all over de airwaves yesterday. Now McDowell's gone apeshit. He gave de hacks an interview dis mornin to set de record straight, and he also insisted dat I back him up in de Dáil. So I had to pay tribute to his work as AG and minister on de record of de house today. And even dough I didn't use de full script he supplied, it still sounded like me oration at de grave of Jack Lynch.

THURSDAY

De good news is dat de Fianna Fáil rebellion on de smokin ban appears to have been stubbed out. Dere was token opposition at last night's parliamentary party meetin, but Noel Davern – de Dan Breen of de anti-ban movement – has assured us dat Sout Tipperary will remain loyal to de Government. De opposition at de meetin would probably have been stronger, only de bastards kept havin to go outside for a fag.

FRIDAY

I gave a wide-rangin interview to de Irish Times today in which, among udder tings, I said I intended to retire from politics at 60. But as I told de interviewer, I foresee a future role for meself in sport. In fact, me secret ambition is to manage de Dubs, eventually. I tink I could revolutionise de approach to de game, by gettin away from de whole adversarial ting, and instead buildin consensus, involvin de opposition more, and tryin to agree outcomes to games dat would benefit all parties equally. Anudder area I could get involved in, as I told de interviewer, is horticulture. I have a lot of experience. Bein leader of Fianna Fáil is a bit like bein in charge of a vegetable patch (in more ways dan one): it's a full-time job keepin de weeds down. So if me retirement target should be achieved, er, earlier dan planned, hopefully I'll have me own TV gardenin series to fall back on. De rest of de interview was mainly by way of apologisin to de people for de fact dat half de country is dug up at de moment, and to promise dat we'd fill it back in before de next election.

SATURDAY

Off to Rome for de EU summit. It's always a pleasure to visit de Internal City, wit its fantastic architecture, even if we couldn't find a pub anywhere dat was showing de Under-21 final from Navan. I had to interrupt me meetin wit Blair to get updates, but tanks be to God de Dubs won anyway, beatin Nordern opposition for a change. As I said to Tony, British domination of de All-Ireland championships is a growin problem for de sout. Basically, dat whole Nordern confidence-buildin ting seems to have gone too far, and it might be time for a few confidence-reduction measures. So Blair said he'd see what he could do to disimprove de sports facilities up dere. Meanwhile, we also decided to press ahead wit November elections. De Provos are at last ready to make a final gesture on disarmament. I tink deir feeling is dat, at de rate we're diggin up de country, it's only a matter of time before we find de arms dumps anyway. So in an historic compromise, we're going to merge de IRA wit de NRA, and use de Semtex for road-fill.

MONDAY

Every time we tink we have de Nort sorted out, sometin happens to screw de whole ting up. I knew leavin for Belfast last week dat dere was a problem. We had an agreement wit General de Casteroil dat he'd brief me at six turty on Monday evenin, or as soon as de cement was poured into de bunker, so I could see if dere were any wrinkles dat needed to be ironed out. But den, of course, de Provos took him to a bog in Sout Galway where dere'd been a lot of rain recently, and when de digger started in, de whole feckin ground under dem shifted. De general lost his mobile phone and his wellies, and he had to be dug out of a bog-hole himself before dey could get on wit de destruction of arms. From what he was able to tell us, I was pleasantly surprised at de range of stuff de IRA got rid of. De idea of includin de collected speeches of Caoimhghín Ó Caoláin was a nice touch, I taut.

TUESDAY

As a contribution to peace in Oireland, de Dáil has been decommissioned for a week. It's been a whole munt since de end of de summer holidays, and de Fianna Fáil backbenchers were exhausted – ye'd be amazed how tirin it is sittin around on yer hole doin nuttin. So we gave dem a well-earned break for Halloween, to spend more time wit deir families, and less time plottin wit each udder behind me back. An even bigger advantage of de holiday is dat I don't have to do de usual question-time shite, so I was able to spend time today concentratin on de Nort and tryin to put togedder some last-minute moves dat might save Trimble's arse. Speakin of moves, I see on de news dat de bog in Galway is still slidin. Accordin to Jim Fahey, it's now trettenin roads and bridges. If he knew how much Semtex was in dere, he'd realise dere was more dan roads and bridges trettened. We should probably warn de poor bastard. But dat would infringe de terms of de agreement wit de Provos.

WEDNESDAY

De vintners are gettin desprit. After munts of hidin behind sophisticated press releases, dey cut loose today at a mass meetin in Portlaoise. From de bit I saw on telly, it looked like a rally of de Ku Klux Klan: if Frank Fahey had walked in in de middle of it, dey would have dragged him out and hung him from a tree. Some of de speakers were over de top, to say de least. One of dem accused de Government of teetotalarianism (er, "totalitarianism"? – Ed) and claimed de country was bein run by "Adolf Ahern and Mussolini Martin". I know I'm a famously carrismatic figger, and a brilliant public speaker; but in fairness, I tink de comparisons wit Hitler end dere. Still, now dat Mussolini's ban is provin so poplar wit de genral public, I'm happy to be part of de Rome-Berlin axis, or de Dublin-Cork one, anyway. I have to hand it Mickey, de helt service is a disaster, but de only thing people will remember come de next election is dat he was the man dat banned smokin in pubs. Dere's a lesson dere for all of us.

THURSDAY

Blair was on de blower dis mornin about de Nort, so I took de opportunity of commiseratin wit him over de resignation of Ian Duncan Doughnuts. It's always a big blow to lose a leader of de opposition as incompetent as dat. I told him I went trew de same crisis when Michael Noonan – who was very similar to Duncan-Doughnuts, in bein baldy, as well as useless – was taken from us so cruelly. All good tings come to an end, I said. And den again, sometimes dey don't. Maybe he'd get lucky, I suggested, and de Tories would elect an Enda Kenny, someone wit a good head of hair but nuttin under it. "Enda Who?" says Blair. "I couldn't have put it better meself," says I.

FRIDAY

When I saw de strange lights in de Nordern sky last night, I taut de IRA had finally bitten de bullet and blown up all de arms dumps in Donegal and Monaghan. But den I read in de papers today dat it was only de angora borealis – a phen … a phenom … eh, an event caused by a massive explosion on de surface of de sun. And even if de Provos had been responsible for DAT, and Genral de Casteroil had been flown to de sun on a rocket to witness de event, his report would be so low-key dat de unionists would insist it should have happened on de moon instead, for greater transparency. I'm not sayin de genral understated last week's event, but put it dis way, I wouldn't send him out to sell fireworks in Henry Street.

SATURDAY

Jayzus, what a night. Dere's so much fireworks now in de run-up to Halloween dat ye'd tink dere'd be nuttin left for de day itself. But Drumcondra was like de bleedin Left Bank *(er, "West Bank"? – Ed)* until four in de mornin. In fact, given de success of de State's fireworks ban, de publicans should stop complainin about de anti-smokin legislation, and order extra cigarette machines instead. Anyway, durin a lull in de fightin, a few kids knocked on me door doin "trick or treat". But in keepin wit McCreevy's instructions, I explained to dem dat dere'd be no treats for anyone until de public finances improved, and while I'd like to make an exception for dem, we all had to share de pain equally, etc, etc. One of de youngsters trettened dat if I didn't cough up, I'd be gettin sometin unpleasant in me letterbox. But I said his Da would be gettin sometin unpleasant in his – de explanatory guide to Budget 2003, to be exact. After dat, dey ran away screamin.

MONDAY

I know he's been on de run for a while, so ye'd expect him to look a bit rough. But it was still a shock to see dose TV pictures of a patetic, bedraggled old man, cornered like a rat. Poor Rambo. Dere's just no hidin place from de Criminal Assets Bureau dese days. I never taut I'd see him facing charges in de Bridewell, and applyin for de free legal aid. In fact, I taut de only way he'd ever be brought to justice was if I made him Minister for it again, and gave him a driver. I wouldn't mind only I never found anyting on him, despite climbin every tree in Nort Dublin. Of course it's a densely forested region, and I suppose I might have missed one.

TUESDAY

De victory in de Miss World is anudder triumph for de Government's economic policies. Time was it woulda been untinkable for an Oirish bird to win de competition: dere was years when we couldn't even make de qualifyin standard. Under the Fine Gael-Labour government of de 1980s, it wasn't just de economic figures dat looked bad. But tanks to Ray McSharry's 1987 budget, we went from de Nolan Sisters to de Corrs in de space of a decade. Now Oirish people are better lookin dan at any time in deir history. Rosanna Davison is a case in point. Wit a fadder like Chris de Burgh, she should have been a candidate for help from the Combat Ugliness Agency. But now look at her.

WEDNESDAY

Tom Parlon might have got away wit claimin dat he'd single-handedly delivered decentralisation to Boglands Central. Everybody knows he has a neck like a jockey's bollocks, and in politics dis is widely admired. But he went too far in suggestin dat, compared to him, Biffo was a waste of space as a representative for Laois-Offaly. Biffo's first reaction was to go after him wit a hurley. Luckily, we were able to calm him down eventually on de basis dat McCreevy would set de record straight in de Dáil. And fair play to Charlie, he put his back into it. I nearly felt sorry for Parlon havin to sit dere and take it. Ye could almost hear him squirm (I know de sound from Michael Smitt, de time I told de Dáil he was 100 per cent behind de Hanly Report). But it's a useful warnin to de PDs not to be gettin above demselves.

THURSDAY

I'm a great lover of de oul literature, as everybody knows. So I was genuinely honoured today to unveil a new sculpture on de Royal Canal of de legendary Brendan Behan, autor of de Borstal Boy, de Square Fella, and of course de Ballad of Reading Gaol. As I said in me speech, Behan lived most of his life on de Nortsoide (of Kimmage), and was very close to Drumcondra (while he was in

Mountjoy). So we shared a special infirmity *("affinity"? – Ed)*. And derefore it was all de more disappointin dat, after I spoke, one of de family got up and said dey never wanted me to unveil de statue in de first place. I had as much to do wit Behan's spirit, he suggested, as Tom Parlon had to do wit decentralisation. Dat's gratitude for ye. Feckin Behans. Dey were all de same, anyway.

FRIDAY

Off to Brussels for de EU summit, aldough I might as well have spent de day doin me Christmas shoppin for all de progress we made. Germany and Poland couldn't agree on de new votin arrangements, and after sittin around twiddlin me tumbs all afternoon, I decided dere was something to be said for de old system, under which de Germans settled deir differences wit Poland by invadin. Now it's up to us to finalise de new constitution, but I'm not worried, because we have a secret weapon. We're gonna lock all de leaders up in a room with Dick Roche, widdout an anastetic. After listenin to him for a few hours, dey'll sign anyting we put in front of dem.

SATURDAY

Now dat de Yanks have doled out de contracts for de reconstruction of Iraq, I've decided to subtly reposition meself on de war. De new line is dat we were against it all along. We've taken legal advice on dis and de lawyers say it's OK because, havin studied me speeches from last February, dey haven't got a feckin clue what I was sayin. De udder reason for de switch is dat de war is clearly turnin into a disaster. It's obvious now dat Saddam is never going to be caught. And I wouldn't be surprised if, after de inevitable American witdrawal, he makes a comeback. So all in all I tink dis is a good time to reveal dat, in fact, we were utterly opposed to military intervention in Iraq, from de very start.

SUNDAY

Shite. First Rambo, now Saddam. At least Rambo never had to live in a hole (if you don't count Swords). But I never taut dey'd take Saddam alive eider. I see he was down to his last million dollars: he'll probably be applyin for de free legal aid too. Anyway, I tink it might be time to subtly reposition meself on de war, again. Luckily, de army officer dat caut Saddam is one of ours. His fadder's from Clare – a point I drew attention to on de Christmas card I just sent to de White House. I also mentioned dat Clare was de location of Shannon Airport, which of course we made available to de war effort at great risk to de Government's popularity. But I'm not complainin, I said, because de capture of dis wicked tyrant "is de final vindication for all of us who stood shoulder to shoulder in de coalition of de willin". I don't know if Dubya will fall for it, but it's wort a try.

MONDAY

De great moment has arrived. After many years of careful preparation, I have finally reached de barnacle *(er, "pinnacle"? – Ed)* of me political career. De next six munts will define not only me own personal legacy to histry, but also perhaps de fate of de European project itself. Tanks to Silvio Maccaroni and his pals, it won't be easy. I don't know what we ever did to deserve comin after de Eyetalians in de EU presidency relay race, but de bastards always seem to drop de baton on us. It's touch-and-go now whedder we can preserve a single-speed EU, radder dan de two-speed, or multiple-speed version tretten by de French and de Germans. And if Mini Brennan succeeds in provokin CIÉ and Aer Rianta into a combined strike, Ireland could be reduced to a single speed – stationary, to be exact – for de duration of de presidency. But wit de help of God, and me legendry negotiatin skills, it'll be all right on de night.

TUESDAY

De lads from Foreign Affairs have been briefin me extensively, to avoid any repeat of Maccaroni's tendency to put his foot into it at every opportunity. So before I met Romano Prodi today at Dublin Castle, for example, I was warned to steer away from European issues, and stick to areas where I was comfortable – like Nordern Ireland. Sure enough, when Prodi apologised for publicly disagreein wit me, I told him to tink nuttin of it. I was well used to bein abused by Prodi's, I said, because Nordern Ireland was full of dem. I taut dis was a good line meself, but when he demanded clarification, one of de DFA lads kicked me on de shin, so I changed de subject.

WEDNESDAY

Meanwhile, back on de domestic agenda, de enlargement of Kildare and Mead, and de resultant change in constituency boundaries, is causin a lot of concern. De proposals will certainly have serious consequences for some, as Biffo was explainin last night in de bar. In de same week dat we heard how tousands of animals could become extinct because of global warmin, he pointed out, dere is now a danger dat we will lose some of our rarer TDs as well. Here, Biffo slipped into his hilarious David Attenborough impression, describin de distinctive head-plumage of de lesser-spotted Donie Cassidy: which, because of de absorption of its native habitat (Castlepollard) into de new Mead West constituency, is now a tretten species. By de time Biffo had done Batt O'Keeffe and John Ellis as well, we were all in stitches. But of course we shouldn't be laughin. De environment is a very serious issue.

THURSDAY

Me tactic in public is to play down de chances of any kind of agreement on de problems facin de EU. But dat's just like Alex Ferguson talkin up de opposition before a big match. De trute is I can't wait to get at de disputin parties and knock deir heads togedder. And today I had a visit from de Belgian PM, me old friend Guy Thermostat *("Verhofstadt" – Ed)*, to discuss de nuts and bolts. It's all about grasp of detail at dis level: ye have to know yer IGCs – or inter-governmental conferences – from yer QMVs – or quality bus corridors *("qualified majority voting" – Ed)*. By coincidence, after meetin Guy, I had to go out to Merrion Square to launch a fleet of Dub buses painted in de EU colours, and dis gave me a cunning idea for breakin de current impasse. De way I see it, we could have a one-speed Europe, but wit France and Germany allowed to use de fast lane between seven and ten in de mornin. I tink dis could be a winner.

FRIDAY

As part of me new responsibilities, I'm expected to solve all de world's conflicts, or at least to present a unified EU position on dem, which is about de same ting in terms of difficulty. To underline dis point, me visitors today included de Palestinian foreign minister, who was askin for our support in implementin de road map for peace. De problem is, we've been so supportive of de Palestinians in de past dat de Israelis have often accused us of bein psychosomatic *(er, "anti-semitic"? – Ed)*. But I told him we'd do our best, anyway, and asked him to give my regards to President Marrowfat, who is still under siege at his headquarters in Ramallah. Den I had to fly off de Berlin, for a meetin wit Gerhard Shredder. It's all go when yer de EU president.

SATURDAY

Even wit our great responsibilities on de world stage, it's business as usual at home. And despite de impendin legal challenge, de Government (or at least Mickey Martin) is determined to press ahead wit de smokin ban, in March, or April, or maybe May. June or July might be even better. Dat way, we could postpone de mass outbreak of pneumonia among doorway smokers until next winter. And it would also get us over de EU presidency, in which nicotine is traditionally an important negotiatin tool. De trute is, treaty talks have always been done in smoky rooms, and dis is no time to be departin from precedent. No matter what Mickey Martin might tink, we're plannin to get de Poles and de Spaniards and de French and de Germans togedder in a pub somewhere, and trash someting out. Dis is where de smoke-filled atmosphere is important. It's vital dat none of dem see de small print before agreein de deal, and dat dey don't notice deir clothes smellin until after dey get home.

MONDAY

I have a certain sympatty wit Alex Ferguson in de Rock of Gibraltar row, especially since JP put his fifty million donation back in his arse pocket. Me and Alex speak de same language, which is probably why people can never understand a word HE says, eider. And of course nobody wants to see a great club like Manchester United tear itself apart *(speak for yourself – Ed)*. But suggestions in de papers dat I'm actin as a go-between in de case are wide of de mark. Ye'd tink I didn't have enough be doin as Taoiseach and President of Europe, flyin around de continent negotiatin deals wit de Spanish and de Poles and de Maltesers, and de rest of dem. Time was I'd a been on for a shot at becomin de hero of Old Trafford. I'd have urged de United board and Coolmore to meet half-way (which would be Drumcondra, near enough). But dat was den. Now, it would be beneet my dignity to get involved in horse-tradin. Of de kind involvin horses, anyway.

TUESDAY

De Cabinet meetin agreed de Rottweiler's plans to close Mountjoy in favour of a new prison on a greenfield site near Dublin. Inevitably, McDowell has his beady eye on Abbotstown. He outlined for us his vision of "Crime Campus Ireland", a state-of-de-art corrective facility where all our elite criminals would gadder. De CCI would have evryting a modern criminal needs: gyms, stone-breakin facilities, etc. But what would make Abbotstown ideal, de Rottweiler says, is its complete lack of transport infrastucture. If dere was a jailbreak, de escapees would have no chance of gettin out of de area before de autorities called in reinforcements. I tink he's only takin de piss. But as always wit de PDs, ye can't be sure.

WEDNESDAY

Dere's a certain amount of nervousness in politics about de new electronic vote system. We all remember de harrowin scenes of Nora Owen in tears after discoverin – widdout any prior warning, tanks to de cold, mechanical computer calculations – dat she'd lost her seat. But de system can't always be expected to work as well as dat, and dere are bound to be SOME problems. De Opposition are insistin dat dere should be a "paper audit trail" in case of mechanical failure, and aldough we in Fianna Fáil are not normally entusiastic about paper trails of any kind, I tink dey have a point.

THURSDAY

John Hume's retirement from politics is de saddest news I've heard since de det of Mudder Teresa. No man has done more for de cause of peace in Oireland. Not even me, an dat's sayin sumtin. Whenever I hear Grizzly Adams goin on about inclusivity, an parity of esteem, an de need for an agreed Oireland and all dat shite, I remind meself dat John Hume was makin de same speech turty years ago. An God knows, he made it often enough since. In fact, I noticed wit concern dat in his press conference, he didn't say anyting about de speech retirin. In any case, his decision has paved de way for Bairbre de Bruin to become an MEP. Oh well. Ireland's loss is Europe's gain, and all dat.

FRIDAY

I don't know de full details of Mandy's libel case, but apparently it relates to a joke about de notorious 1964 Portillo Affair *(er, "Profumo" – Ed)*, involvin call girls, dat rocked de British government to its foundations. Back in de dark days of de Rain-Cloud Coalition, when Mandy was de FF press officer, she joked to some hack dat she wouldn't be de first Mandy to bring down a government. She mightn't be de last, eider, if Blair brings back Peter Mandelson yet again, as he eventually will – but dat's neider here nor dere. De hack den illustrated de story about our Mandy wit a picture of one of de 1964 women in de nude: de vague implication bein – Mandy says – dat she would use similar tactics to bring down Bruton's Coalition. Ye'd really have had to love yer country to even tink about it, is all I can say. I just hope it's a short case, because in de meantime, I'm missin a press secretary. Of course, Government policy towards de media is to tell de b*****s nuttin anyway, so we'll probably survive a couple of days widdout her.

SATURDAY

Ye'd tink dis whole Gilmartin affair would be very embarrassin for me, especially as it looks like I'll have to appear before de Tribunal durin de EU presidency. But if anyting, it's made me more popular wit de udder EU leaders. Silvio winks at me evry time we meet lately, and Jacques rang durin de week to say how unfair it was dat a sittin premier has to give evidence before a judicial investigation. It wouldn't happen in France, he says. I won't have much to tell dem anyway. I have no memory of meetin Gilmartin, even if Mammy O'Rourke says I was in de room. But if I was dere, de view must have been obscured by Pee Flynn's eyebrows, because I saw nuttin, and I know even less. Tankfully, Gilmartin has made no allegations of wrong-doin by me, which is only right. In de 1989 Government, I was like a goldfish in a shark tank.

MONDAY

If Gerry Adams says he was never in de IRA, den of course I believe him. I also believe in de toot fairy. I believe Enda Kenny is electrifyin Fine Gael, as promised, and I believe Osama bin Laden is an active member of de Legion of Mary. I also tink Elvis is alive and well and playin Tuesday nights in Slatterys of Capel Street. No, really, I don't doubt for a minute dat Grizzly is tellin de trute. I hope dat, for his part, he will believe me when I say dat I was never in Fagans pub in my life, contrary to de rumours, and dat I've never been in de same room as a pint of Bass, anywhere.

TUESDAY

I'll tell ye anudder ting I was never in – seriously – and dat's de room where Tom Gilmartin says he had a meetin wit meself, CJH, Pee Flynn, Rambo, Liam Lawlor and udders in 1989. I have to admit dat some of Gilmartin's details do have a ring of trute, dough. When he says dat de people he was dealin wit made de "effin Mafia look like monks", dat does sound a bit like de 1989 Cabinet, right enough. Also de suggestion dat someone told him he could end up "in de Liffey" is just about believable. Certainly, dere was a more robust approach to government business back in CJ's time, and de Liffey was always an option. But I tink it's more likely dat what Gilmartin was told was dat he could end up "in Liffey Valley (wit a big shoppin centre)" and dat he just misheard it. Yeah, I'd say dat's what he heard at de meetin. Eh, not dat dere was any meetin, of course.

WEDNESDAY

Ever since we decided to turn Oireland into Europe's dirigible hub *("digital"? – Ed)*, de Government have been embarrassed by de continued use of paper in elections here. De shame of it. We're determined to remove dis stain on our reputation, once and for all, and to drag de country into de 21st century. But de knuckle-draggers on de opposition want to keep us in de stone age, scratchin ballot papers wit pencils, one, two, tree, and den squeezin dem into ballot boxes to be counted manually for days on end. It makes me sick just tinkin about it. Unfortunately, de forces of darkness have successfully exploited public fears about de technology. Which is why, in order to introduce discrepancy *(er, "transparency"? – Ed)* into de new system, our independent commission – specially chosen by de Government – is so important. It includes some of de most prominent people in Irish society, aldough de names escape me at de moment. And it will have far-reachin powers, includin de power to pull de plug on de system if necessary. Of course, we've told dem dat if dey ARE pullin any plugs, dey should always press "save" first.

THURSDAY

De new guidelines on rural housin are not a prescription for unlimited ribbon development, as critics claim. Dey are an honest attempt to balance de demands of conservation wit de maximum possible number of votes in de fortcomin local elections. Dis means dat anyone wit roots in a community will be able to build dere, subject to de normal plannin requirements, such as road safety, proper sewage, access to at least two county councillors, etc. For too long, people in rural Ireland have been dictated to by deir so-called betters in Dublin. Now, finally, we're givin dem a break. And de way I see it, if dey live in rural Ireland – God love dem – dey need all de breaks dey can get.

FRIDAY

Me openin address to de Ard Fheis was completely given over to helt, which I tink demonstrates to our critics on dis issue just how much of a priority de government has given to de need to nip any independent hospital candidates in de bud. De message of me speech was dat de Hanly Report will not have any adverse effects on emergency services – by which I mean services, de absence of which might lead to de emergence of a hospital candidate. We tink dis is one of de key battle-grounds in dis election, de udder of course bein de need to stop de Shinners eatin any furder into our base. Dat's why ye'll also hear lot of stuff at de Ard-Fheis about us bein de real republican party, de party of de Irish language, de true Gaels, de direct descendants of de men of 1916, etc. Dis is de message I'll be drillin into our 800 local candidates (one for every year of British oppression), as I send dem out to fight for Oireland.

SATURDAY

I'm not dat big into rugby, but I watched de Twickenham game on telly dis afternoon because dere was nuttin else on (unless ye count Zero's conference speech: when we were doin de schedules, we put him on at de same time as de match, just for badness). And it was grippin stuff, especially when dat lad Gordon Dempsey went over in de corner. De result set up de rest of de Ard-Fheis nicely. In between Brit-bashin, we pulled a few vote-winners outta de hat: McCreevy's clamp-down on tribunal lawyers, Mini Brennan's 600 million for de Mad Cow Roundabout; me own announcement of de 200-euro old-age pension by de next general election. And, of course, Cullen's speech about rural housin went down like mudder's milk. Personally, I preferred de days when Biffo used to do de kick-de-opposition speech as me warm-up, before he turned into Henry Kissinger. But overall, I tink de day was a big success. De grassroots lapped it up, anyway, and we sent dem home sweatin, aldough dat could have been because de hall was overheated.

MONDAY

De first week of de smokin ban, and predictions dat de measure would result in mass killins of pub workers have not materialised. On de contry, it seems to be a roarin success. So I tink it's time to pay tribute to de man who made it happen, de man who stood up to de smoke lobby when udders wavered, who risked everyting on a measure dat he believed was de right ting to do. In fairness, dough, it wasn't just me. Micheál Martin deserves a bit of credit as well – but enough about him. De important ting is dat de country is today a heltier place dan it was yesterday, a point I underlined by visitin de Mater's lung unit dis afternoon. In de midst of all de arguments for and against, we mustn't forget what de whole point of de ban was: ie, to distract attention from hospital waitin lists. Eh, no, I mean to protect de helt of workers from de known risks of environmental tobacco smoke. Yeah, dat was it – I forgot for a minute.

TUESDAY

When I heard a Waterford TD had lit up a fag in de Dáil bar, I immediately taut it must be Cullen. He's been very ratty since de ban came in. I was resigned to de likelihood one of de back-benchers embarrassin me by smokin a cigar durin Leaders' Questions or someting, but if it hadda been Cullen, it woulda been a lot worse. It could have been de signal for a national rebellion, like when De Valera's lads took over de Four Courts in 1922. So, anyway, it was a big relief when I heard it was only John Deasy, de Blueshirts' spokesman for head-banging. I even had him in de sweep dat Biffo organised for first TD to be caut smokin, so it was a good result all round. Not dat I'm unsympatetic. In fact, when we allowed exemptions from de ban for prisoners and psychiatric patients, I believed dere was a case for includin de Fine Gael parliamentary party as well, on humanitarian grounds. Dey were sufferin enough as it was, I taut.

WEDNESDAY

No Leaders Questions today tank God. Instead, it was off to France to address me udder parliament – de European one. It's always a pleasure visitin Salzburg *("Strasbourg" – Ed)*, but especially today, because I was performin a lap of honour after de success of de EU summit. Negotiations on de constitution are back on track. We've set June 18th as a deadline for agreement on all outstandin issues. And such is de optimism now dat we already have a draft version of de so-called Fagan's Treaty (in keepin wit tradition, it'll be named after de venue of de signin ceremony) ready to go.

THURSDAY

An EU President's work is never done. I was just knockin off last night when I got a call from de Turkish prime minister, Mr Cardigan *("Erdogan" – Ed)*, askin me to

De latest exchequer figgers are a welcome sign of de economy's underlyin strent. Of course, dis government will not abandon its fiscal responsibilities. But de surplus does allow us to relax de purse strings for priority projects: eg, buyin de local elections. Heh, heh.

De Composer and Auditor General claims de deal Woods did wit de religious orders could cost de State a billion. When I tink I could have built me Bertie Bowl for dat, it breaks me heart.

I'm missin a press secretary at de moment. Of course, Government policy towards de media is to tell de b******s nuttin anyway, so we'll probably survive a couple of days widdout her.

When Ratso asked me how me own "situation" was, dere was an awkward moment. I didn't know whedder he was referrin to de relationship between me and de Widda Bogle, or de one wit Harney and de PDs. In de end, I fudged it, and said I hoped we'd be togedder "for a couple of years anyway".

I considered interruptin me holiday when de news came trew of a terrorist plot in England. I decided in de end dat it would have a calmin effect on de population if Mary Coughlan handled de press interviews, since de public would reckon dat if dere really was a problem, dere's no way she'd be left in charge.

Wid de reshuffle rumours in full flow I dropped a hint to Seán Haughey dat if he baut anudder new suit, dis one wouldn't be wasted. De poor hoor was off to Louis Copeland's like a flash.

Galway is always mobbed durin de racin festival, but dis year is mad altogedder. Every chancer in de country is here – an dat's just de Fianna Fáil tent.

With Cecilia now in the money, it's a bloody good ting we changed our minds about abolishin de artists' tax exemption in de budget.

intervene to prevent de collapse of de UN talks on de unification of Cyprus. Dis is a complex issue, and luckily I'd read up on it a bit. Because of its strategic location in de Mediterranean, Cyprus (or "Malta", as it's sometimes known) has been invaded many times. But de current division between Greek and Turkish sectors dates from 1974 when de Turks invaded in response to de Greeks' failure to stop Demis Roussos makin records. Ever since, attempts to broker agreement have foundered on de ancient mistrust between de two peoples. Mr Cardigan said dat my success wit de Good Friday Agreement made me de ideal person to mediate. Udderwise, he feared a repeat of de historical double-cross where de Greeks built a wooden horse as a gift to de Trojans, who didn't know what was inside until it was too late. Sounds a bit like de unionists and de Good Friday Agreement, I taut to meself. But I told Mr Cardigan to leave it wit me.

FRIDAY

Wit all me great responsibilities on de world stage, it's important I don't take me eye off de ball at home. Dat's why I'm preparin for a U-turn on de decision to witdraw benefits from widows. De Opposition may be shite, but it's still an election year and we don't want to give dem any candelabras, as de French say *(er, "cause celebrés?" – Ed)*. Enda Kenny reminded de Dáil de udder day dat when de Blueshirts took a shillin off de pension in 1929, it haunted dem for 60 years afterwards. I tink 60 years is a bit of an understatement – we were still mentionin it on de doorsteps at de last election – but I know what he means. De udder important issue is de new national pay deal. SIPTU trew a wobbly durin de week over Harney's tret dat she'd pull de plug on the Government if we didn't go ahead wit de break-up of Aer Rianta. I don't know about dat. De PDs are so committed to competition, maybe dey'll break up demselves, into de Parlon and McDowell factions, and give de consumers more choice. In de meantime, I'm plannin de steer a middle course on de airports issue until summer, by which time Mini Brennan will be de new EU commissioner. Wit his Napoleonic tendencies, I tink only Europe is big enough for him at dis stage.

SATURDAY

Great news in de latest exchequer figgers, wit revenue layin an easter egg, and spendin well below projections. Dese are timely figgers, comin as EU finance ministers meet in de white elephant enclosure at Punchestown. But even apart from dat, dey're a welcome sign of de economy's underlyin strent. Of course, de need for prurience *("prudence"? – Ed)* still remains. Dis government will not abandon its fiscal responsibilities. But de surplus does allow us to relax de purse strings for priority projects: eg, buyin de local elections. Heh, heh. No wonder de Blueshirts are findin it hard to give up de fags.

MONDAY

Dramatic news from Sout America, where de Colombia Tree have been cleared of trainin gorillas *(er, "guerillas" – Ed)* in de jungle. Dey've been done on de lesser count of travellin wit false passports. But deir acquittal on de main charge is a surprise considerin de hints dropped by de Colombian Minister for Justice, Miguel Macdowellio, dat dey were "guilty as hell". Dis was also de view of de nordern unionists, who would have been disappointed wit any sentence more lenient dan de firin squad. Even so, the fact dat de tree have been cleared will boost me efforts to restart de peace process, which are continuin despite claims to de contry by de depitty chairman of de policin board, Denis Bradley. I have great time for Denis, but I respectfully suggest dat he's a complete b******s for sayin I wouldn't talk to de Shinners because I was "in a huff" wit dem. It's outrageous to tink I would allow me personal feelins get in de way of someting as important as dis: when in fact de only reason I wouldn't talk to dem is because we're competin for votes in June.

TUESDAY

McDowell briefed de Cabinet on de security arrangements for de big weekend, and de tret posed by a group called de Wombles. Dese are hard-line British anarchists, opposed to globalisation, capitalism, and washing of any kind. Many of dem are expected to be armed wit serious body odour, and fleas cannot be ruled out completely. It's a serious tret, so all Garda leave has been cancelled for de weekend and a wing of Cloverhill prison has been cleared to deal wit de trouble-makers, who will be given fair trials and jailed (but not necessarily in dat order). De inmates removed from Cloverhill will be given Garda uniforms and discretely handcuffed to udder Gardaí on Saturday, to boost de security presence on de streets.

WEDNESDAY

On a personal level, I feel a certain sympatty wit Beverly. But on de level of a leader already facin a drubbin in de June elections, I have moved decisively to ensure dat, hencefort, dere will be a forty foot pole between me and her at all times. Her activities as a bank official were clearly not compatible wit Fianna Fáil ettics. But arguably even more serious was de fact dat RTÉ got filmed evidence of me canvassin wit her in Castlebar durin de last genral election, which meant I had no choice but to cover me arse now. I know she's very popular wit de local grassroots, so I may have to stay out of Mayo for a while. Luckily, dis is not a major sacrifice.

THURSDAY

I've also taken a tough line against de misuse of departmental resources for election purposes, dereby deliverin a stern rebuke to Noel Dempsey and Frank Fahey. When you're in power as long as us, de lines can get blurred between constituency work and de minister's office. But rules is rules, so when Inda Kinny raised de matter in de Dáil yesterday, I had no hesitation in agreein wit him and hangin de lads out to dry. It caut him on de hop, I tink. But de trute is, I was a bit worried about Inda, who was just about to embark on a two-day tour of Ireland in a small aeroplane. I get on well wit Inda, and I wouldn't like to lose him. De election campaign could be hard enough as it is.

FRIDAY

Inda made it down safely, but it's not all good news. Despite de care we took in choosin de membership, de e-votin commission has recommended against usin de machines on June 11th – and us after already spendin a couple of million on assurin de public dat de technology was a hunderd per cent reliable. Cullen has emerged from dis lookin like a second-hand car salesman. Aldough, in fairness, ye had to admire his neck in media interviews today. He made Beverly look apologetic by comparison. When anyone mentioned resignation, his attitude was no, he wouldn't be acceptin any resignations, de commission members would all finish de work dey were appointed to do, etc. Dis is de official line we've agreed on: dat it's de commission needs more time, not de machines. A bit of adjustment wit deir software and dey'll get de right answer next time.

SATURDAY

It's been a bad week on de domestic front, but as de leader of Free Europe, nuttin could ruin me big day today. As Pat de Cox said at de press conference dis mornin, dis is a moment when hope and hysteria rhyme (or sometin like dat, anyway. I wasn't listenin to him – he's a ferocious windbag). And as I welcomed one head of state after anudder at Farmleigh dis afternoon, I taut to meself: Bert, you've come a long way for a lad from de nort inner city. De security plan worked a dream, by de way: dere were so many guards on de beat in Dublin dat it looked like we'd kept one of our election promises. But today was all about de new EU states, and de flag-raisin ceremony at de Áras was very emotional. I taut dey mighta got Westlife to sing de Beethoven ting – and jazz it up a bit – radder dan de RTÉ choir, but dat's only a minor criticism. Den it was back to Farmleigh for de dinner and a bit of music. When we got word of de riots at Ashtown Gate, we got de sound enginners to turn up de volume, just in case. But McDowell was able to report soon afterwards dat de matter was well under control. De cops got to use de lawn sprinklers dey borrowed from de PSNI, he said, and dey were delighted wit demselves.

TUESDAY

De end of de EU presidency draws near, and de grim reality of a return to domestic politics hovers over me like a pigeon waitin to take a dump. I'm so used to bein an international statesman now dat, widdout such a role, I'll feel naked. Dat's why I'm beginnin to tink seriously about dis EU job. When it first came up, I couldn't see meself bein outta de country for up to four nights at a stretch, evry week. But now I look at Oireland and it's like I'm a stranger in me own land. It hit me de most strongest last week in Croker when I realised dat de Dubs were gonna be beaten by Westmead – for Jayzus sake! – and yet I didn't feel any real embarrassment. Even me native city seems different to me lately. It looks like Gay Mitchell will top de poll in de Euros, for example: I mean, what's dat about? I tink what I'm tryin to say is dat I feel I've grown a lot in de last six munts. Whereas Oireland just got smaller.

WEDNESDAY

Time was, too, when I wouldn't give much taut to clothes. But de new me is different. So when I was packin for de G8 summit dis mornin, I made a special effort. Maybe it's part of de liberation I feel as a world leader, but I finally broke open de silk boxer shorts dat Celia bought me a few Christmases back. I also tried on de yella jacket-and-trouser ensemble dat Jim Fitzsimons gave me when he was clearin out his wardrobe in Brussels. He had loads of dapper outfits dat he never got around to wearin, and he taut dis one would look good on me. De invite for de G8 said to dress "smart casual", whatever dat is. But I know de venue's very tropical, so I'd say de udder leaders will be in Hawaiian shirts and de like.

THURSDAY

De bastards all wore dark suits, as it turned out, but I tink me choice was judged a success. "Pantalons tres interessant!" Chirac said, which I believe means: "Nice treds!" De summit was a success too. We kept it fairly simple, so Bush could follow evryting. But we touched on all de issues: Iraq, oil prices, world trade. Den de subject of de EU job came up, and I played it cool. Blair joked dat he'd prefer an English-speakin candidate but he'd accept me as a compromise. As rehearsed, I said de job was "not on my agenda at dis point", which is de phrase Biffo came up wit for me before I left (when I was tippin him off dat dere might be a job vacancy for Taoiseach soon). But I added, after a pause, dat if Europe felt it needed someone wit proven negotiational skills, from a country dat represented de outstandin success story of de EU, a country dat had maintained good relations wit America – I nodded to Bush – well, maybe I'd have to consider de offer. At dis point Jacques Chirac smiled and touched me arm de way he does. He said dat while he was a great admirer of mine, France would have to insist dat any EU president spoke at least basic French. I nodded in agreement. "Naturellement," I said.

FRIDAY

I flew home trew de night, and was back to Drumcondra in time to vote first ting after breakfast. De nuns were out in force on Church Avenue, as usual, and overall it looks like bein a respectable turn-out. Dat's de good news. De bad news is dat we're gonna get a good kickin from de electorit. Even me brudder Maurice tinks he could lose his seat on de council – because of de Ahern name. De Shinners are cleanin up all over de city, he says, bitterly, and dere'll be no more Fianna Fáil lord mayors for a while. Maybe dat's just as well, dough, after what happened de current one. Poor Royston. Even before pollin day, evrybody knew he was f***ed. He was never de sharpest tool in de box. But in hindsight, de only way he was goin to win was if some loyalists hijacked his car, drove him up de Dublin mountains, and held him at gunpoint until de campaign was over.

SATURDAY

Up to Parnell Park dis evenin to watch de Dubs go trew deir paces against London. Apart from dat, I stayed indoors all day and kept me head down. De news from everywhere was even worse dan we feared. Gerry Collins is down de tube in Munster. McDaid is up de Swanee in de Nort-west. Meanwhile, de locals are a wash-out. We've lost Dublin, Limerick, Monaghan and God knows where else. Nicky Kehoe got tree-and-a-half-tousand votes in Cabra, which means he'll be bitin me bum come de next genral election. And if it's not Shinners toppin polls, it's Blueshirts. Who'd a taut we'd ever used de terms "Gay Mitchell" and "popular" in de same sentence? I'm tellin ye: I don't even know me own country anymore.

SUNDAY

Cullen says we're headin for de worst result since 1927. But dere is some good news. Our strategy of makin all de counts as slow as possible is borin de media to tears evrywhere, so maybe de f***ers will tink twice before dey oppose electronic votin again. I stayed well clear of any of de count halls meself, of course. And dere was a bit of welcome relief in de football on de telly dis evenin. Dis looked like bein anudder bad result when England led on first preferences. But de French came trew on transfers in de end, tanks be to God. De udder good news is dat tousands of people turned up in O'Connell Street dis mornin for de free James Joyce breakfasts. And ye know, it's very apt dat we should be celebratin de centenary of Doomsday *(er "Bloomsday" – Ed)* dis week. After all, he was a Dub who left Oireland for Europe. When de country of his birt got too small for him, he opted for "silence, exile, and cunning". Cunning is my middle name, of course. And I have no problem stayin silent when it suits me. But as I was sippin me pint in de Brian Boru tonight, de question I was wrestlin wit was dis: Could I really hack de exile?

MONDAY

It's going to be some week. I've got to meet God knows how many bleedin backbenchers to reassure dem dat deir seats are safe. I've no idea what I'm goin to say to dem but the old way of treatenin dem with Biffo just doesn't seem to work any more. I tink Biffo is best kept on a short lead dese days. He's made it a little obvious dat he wants me job and I don't want to be askin them to do me any favours. I'll probably tell the backbenchers to take a page out of Greece's buke in the European Championships. Like de Greeks, dey're a limited bunch at the best of times but when dey come together under the leadership of a master tactician, dey can perform miracles. Of course I realise dat after the elections we're really more like France – the cocky holders who got stuffed by lesser opposition.

TUESDAY

De talk is all about reshuffle. At least it keeps de lads on deir toes, but who am I gonna send to Brussels? Fianna Fáil have as much chance of wining a by-election as England have of winning a penalty shoot-out. I've de same problem as Sven with various fancy dans dominating the Cabinet midfield – Cullen, Brennan, McCreevy – glory holes de lot of em. No matter who I send, we'll get stuffed in the election. Hickey says we might hold Kerry South but Zero's not a bad lad. I'd love to send Brennan but his seat's about as safe as Tommy Lyons'.

WEDNESDAY

Dere's quite a few lads I'd like to see sleepin with de fishes after a six-hour parliamentary party meetin. Six hours! It felt as long as me European presidency and the stink of sweat was something else. Anyway, I knew I'd have to bring something to de table. When I came out of the toilet I didn't want to be just holdin me lad in my hand. So, I turned to de old Fianna Fáil manual and told em dat we'd start pourin money into health, education, whatever you're havin yourself. Some members of the party remained a little unconvinced but de bulk of em just wanted to hear something nice to tell de constituents. Leadership is all about keeping the troops happy, udderwise dey get to tinkin about life with Biffo in charge. Kids are always quieter when dey've got de crisps and can of Coke.

THURSDAY

If it's not de ESB it's Aer Lingus. What is it with de State sector. I spend six munts runnin Europe and when I get back dey're eider queuin up to go on strike or to run off with the family silver. One ting is certain: I'm not havin an electricity strike – de Dubs are playing in Portlaoise for God's sake so I'll have to watch it on de box. As for Aer Lingus, I know we have to play dis very carefully. I've already got a massive pain in me hole from Aer Rianta (Brennan should be sent to Siberia not Brussels) and now I'm hearin about airline embryos *(MBOs? – Ed)*. If de public tink we're planning on creatin more fat cats after Eircom we'll be for de high jump at the election, SSIAs or not. I'll set up a review committee to examine de feasibility of blah blah blah. Dat should buy me 18 munts.

FRIDAY

Europe is looking like a foreign country already. When I was king dey were eatin out of me hand but now I can't even get me own lads to change parties in Strasbourg. Apparently we're still members of the Nazi Fascist Baby-Eating party (not de PDs apparently but sometin like dem). Anyway, I can't be worryin about Euro politics now, I've bigger fish to fry. Feelin a bit mischievous, I mentioned retiring from politics again. It gave Biffo a new lease of life and he was bouncin around like a baby hippo. Of course I plan to stay around til I'm 60 but if he believes dat I'm sure he'll put me in a headlock some evening.

SATURDAY

I got de press lads to ring de Mirror newspaper and correct de story about me headin off to Monte Carlo for Seán Dunne's birthday party. I had originally said yes but I taut he'd said Carlow. Five days on a yacht wit not a drop of Bass in sight is not really for me! Maybe in de old days it would have happened – Celia would've made me go and she'd have got de new wardrobe for herself and put me in some casual gear (aldough I've got me own yellow trousers for such occasions now). Dunner is a good party supporter and he knows how to throw a decent bash but I'm just tryin to reconnect wit me people and de south of France is not de place to do it. It's hard enough keepin Biffo at bay without people tinkin dat decent skin Bertie has turned into flash Harry. Anyway, de papers were more interested in the Dáil bar bein illegal. De amount of lads who give it a miss since the smoking ban, it's a miracle it's solvent, never mind legal.

SUNDAY

As if tings aren't bad enuf with Brennan and the airport baloney I've got to spend Sunday listenin to Mother O'Rourke puttin de boot into de Government on de same issue. She's not one to forget easily. I'm startin to wonder if Donie was worth the trouble. Worse still, she only came on de radio after Inda Kenny was given a solo run about how marvellous he is, with his bleedin' tiny party. You'd tink he was de one who'd just saved Europe from extinction. You'd tink he was de one who found an agreed new EU president. You'd tink he had just led de most successful European presidency ever! Dey say a good Samaritan is never recognised in his home town. Maybe I should've gone to Monte Carlo after all.

MONDAY

De Attens Olympics are a lesson to all dose people who said Oireland had no right to bid for Euro 2008. Shortage of facilities has not stopped de Greeks. I see de poor bastards were reduced to holdin de women's shot putt competition in de ruins of a 2,500-year-old stadium, for Jayzus' sake. And to tink we were criticised for proposin to have games in Lansdowne Road, which is barely half dat age. But despite deir lack of venues, and deir early setback in de synchronised motorbike crash event, de Greeks have done a good job. I just wish I could say de same ting for de Oirish team. It's been a trail of disaster so far. But we have to look on de bright side, and Zero – who phoned me last night wit a progress report – says de rowin team are certainties for a medal. He's enjoyin himself anyway: he was just back from a visit to de Apocalypse *(er "Acropolis?" – Ed)* when he rang. He says it'll be very nice when it's finished.

TUESDAY

Speakin of ancient monuments, de decision by Joe Walsh to retire as Minister for Agriculture has made de reshuffle dat bit easier. Hopefully de udder Pillar of Hercules – Michael Smit – will voluntarily remove himself as well, and save me havin to shaft him to his face. He must be able to see de writin on de wall – short of sprayin it on his house wit an aerosol can, I couldn't make it more obvious. But I'd radder not have to sack him, because ye have enough enemies in dis game widdout addin to dem unnecessarily. McCreevy is still not speakin to me over his Brussels "promotion", even dough I got him one of de big jobs. I know I screwed him. But he's on de pig's back, financially. He can retire in a few years' time and devote himself full-time to backin horses. It's not de worst way to go. Ye'd tink he'd be just a little grateful, de Kildare b****x.

WEDNESDAY

Mini Brennan rang first ting dis mornin, all excited, wit de news dat de Port Tunnel has broken trew up at Whitehall. Dat's all de diggin done, he says. It's only a question of wirin it up now and Bob's yer uncle – de trucks will be off de streets before ye can say: "ten-four, good buddy, dis here's a rubber duck, c'mon". I congratulated him and told him to keep up de good work. He asked me if I had any opinions about "the height issue". So I said dat de fact he was a bit on de short side was neider here nor dere – nobody held it against him so long as he did a good job, and it wouldn't be any part of me considerations when I sat down to pick de new Cabinet next munt. But apparently he was only talkin about de height of de tunnel, and whedder we should raise it to facilitate super-trucks. Me and my big mout! So I told him I had no feelins about dat eider, but dat if he did want to avoid de expense of increasin de tunnel height – an admittin we made a balls of it in de first place – we could always ban de super-trucks altogedder and say it was for environmental reasons. He said he was tinkin de same ting.

THURSDAY

De word on de street was dat Smit would not be goin peacefully. And sure enough, I see in de Oirish Times today dat sources close to de monsignor are sayin I'll have to "take him out". De same sources are boastin about his record in reducin de cost of Army deafness settlements. And dey also question me judgment – obviously wit his encouragement – in flaggin de reshuffle a year in advance. De nerve! I only flagged it a year in advance so f***ers like him could make plans for deir retirement. So much for me social conscience. I taut Smit was sufferin from a bit of Army deafness himself de way he missed all dose hints I was droppin about de need for him to take up golf or someting to keep himself busy next year. And after all dat he says I'll have to "take him out".

FRIDAY

Oireland's Olympics are goin from bad to worse. Zero rang me dis mornin to say dat even de rowin team – our best chance – have revised deir ambitions downwards. Dey'll be happy now if dey can just avoid drownin. Dere's no good news anywhere else eider. Our high jumper couldn't have cleared de bar last night if dey'd allowed him use a pole vault. Our walkin team is a complete non-runner. And it looks like old fadder time has caut up on Sonia. She just about qualified in her heat tonight, but if she makes it into de top tree in de final next week, it'll be a miraculous medal and no mistake. De sooner we get football and hurlin into de games de better. I must talk to Hickey about dis when he gets back.

SATURDAY

De only consolation, as usual, is dat de Brits are crap too. But when Blair rang me dis evenin, I had to congratulate him on de historic achievement of deir rower, Mattew Pinhead, in winnin his fourt Olympic gold. He didn't even know about it: he's still in Sardinia, and de telly in Silvio's pad doesn't get de BBC, apparently. He asked me if I'd seen de pictures of Berlusconi wearing a banana *(er "bandana" – Ed)* on his head, and I said no, but nuttin would surprise me about Silvio at dis stage. Den it was on to politics. I briefed him on de latest developments in de Nort, in de run-up to next munt's conference. De word is dat Grizzly is gettin ready to ditch de Provos once and for all, I said. Robinson is gaggin for de first-minister job. And, addin to de sense of optimism, Paisley is still sick. "I hope it's nuttin trivial," says Blair. "And so say all of us," says I.

MONDAY

I don't know about anyone else, but I'm really enjoyin dis Cabinet reshuffle. Critics tink I shouldn't have flagged it so far in advance, but dat's de whole point. I've had no critics dis summer – at least widdin de party – because de bastards are eider worried about deir jobs, or worried about screwin up deir chances of a job. Even Ned O'Keeffe has been bitin his lip lately, in de hope of a glorious comeback. It was cruel of me to put de word out dat he might be in for a recall, but sure ye have to enjoy yerself when ye can. Besides, when I arrived back at me desk dis mornin, I found it weighed down wit goodies. Dere was an apple from Dick Roche, a box of chocolates from Willie O'Dea and a big bunch of flowers from Mary Hanafin (forget-me-nots, I tink). And best of all, dere was an anonymous document from de Department of Defence wit de latest figure on Army deafness pay-outs, which is much lower dan originally expected. Very touching, dat. I have a birtday comin up next week, and at dis rate it should be a good one.

TUESDAY

We were plannin a State reception for de Olympic team. But Macca wanted to have dem up to de Áras as well, so we decided dat two parties would be overdoin it. In fact, one party is overdoin it, de way most of dem performed in Attens. But de games ended well anyway. Fair play to Cian O'Connor, jumpin clear wit all dat weight of national expectation (not to mention Tony O'Reilly) on his back. Den, on top of de success in de showjumpin, we had Fadder Cornelius Horan's heroic performance in de Marraton, where he won de gold medal – albeit for Italy.

WEDNESDAY

De first post-summer Cabinet meetin was a routine affair, except dat de smell of male sweat was even heavier dan normal. McCreevy presented his last set of exchequer figgers, and said a few words about his departure for Brussels, makin it sound like he was Scott of de Antarctic leavin de tent. De figgers are good, tankfully, so we have plenty of room for manoeuvre in de budget. I warned evryone – includin Charlie – not to speculate publicly about it, but de f****r went straight out anyway and told de media dat de budget would be presented by Santa Claus. After de meetin, Smit sidled up to me and apologised for any "misunderstandings" dat had occurred over de summer. You know what dose bastard journalists are like, he said, dey twist yer words. He asked me if dere was anyting he could do to make it up. So just for de crack, I mentioned how in de old Soviet Union and China, people sometimes went on television to confess deir crimes. I didn't mention to him dat dey still got shot, anyway. But he went off looking very hopeful, and I heard him askin Dermot Ahern if he had a mobile number for anyone in Prime Time.

THURSDAY

Spent de day puttin de final touches on our special two-day parliamentary-party meetin, which is to be held in Cork next week. De feelin in Fianna Fáil is dat we've maybe lost touch a bit wit de common man lately, so where better to put dat right dan in de luxurious surrounds of Inchydoney Spa Hotel? Two days of pampering, massages, hydroterapy, transcendental mediation, yoghurt *(er "yoga?"* *– Ed)*, and whatever yer havin yerself. De treatments are designed to relax evry part of de mind and body, apparently. I always find dat seven or eight pints of Bass can do much de same ting, but dere ye are. De main ting is dat de two days will be a chance for us to detoxify, to rid de system of de poisons dat build up as a result of daily contact wit de PDs – eh, I mean as a result of de pressures of modern life. Hopefully, we'll be able to re-establish contact wit our inner selves, find out de tings dat really matter, and remind ourselves dat dere's more to life dan materialism. After dat, we'll get on wit buyin de next general election.

FRIDAY

Speakin of spas, Smit's performance on Prime Time was a tour de france. It was like listenin to Dessie Connell apologisin for de church's mishandling of abuse allegations in religious-run schools. Of course Biffo's impersonation is even better – he had me in stitches on de phone dis mornin doin a re-run of de highlights, complete wit his Tommy Gorman-style analysis of whedder Smit had done enough to get himself back into de team. I wasn't able to enlighten Biffo in dat regard. Even I've stopped tryin to guess what Bertie Ahern will do until after de decision is publicly announced – I've been caut out too often in de past. But whatever happens, I (nearly) admire Smit at dis stage. If de worst comes to de worst, true to de traditions of de Defence Forces, at least he went down fightin.

SATURDAY

While de Inchydoney jaunt is top of de agenda for de moment, preparations are also intensifyin for de Leeds Castle talks dat will hopefully get de Nordern institutions back on track. Dere've been two worrying omens for de peace process in recent days. On de one hand, Bill Clinton went into hospital. And on de udder hand, Ian Paisley came out. De latter incident casts some doubt on whedder de DUP are really serious about a deal. From our contacts with de Peter Robinson camp, we were given to understand dat de big man was on life support and dat, if de opportunity arose, Robinson would personally pull de plug. We told him dat, as chairman of de international decommissioning body, dis would be General de Chastelain's job. But Robinson's people said dey'd radder take care of it widdin de party. Now we just don't know what's happenin.

MONDAY

I am writin dis in me hotel in Koala Lumpur, de capital of Malaysia (or possibly Thailand). Anyway, me tour of de Pacific rim is goin well. We had de EU-Asia summit in Hanoi over de weekend, which was a big success despite tensions over Myanmar. I didn't feel de tensions meself, personally – me officials are dere to protect me from dat sort of ting. But dey told me about dem afterwards, when dey also explained where de f**k Myanmar was. We tried to arrange a bilateral meetin wit de Chinese premier, Wen Jiabao, on de margins. Unfortunately de margins were booked out – dey're always very popular at dis sort of ting – so we had to have it on a sofa in de conference centre instead. We discussed trade, climate change, terrorism, and any udder business. Den Wen started on about feckin James Joyce again. At which point, I looked at me watch suddenly and says "Jayzus – is dat de time?" – before pretendin to dash for de airport.

TUESDAY

Dermot Ahern rang me from home wit de final draft of his future-coalition-wit-Sinn Féin speech, or Operation Hokey Cokey as we're callin it. De plan is dat we'll put our right leg in and (in clarifyin comments later dis week) our right leg out on de issue. Dependin on how dis is received, we'll put our right leg in and out again next week: den in, out, in, out, before eventually shakin it all about. Dere are a couple of different reasons for our tinkin on dis. First, de refusal of all suddern parties to consider coalition wit de Shinners is givin de DUP an excuse dat we need to remove. Second we have to keep manners on de PDs, who'll be buildin an independent profile (probably widdout proper plannin permission) between now and de next genral election. And turd, in de Fianna Fáil tradition, we have to keep our eyes on de main chance, which – after 2007 – could be de Shinners.

WEDNESDAY

De tour of Asia continues. Our latest stop was Singapore, where I had a useful meetin wit prime minister, Lee Well Hoong *(er "Lee Hsien Loong" – Ed)*, at which we bote agreed to increase trade between our countries. Basically, dey're goin buy more of our hi-tech computer stuff, and we're goin to import deir total ban on chewin gum. De udder highlight of de visit was dat de Botanical Gardens named a new flower after me. "So long as it's not a tulip," I says to dem, "because we have enough tulips in Fianna Fáil already."

THURSDAY

Today, we began de long flight home wit a stop-over in Bahrain, to highlight business opportunities in de Arab world. I met de prime minister, Sheikh Khalifa

Bin Salman al-Khalifa, and I paid a courtesy call to de king, Sheikh Hammad Bin Isa al-Khalifa. De al-Khalifa boys have it all sown up here, and nobody seems to mind. Maybe I shoulda made me brudder Noel de Minister for Foreign Affairs, de way I originally planned. I tink de Bahrain visit was a success, aldough de protocol in dese Arab states can be a pain in de hole. I was very glad when we got back on de plane for home and de stewardess asked me what I'd have to drink. "Someting strong," I told her: "I've a bad case of de sheikhs."

FRIDAY

It's good to be home, especially wit de papers full of Enda Kenny's botched reshuffle. Michael Ring is a bit like John Deasy. It's dangerous havin him on dc front bench, but it's more dangerous not havin him dere. I reckon Inda will be so busy watchin his back for a while dat his front will be even less of a tret dan it was. But it was back to work for me dis mornin, and I rang Iveagh House first ting, before launchin de second part of Operation Hokey Cokey. De gist of me clarifyin statement was dat we wouldn't touch de Shinners wit a 40-foot pole. But after discussions wit Dermot, I amended de pole-lent to 20 foot.

SATURDAY

Up to Farmleigh for a meetin wit Kofi Annan. We discussed a wide range of issues, includin de appointment of Conor Lenihan as junior minister wit responsibility for overseas development. Kofi argued dat Africa had enough problems already, but I assured him dat Conor's promotion was not just a case of de Government wantin him to spend more time abroad. "He has great, eh, energy," I said. We also discussed Iraq – we agreed it was a bad situation – and Sudan, which we agreed was a terrible situation altogedder. Finally, he asked me if Oireland remained committed to reachin de UN aid target of 0.7 per cent of GDP by de end of 2007, and I told him dat it was one of our two main national priorities, alongside de drainin of de Shannon. He seemed happy enough wit dat.

SUNDAY

As usual, Mansergh wrote most of me Bodenstown speech. But dis year's address was a key part of de Hoeky Cokey strategy, so I was up half de night makin amendments. De main teem was dat dere can be one Army in de State and it's not P O'Neill dat speaks for it; it's, eh, W O'Dea. In fact, de Shinners are ready to play ball if de Paisleyites do too, and de next fortnight will be crucial. De final details of de "demonstrable" act of decommissioning have yet to be worked out: de DUP wants it to be on terrestrial television, whereas Sky are insistin on pay-per-view. But we're reasonably confident it's goin to happen widdin two weeks. And dat come Halloween night, at long last, de Provos will go out with a bang.

EL DIARIO DE UN
SOCIALISTA DEL CAMINO NORTE

THE STORY SO FAR: *In the spring of 2004, two idealistic young men set out on an exhausting six-month tour of European capitals, carried only by "La Poderosa" (the Powerful One), their battered old government jet. For Bertie "Che" Ahern, it would be a voyage of discovery in more ways than one. Moved by the terrible poverty witnessed during an endless series of State dinners, Che and his friend "El Biffo" return home as changed men, dedicated to the overthrow of capitalism, and in particular the hated Partido De Los Democratas Progressivos.*

MONDAY

De overtrow of management at Aer Lingus has been a mighty victory for de workers. In de favelas of de nortsoide, wild celebrations have continued for sevral nights now. De sound of joyful gunfire still rings out across Drumcondra, clearly audible even here in Fagan's Taverna, above the happy chatter of proletarian men and wimmin as dey escape for a few hours from de grind of deir daily lives. But if you listen hard enough, anudder sound can be heard, from sout of de river. It is de sound of de rulin classes quakin in deir boots! "The great only appear great because we are on our knees," quips Mick de barman. I smile and push an empty glass across de counter. "De great only appear great because we haven't drank enough beer yet," I say. "Put on anudder Bass dere quick."

TUESDAY

All revolutionaries live wit de constant tret of discovery, and I am no exception. I too fear de knock on de door in de middle of de night. Biffo says me cover as de leader of a conservative government is so cunning, dat nobody will ever cop me radical intentions until it's too late. But de rulin classes are cunning too, and deir henchmen are evrywhere. Tankfully, my recent interview gaffe – when I revealed meself as a socialist – has been dismissed as a joke in most quarters. Still, suspicions must have been raised, and I sense dat my situation is now more precarious. Evry day I enter Government Buildings, half expectin de hand on de shoulder and de one-way trip to de headquarters of de Secret Police, where McDowell himself will be waitin wit de electrodes. But somehow I must keep me nerve, at least until de budget.

WEDNESDAY

Biffo's cover is equally clever, and equally dangerous. As Minister for Finance, he even has de power to transfer large resources to de poor. But his actions are under close scrutiny, especially from – excuse me while I spit – right wing economists. Like me, he must hide his revolutionary intentions under de guise of a pro-capitalist approach, however much dis hurts. De upcomin budget is our first big chance to reverse de dark years of McCreevyism. But de PD spies are evrywhere, so today we must meet at a secret location to discuss our plans. Unfortunately, de meetin ends prematurely when Fadder Seán Healy rushes into the room to say that the secret police have been seen in the area and the house is no longer safe. He ushers us out a back entrance to a waitin car, pausing only to make the sign of the cross over us. "May God protect you," he says, as we are driven away – me lyin flat on de floor of de car.

THURSDAY

We are not alone in struggle. Dis mornin, we receive a telegram from Havana! El Commandante writes: "Fraternal greetings to our brothers in Ireland. Our wishes for your success flow across the Atlantic Ocean as surely as the Gulf Stream warms your green shores. We are with you in your great efforts. Viva la Revolucion! Yours in socialism – Fidel.

P.S. But what the hell were you thinkin about with that smoking ban?"

SATURDAY

Grizzly Adams rings me wit de final details of de IRA wind-up. "It's kinda ironic," he says: "Here's us endin a revolution, and there's you and Biffo startin a new one." A chill runs down my spine. How much do the Shinners know? Is dis a bluff, or has Aengus Ó Snodaigh's pal been trackin our movements too? "A word of advice," says Grizzly. "I wouldn't be meetin Biffo again in Fadder Healy's house if I were you – the PDs are on to it.

SUNDAY

I decide to hold de final pre-budget meetin wit Biffo in me office in Government Buildins. It's so obvious, nobody will tink of it. Again I outline me broad priorities. Dese include de immediate nationalistion of banks, de seizure of all private property, introduction of a 98 per cent welt tax, forced sterilisation for McCreevy's stallions, and de establishment of collectivised farms. Biffo favours a more gradulist approach, however, arguin dat if we tried all dis at once, de PDs might suspect something. After much debate, we agree a ten per cent rise in social welfare payments, as a preliminary measure. We shake hands, and Biffo leaves trew de secret tunnel. As I walk out into Merrion Row, a chill November breeze grips me, but I do not feel cold. It is de wind of freedom, and it is blowin also trew de corridors of de rich and powerful. It whispers in my ear dat we will win soon.

MONDAY

We haven't had de official verdict from de PSNI yet, but even de dogs in de street know who carried out de Belfast bank raid (only dey've been warned dat de first one to bark will be neutered). We know it's not de loyalists, who – let's face it – couldn't organise a hold-up in a bra factory. And de Nort has not yet developed into de sort of mature, self-confident democracy dat's capable of sustainin large-scale civilian crime. So it can only be de Provos. Maybe we should have seen de signs durin de talks in November. I remember at one point we were discussin de Shinners' future role in de police force, and de DUP were concerned about known IRA men gettin high-profile positions in de PSNI. "We don't want P O'Neill as chief constable," was how Peter Robinson put it. But de Shinners said not to worry, dat P O'Neill was currently studyin for a career in de financial services sector – or "a big bank job", to use deir exact words. De true meanin escaped us at de time. We all just wished him well in his exams.

TUESDAY

De problems at Aer Lingus have been worsened by news dat Willie Walsh and de boys are plannin to establish a new low-cost airline. Dis makes de Monicagate affair even more unfortunate in its timing. As it is, I may have no choice but to establish a new, low-cost Minister for Transport in de near future. De current one is too much associated wit de luxury end of de travel market, which is not what de consumer wants. Also, his baggage-handlin charges are becomin a major drain on Government resources. No, I tink de only answer is to introduce more competition into de Minister for Transport sector, and to open up a new route for Cullenair: from de Cabinet to de back-benches.

WEDNESDAY

De first Government meetin of de new year was a sombre affair. We held tree minutes' silence for de tsunami victims, and den agreed to increase de Irish aid package once de UN works out what it needs. On a lighter note, we okayed Dick Roche's proposal dat we lift de cap on de size of retail developments to allow Oireland's first IKEA store go ahead. When Dick said de company wanted to build one along a motorway somewhere near Dublin, Biffo suggested de "Hill of Tara" as a possible site. But when de laughs died down, Dick said Ballymun was a more likely venue. After de meetin, Biffo asked me if I was considerin liftin de cap on de size of the Minister for Transport. De last two have been very small-scale units, he pointed out. I told him I'd do whatever was best for de environment

THURSDAY

De Provos' denial of responsibility for de Belfast heist might be as wortless as a new Nordern Bank 50 pound note, but at least P O'Neill's statements are consistent. Dis is more dan can be said for de bankers. First dey gave incorrect serial numbers to de police. Now, weeks after de raid, dey say it was £26.5 million dat was taken, not £22 million. Maybe dere's a split in deir movement. But if so, de question is who is now in control? Is it de Official or Provisional wing, or has a Continuity Nordern Bank emerged to carry on de struggle? Maybe de PSNI will tell us; aldough considerin dey know nuttin about de raid udder dan dat de Provos did it, I wouldn't hold out much hope. I wouldn't be too confident eider about Hugh Orde's claim dat dis was de biggest robbery of "waste-paper" in history. De IRA have shown dey can launder everyting from guns to diesel, and de evidence is dat dey've already taken de bank and de PSNI to de cleaners on dis one.

FRIDAY

I rang Blair first ting dis mornin and asked if he was worried about de peace process. "Not really," he said, "I don't think Gordon will try anything before the general election." He wasn't nearly as optimistic about Nordern Ireland, dough. When de talks stalled before Christmas, Blair said we were like mountain climbers takin a breeder before de final assault on de summit. Den a feckin £26.5 million avalanche fell on us and buried us up to our necks. So we agreed today dat, as a first step, dere'll be no more mountaineering images. Secondly, we agreed dat however long it takes de Provos to launder de money, de laundry job on de Shinners will take even longer. When de wash-cycle is finally completed, we'll still have to hang dem out to dry for a while. So all in all, it'll probably be 2006 before we have a go at solvin de Nort again. I just hope Gordon Brown is as committed as Blair was.

SATURDAY

As if de New Year wasn't grim enough already, today I had to watch Man Utd strugglin to get a nil-nil draw wit someting called Exeter City. Alex Ferguson apologised to de fans afterwards, as well he should. Puttin out a team like dat and callin it United makes de Nordern bank job look like an honest day's work. But dere's not much light relief anywhere at de moment. Between de Asian disaster and de wedder and everyting, dis has been a miserable start to January. Not even today's launch of de "Cork City of Culture" could lift de gloom completely. It's a very amusin idea, admittedly, and whoever taut of it deserves credit. But it's still hard to laugh.

MONDAY

De rottweiler has been in a state of high excitement lately, but any time I ask him what's goin on, he won't tell me anyting. "Loose talk costs lives," he says, tappin his nose. I tink he may be plannin a spectacular of some sort against de "Provisional Movement", as he calls it. I made de mistake de udder day of referrin to Grizzly & Co as de "Republican Movement" and he gave me a lecture about how I shouldn't use dat term about dem. "The Government is the real republican movement in dis State," he said. "Tiocfaidh Ár Lá!" says I. "I'll see ye at de Army Council meetin tomorrow."

TUESDAY

De Army Council meetin was dominated by a debate about de by-elections. I was hopin to keep dese until after Easter, partly because I've given up canvassin for Lent. But de Opposition were trettenin a campaign of destruction *("obstruction"? – Ed)* in de Dail if we didn't call dem now. Dis could have been a real pain in de hole. If dey were goin to be callin votes evry five minutes, I'd have to hang around Leinster House all day, which means I could miss important pub openins and de like. So I told de Cabinet, Feckit, we always lose by-elections, anyway, so we might as well lose dem before Easter as afterwards. Biffo reminded me dat we didn't even have a candidate in Kildare yet. But I said dat if we called de poll for March 11th, de resultant panic would concentrate evrybody's minds.

WEDNESDAY

In a sinister development, somebody has fired a shot at de Rottweiler's holiday home in Roscommon. Dis could be de first recorded case of de Provos carryin out a punishment attack on a house. But accordin to de Guards, dere's a wide range of suspects, and not even crazed architectural critics can be ruled out at dis stage. Dese are turbulent times. No sooner had we learned about de assault on de front of McDowell's house, dan news came trew dat de back of Ivor Callely has also been attacked. Damage is believed to be extensive, but de good news is dat dere's a definite suspect. Gardai are lookin for a man of about 5 feet 4 in height who answers to de name of "Minister" (for now anyway). At least nobody can say he didn't pick on somebody his own size.

THURSDAY

Dramatic developments in Cork, where gardai have swooped on a house full of hot money. De move follows de arrest of tree lads yesterday in Heuston Station wit a Daz box (economy size) full of cash. It's too early to say if dis is a launderin operation. But de money was bluey-white, apparently, and when approached, de men refused to swop it for two boxes of Brand X. Dere were also arrests overnight in various parts of Cork, and today dere were raids in Dundalk, Westmead, and Offaly. I haven't seen dis many culchies implicated in de movement of large amounts of cash since de last episode of Winnin Streak. Apparently some of dose arrested are Shinners. De home of Phil Flynn – who has always been very sound on de national question – has also been raided, aldough Phil has not been arrested for anyting. A statement phoned to a newspaper tonight claimed de raids on behalf of de Republican movement (Ranelagh Brigade) and promised dere would be more such attacks until Ireland was crime-free.

FRIDAY

De raids have continued. We taut de money found yesterday was hot until, today, de guards discovered a lad settin fire to a bundle of cash in his back garden in Cork. Turty rounds of ammo for a Kalashnikov rifle were also found. Phil Flynn has bitten de bullet (not one of de Kalahsnikov bullets, obviously, or he'd have no teet left) and resigned from de government's decentralisation committee and udder boards. De cops say de investigation could go on for munts. But McDowell is on a high. As high he's been since he climbed dat lamppost during de 2002 election, in fact. And nuttin would do him today but go up to Garda HQ and congratulate de lads in person. I tink he's havin medals struck for de participants. By contrast, Gerry Adams has had to curtail his visit to Spain's Basket Country, where he was promotin his buke. Poor old Grizzly. I know de Provos always favoured a British witdrawal. But at twenty-six-and-a-half million sterling, dey just witdrew too much.

SATURDAY

It's very unfortunate for de Shinners dat dis should all happen in de middle of a by-election campaign. Very unfortunate. But dere ye are – de political process is full of ups and downs, as dey'll discover if dey ever join it full time. Come to tink of it, my schedule is full of ups and downs too, even on a Saturday. Today it was up to Navan and down to Naas, as de elections put de kibosh on any chance of a quiet weekend. At least we finally have a candidate in Kildare – Tom Kitt's sister, no less. But if ye were dat slow away in a sprint at de Curragh, dere'd be a stewards' inquiry. Anyway, I did me bit for de campaign effort and – tanks to de evenin kick-off – I was back in Drumcondra in time to watch United beat Everton in de Cup. De Reds are probably de only winners I backed today, but we'll know in tree weeks time.

MONDAY

It looks like certain people knew at least two years ago dat de nursin homes charges were illegal. But de question is who? Apparently de issue came up at a pre-Christmas meetin in 2003 between Department of Helt officials and de Tree Wise Men – Mickey Martin and his junior ministers Ivor and Tim. De ox and de ass probably attended too. But nobody seems to have noticed de baby Jesus. Mickey says he missed some of de meetin. Ivor was dere trewout, but insists dere was nuttin discussed dat rang "alarm bells". Maybe dey were ringin, all right, but wit de season dat was in it, he mistook dem for jingle bells. Eider way, we can all hear jinglin now, and no mistake. Evry chancer in de country will be crawlin out of de woodwork wit claims against de State for elderly relatives dat dey didn't know existed. Of course, dat's not to take away from de genuine cases. In fact, payin out in dem (before de next general election) is de Government's priority. Dat and findin a fall-guy.

TUESDAY

Needless to say, de Opposition were givin me grief about de issue on question-time. But, eh, I was quick to remind dem dat de whole debacle started way back in 1976 when – let me see, now – oh, yes, dere was a Fine Gael-Labour coalition in power! Luckily dey backed off at dat point. Or I'da reminded dem dat in takin money off old people in de 1970s, de Blueshirts were continuin a proud tradition begun in 1929 when dey cut a shillin off de old age pension. Ye don't get to be leader of Fianna Fáil widdout havin a long memory.

WEDNESDAY

More bad news on de financial front. Under tret of a rulin against us by Brussels, we've had to cancel a hunderd million euro in aid to one of Intel's new microchip projects in Leixlip. De company says it will now have to review furder investment in Oireland. De chips are down, ye could say. Dis is very bad news for Nort Kildare – which is a wholly-owned subsidiary of Intel at dis stage – and in de middle of a by-election too. But it's bad news for de Government's whole job strategy as well. De attractiveness of Oireland to US companies is based on tings like de easy availability of greenbacks – eh, I mean, greenfield sites. If we stop lookin after de Yanks in de manner to which dey've become accustomed, before ye know it, we'll lose our position as de 51st state of de union, and we'll be stuck wit bein full-time members of de EU instead. De sooner McCreevy sorts out dose communists in de Commission, de better.

THURSDAY

Over to London for a quick meetin wit Blair. Nuttin much to discuss. De fall-out from de bank job and de McCartney murder continues to leave de Shinners beyond de pale, and Big Ian's conciliatory statements – to de effect dat he'd consider touchin dem wit a 40-foot pole again if conditions were right (two moons in de sky, hell freezin over, etc) – are for de longer term. Blair asked me if dere was any danger of de hard men returnin to war. So I said dat no, based on all de available intelligence, McDowell was still observin his ceasefire. Apart from de odd skirmish, dere hadn't been any major statements from him for almost 24 hours. We agreed dat de Shinners were comin along nicely, but dat we should turn de heat down a bit and let dem simmer for anudder while.

FRIDAY

Dramatic developments. Grizzly has suspended seven of de McCartney suspects, on de eve of deir party conference! A few years ago, de gang would have arrived at de Ard-Fheis in triumph and probably got a standin ovation from delegates. But tings have changed, big-time: especially in de States. No invite to de White House dis year, and no lucrative fundraisin dinners eider. Dis at a time when, tanks to setbacks in de party's financial services sector, de Shinners are in de red for de first time in decades. Someting had to give – hence Grizzly's unprecedented move. Of course, members of de republican movement have been suspended before. But dat was usually upside down in a bat-full of water, while bein questioned by de nuttin squad. So dis is a big departure. Needless to say, McDowell is beside himself at de Shinners' surrender. He wanted to organise a cavalcade of tricolour-waving Government supporters to drive up and down outside de RDS dis evenin. But luckily I was able to talk him out of it.

SATURDAY

Got de Travers report last night from Harney. Only had a flick trew it so far, but it looks like Mickey Martin might be safe at least. Pity. Dere'll still be plenty of fall-out, dough. Harney was supposed to be goin to San Francisco next week as part of de annual St Patrick's Day flight of de wild geese. But I told her, in de words of de song: If you're going to San Francisco, you're sure to have Charlie Bird in your hair. So on reflection, she's decided to stay home and deal wit de flak. I noticed in Grizzly's speech to de Ard-Fheis dis evenin, he referred to us "robbin" old people. His underlyin message is dat de Provos only robbed a bank. De sneaky f****r. Still, dat was some stunt he pulled wit de McCartney sisters. De Shinners certainly have a sense of teeatre. Ye have to hand it to de bastards sometimes.

MONDAY

De lads in Mount Street gave me a rundown on de new fundraisin scheme today. Plans are not yet finalised, but basically it'll operate like an upmarket nightclub, wit a membership structure, a VIP room dat you need a special key for and so on. Bertie's Bordello, dey're callin it, aldough we'll tink of something more official at a later stage. De plan is to have 'seminars' and udder functions, at which members will be able to rub shoulders wit Government ministers and de like. In between mixin wit guests and servin drinks, ministers will do a bit of pole-dancin. Dey may also be available for private, one-on-one dances. But dere'll be no touchin allowed by customers.

TUESDAY

Royston will not be joinin, needless to say. I've already told de bouncers to look out for him and, if he tries to blag his way in, to tell him dat whatever he's wearin doesn't meet de club's strict dress code. He's bein a pain in de hole over dis campaign debt issue, bad-moutin us in de press, trettenin lawyers, and what not. But Fianna Fáil's rule on candidates' fund-raisin are clear, as he well knows. Win yer election and ye get club membership for life, a VIP pass to de inner circle and so on. Lose and you're out in de street queuin wit de rest of de mugs, tryin to pretend you know de doorman. It's a harsh system, but dey're ye are.

WEDNESDAY

Wit all de trouble we go to over fundraisin, I sometime wonder why we don't just knock off a Brinks Allied van like evrybody else. Dere'd be a small risk of gettin caught, I suppose, but we could always just deny responsibility for it. Den again, we tried denyin responsibility for Royston, and look were dat got us. Needless to say, McDowell is fumin over how easy dese money vans are bein robbed, so he's called an emergency meetin wit de security sector to see how dey can improve deir security. Udderwise, as he says, wit a general election only two years off and de Shinners short of cash, no van will be safe.

THURSDAY

It's been a hard week for de Rottweiler. His u-turn over de deportation of Okulun ... Olunkun ... eh, of de young Nigerian lad from Palmerstown was so dramatic dat even I had to admire his footwork. At de Cabinet meetin yesterday, I asked him if he'd ever considered runnin for Fianna Fáil, where his flexibility would be properly appreciated. He took de slaggin well, in fairness. But what he's findin it harder to deal wit are de allegations of compassion. Some commentators are goin so far as to suggest dat he may even be human, after all. "A vicious smear," he said to me, tryin to put a brave face on it.

FRIDAY

Never mind de condition of de Pope. It's de journalists in St Peter's Square I'm worried about. Dey've been predictin de Holy Fadder's demise for sevral days now, and ye'd wonder how long more dey can hang on. If de Pope had gone back to hospital dey'd have got a new lease of life, or at least a change of scenery. But it's like dey've been refused furder treatment. I'm sure it's inspirin for Christians evrywhere to watch dem, wafflin on bravely when dey have absolutely nuttin new to say, and waitin patiently for God or deir news editors to call dem home. Even so, at de mass in de Pro-Cateedral tonight, I offered up a few prayers dat deir sufferin might end soon.

SATURDAY

I was over in Fagans when I heard de news from de Vatican. We held a minute's silence, wit our pints at half-mast, as a mark of respect. Den I spent de rest of de night watchin de coverage. It's soberin to tink dat I was a new TD, still wet behind de ears, when John Paul II came to power. In fact, dose old pictures of him sharin a platform wit Bishop Casey and Fadder Michael Cleary are a bit like de ones of me wit CJH and Rambo. How little de Pope and I knew back den! But in many respects, we've had similar careers. We'll bote be remembered as men of peace. We bote travelled de world spreadin de Gospel (albeit he had a better jet). And we bote sought a middle road between communism and de free market. De Pope helped bring down de Berlin Wall, of course, and I finished de job by welcomin de downtrodden peoples of Eastrin Europe into de EU. OK, he only won de one election. But I hope posterity won't hold dat against him. And you've got to admire him appointin a lorryload of archbishops just before de final bell. Dat's class dat is.

SUNDAY

Speakin of which, de choosin of a new Pope happens in de same mysterious way as a Fianna Fáil selection convention. It's a mixture of politics and divine inspiration. Like de time I was supportin Albert's nomination for president, until de Holy Spirit intervened at de last minute and – when de white smoke cleared – I'd backed McAleese instead. But for all de secrecy surroundin de College of Cardinals, dere'll be a fair bit of horse-tradin beforehand. Berlusconi will be tryin to reclaim de job for de Italians, while Eastrin Europeans won't want to let go of it, and de Franco-German alliance will attempt to exploit de divisions to get deir man in. Much as I'd like to swing it for Dessie Connell as a compromise candidate, I tink dat might be beyond even my powers. Still, I'll do de usual ring around anyway and see how de land lies.

MONDAY

Dis mornin I flew to Moscow, where I joined 53 udder world leaders for ceremonies to mark de sixtieth anniversary of VE Day. It was a proud moment for all dose of us who helped liberate Europe from de evils of Nastyism. Of course, Oireland's role in de effort was mainly limited to logistical support: I tink Dev offered refuellin rights at Shannon for any Russian planes en route to Germany. But, eh, as I reminded Mr Putin today, me own constituency took a more active part in de fightin. So fierce was de resistance in and around Ballybough dat de Gerries bombed de Nort Strand in 1941 in an effort to stamp it out. It didn't work. We held out to de bitter end, and like many a man before him, Hitler learned de hard way not to mess wit Nortsoiders. It's just unfortunate dat de world doesn't recognise de role of Dublin Nort Central in winnin de war. But I was back home tonight in time to mark de occasion wit a few quiet jars in Fagans.

TUESDAY

Had a quick meetin wit Blair in a pub off Red Square yesterday. As I told him, he's one lucky f***er: turty-seven per cent of de vote and a majority of 66 seats! If it was any udder country, Amnesty International would be on de case and de White House would be talkin about de need to introduce democracy. Anyway, we discussed de Nordern elections. As usual, Blair found reasons for optimism: mainly de fact dat our success in abolishin de Ulster Unionist Party would cut down on de number of meetins we need to hold. Unfortunately we didn't manage to obliterate de middle ground completely – de SDLP are still alive. But you can't do everyting. Blair is gaggin for a deal wit de Shinners, aldough, personally, I tink he could have been a bit more subtle dan appointin a Nordern Secretary who was once framed for robbin a bank. Eider way, nuttin will happen now until de after de marchin season. We'll have to wait for de autumn, and see how Paisley responds to de new medication, before we restart talks.

WEDNESDAY

De airport terminal issue is still up in de air, as it were. We were hopin to finally land it at dis week's cabinet meetin. But dere was a report of PD protesters on de runway, so I've advised Cullen to keep circlin for at least anudder week. De passengers are all trowin up back dere, but it's not my fault. Harney's determined dat de two terminals should compete at some level, and my suggestion of an annual soccer tournament didn't help to break de impasse. It looks like we'll have to agree a compromise whereby de Government is committed to buildin a turd, independent terminal if de number of passengers (or flyin pigs) reaches a certain level. Dis should secure PD agreement. But I've told Cullen to keep de "fasten seatbelts" sign on for de moment.

THURSDAY

Me work in brokerin de EU constitution was recognised today when I received de European of de Year award, holdin off a fierce challenge from Royston Brady. Of course it's not all about awards: I'd be perfectly happy just to have a street in Brussels named after me. And de real prize will be seein me constitution approved by all de member states. Dis is by no means certain. As I said in a recent interview wit de influential French newspaper Le Merde, de outcome of the referendum in France will have a crucial influence on de rest of Europe, includin Oireland. Havin said dat, I'm confident de Oirish people will back us when we hold our referendum later dis year. But we have de replay pencilled in for next spring, just in case.

FRIDAY

De Government is very sensitive about de importance of de Hill of Tara, as de ancient seat of de high kings of Oireland. But we were also sensitive of de importance of de M3 to a number of more modern seats – includin Noel Dempsey's. Based on extensive consultation in the area, we concluded dat de high kings were unlikely to vote in the next election; unlike de commuters sittin in traffic jams dis side of Navan. So all in all we've decided to proceed wit de road. As a mark of respect to de tree-huggin community, we've agreed to go around de hill radder dan trew it. And environmentalists can also rest assured dat de project will not be carried out wit undue haste. If the NRA has anyting to do wit it, it'll be sevral years late and at least €100m over budget.

SATURDAY

I'm as big a Man United fan as de next fella. But de way some people are talkin, ye'd tink de club was de soccer equivalent of de Hill of Tara – some ancient monument dat should be protected under de heritage acts and have an interpretative centre – radder dan a plc. Sure, I was hopin meself dat JP and Magnier would take it over. Den, in a few years time when I quit politics, I'd have been a model for de board of directors. And ok, dis Glazer fella looks like a complete muppet. But dere's no use pretendin dat United is anyting udder dan a business. Besides, wit de dosh he's made out of dis, JP could pay for de whole Bertiebowl if (as I still hope and pray) de Lansdowne project collapses at de plannin stage. Meanwhile, I imagine Glazer will make his money by introducin American-style caterin, and de like. De beer at Old Trafford will be weaker dan piss and vastly overpriced. But at least it will match de current team.

MONDAY

It was just like old times when Bill Clinton dropped in to see me dis evenin durin his latest Irish trip. He's on de lecture circuit dese days, doin after dinner speeches at a hunderd grand a pop: money for old shite. But he still keeps an eye on de peace process here, and he's takin a very big interest in de McCartney sisters. Not de sort of interest he would have taken in dem a few years ago – Hillary seems to have him house-trained now, at last – only in deir campaign for justice. Apart from de Nort, we discussed de good old days, before de Jehovah's Witnesses took over de White House. And he told me he expects to be back dere in 2008. He said Hillary was still reinventin herself to suit de new mood in America, but dat in a couple of years' time she'd be somewhere to de right of Bush, which is where de next Democratic president would have to be. We agreed dat ye did what ye had to do to win power, or to hold onto it. "I'm a socialist dese days," says I. "So I heard!" says Bill. We had a good laugh about dat.

TUESDAY

Bad news from de Nort – where the IMC says de Provos are still recruitin new members – and from de West – where de hardline supporters of Beverley Flynn are also continuin to operate as normal, in contravention of orders. We're still confident dat de IRA will respond positively to Grizzly's invitation to stand down. I just wish I could say de same for de Michael O'Morain Cumann in Castlebar, which is refusin to disband. We've told dem dat dey can only continue to exist as an old comrades association. But dey had a meetin of deir army council last night, attended by Pee Flynn, and it looks like dey're determined to fight on. As our mole in de cumann reported afterwards: "They haven't gone away, you know."

WEDNESDAY

Sometimes it seems like de whole world is full of annoying Mayo people. Especially on Wednesday mornins, when I have to put up wit bote Pat Smartarse and Inda Kinny givin me guff in de Dail. Inda was doin de whole law and order ting again today, haranguin me over crime levels in Dublin. De number of crimes is up, he says, and de number of detections is down, and dere are no gardai on de streets. Of course his big problem wit Dublin not de lack of guards, it's de lack of Blueshirt TDs: he's desperate to recruit a few more at de next election. Unfortunately – and dis is what he was able to exploit – de good crime stats for de country as a whole are skewed by de figures for tree Dublin suburbs – two of dem on de Nortsoide. Dat's bad enough in itself. But to have some mucker from Castlebar lecturin me about anarchy in Blanchardstown and Coolock is hard to take ...

THURSDAY

… So when de ERU whacked a couple of post office robbers in Lusk today, I didn't hold back in me expressions of support. Amnesty International called for a public inquiry and de usual bleedin hearts fretted about violation of criminals' human rights. But we've done de focus groups, and as well as de bit of cod socialism, we've discovered dat de electorate wants more of a Ghengis Khan approach to dispensin justice. Which is why I backed de ERU one hunderd per cent and urged de public not to be "weak-kneed". It's all about detection rates, and de rates for Lusk have just increased dramatically. Let's see Enda try askin me about crime levels on de Nortsoide now.

FRIDAY

Today we published de wordin for a referendum on de EU constitution, aldough de way France is shapin, I don't know if dere'll even be a poll. We can pretend udderwise in public, but if de Frogs say no, the constitution will have croaked too. Jacques de Lad rang me last night, concedin defeat. His big worry is dat not only will de French vote no, but dat de Brits – out of pure badness – will vote Yes. Just to embarrass him. Of course, de Nedderlands is headin for a No too, so de chances of me gettin a street in Brussels named after me look slim now. I don't know why people are objectin to de treaty: we designed it in such a way dat nobody – includin us – could understand de feckin ting. But anyway, I've advised Jacques to have a rerun in de autumn. If dat doesn't work, we'll have to renegotiate, and no doubt yours truly will get de job again. I wouldn't mind only I have to do de Good Friday Agreement too. Sometimes I'm tempted to join Clinton on de lecture circuit.

SATURDAY

Spent de whole day canvassin in Dublin Central. I'm gradually ratchetin up de effort because, aldough de election is officially still two years away, ye never know when de PDs might decide to cut and run. We stitched dem up rightly over de airport terminal. So de fact dat dey have de same vested interest as us in waitin for de SSIA scheme to lay eggs is no guarantee dat dey won't jump on de next big issue. I got home from de canvass dis evenin just in time to see Rabbitte rulin out coalition wit anyone udder dan Fine Gael. But dat might change yet. Pat has been in more different parties dan I've had periods in opposition, so nobody would accuse him of bein a slave to consistency. After de next election, if his figures don't add up, I'm sure he'll do de right ting to advance de cause of socialism. I know dat's what I'll be doin.

MONDAY

De IRA statement is now all but finalised and will be released soon, provided dat (a) de marchin season and (b) de Ulster football championship passes off peacefully. We're a bit more worried about de latter, to be honest. Whenever Tyrone play Armagh, de prospects for a split in de republican movement are huge. Dat's why we've re-routed de final to Dublin, again. De hope is dat in a neutral venue, de deep hatred between dese two communities, and de potential for violence, will be reduced. Unfortunately, dere's less room for optimism on de Paisley front. He now says dat regardless of any statement, he will not share power wit Shinners "until the Pope becomes a Free Presbyterian". As preconditions go, dis is a tall one. But I'm not de world's greatest negotiator for nuttin, so I've arranged a meetin wit Benedict de Sixteent dis week to begin exploratory talks.

TUESDAY

Speakin of flashpoints, de RTE series on Haughey has passed off widout major incident, tank God. I was afraid it might stir up old passions (not to mention old footage of me) dat would not be helpful in, eh, movin de situation forward. But it left many of de great mysteries unsolved, hidden in de dark undergrote of Pee Flynn's eyebrows. Personally, I taut de biggest achievement of de programme was in makin CJH seem more human. For years, he's been portrayed as dis big, terrible monster. But as a result of de series, somehow, he doesn't seem as scary anymore. Seein a televised close-up of Pee Flynn has put scariness in perspective.

WEDNESDAY

I was down in Adare last night for JP's Pro-Am dinner. Jayzus, dat's what ye call a fundraiser. People go on about de Fianna Fáil tent at de Galway Races, which is only a glorified chicken-and-chips operation by comparison. It was 25 Gees a table last night, and dat was before anyone spent a penny on de auction, where items included a round of golf wit de supermodel Jodie Kidd. Personally, I can tink of a lotta tings I'd like to play wit her, and golf wouldn't be in de top five.

THURSDAY

Me trip to de Vatican went well aldough, as expected, dere was no progress on de issue of de Pope renouncin "priestcraft" (as Paisley calls it) and embracin Lutheran principles. At least I asked. Udderwise it was a pleasant meetin. Ratso knows all de Oirish lads – Dessie, Diarmuid, Sean Brady, etc – and he told me he kept a close eye on tings in Ireland, genrally. So when he asked me how me own "situation" was, dere was an awkward moment. I didn't know whedder he was referrin to de relationship between me and de Widda Bogle, or de one wit Harney and de PDs. In de end, I fudged it, and said I hoped we'd be togedder "for a couple of years anyway". He said he'd pray for us (I'm still not sure who he meant).

FRIDAY

De bombs in London are a soberin reminder of de tret posed by Al-Queda. After ringin Blair to express de sympatties of de Irish people, de first ting I did was get a briefin from McDowell on whedder dere were any of Hosannah Bin Liner's nutters operatin here. He said dere were a few known supporters, but dat he was monitorin dem "very, very closely", and dat, providin dey didn't move to Donegal, or "somewhere equally impenetrable", he would continue to keep dem under surveillance. He also says we may have to introduce ID cards like in Britain. Dis would help combat de "twin evils" facin western democracy, as he sees it: Islamic fundamentalism, and young lads trying to get a drink.

SATURDAY

From de Carrickmines bypass to de Tara motorway, de Government has incurred de wrat of a lot of tree-huggers lately. But hopefully, Dick Roche's decision to buy de Great Blasket island for de State will show how much we care about our heritage. Aldough dey were evacuated in de 1950s, de Blaskets remain central to understanding Oirish culchure (or so Mansergh says). De people who lived dere suffered a lot because of deir isolation and, trew de work of Peig Sayers and udders, dey passed dis sufferin on to generations of schoolchildren. But it's time to forgive dem now. Dat's why we plan to create an interpretative centre and to restore some of deir former houses as visitor accommodation. Everyting will be done wit maximum sensitivity, especially de national incinerator we plan to build on de island once de sale goes trew.

SUNDAY

Good news and bad news from de Nort. De good news is dat Drumcree passed off quietly, wit no need for a replay. De bad news is dat de Ulster final finished in a draw. It was goin well until a small group of Armagh orangemen breached de terms of de parades commission by penetratin de fiercely nationalist Tyrone defence, to score a late goal. Now de teams have to do it all over again, and de besieged residents around Croke Park face bein locked into deir homes on yet anudder July afternoon. Needless to say, de GAA – who face a potential €1.5 million gate from de replay – are gutted at de turn of events. We can only hope de game passes off peacefully. But Grizzly says tension remains high along de interface, and for now de statement is on hold.

MONDAY

Me holidays were ruined first by de surprise – I swear – return of de Colombia Tree, and den by bad news from party headquarters about de private opinion polls we commissioned, which would put de kibosh on me historic turd term. Neverdeless I was determined to stay on in Kerry, anyway. Den de lads in HQ pointed out dat one of de big findins from de focus groups was dat I was seen as indecisive. Dis is rubbish, of course. But I quickly changed me mind about stayin in Kerry and made an early return to Dublin, so dat I could be seen to be pretendin to do someting about de Colombian situation, even dough I can't tink what. It didn't hurt dat de Dubs were playin Tyrone at de weekend. And a crackin game it was too, wit de crowd on de edge of deir seats right till de end. As I said to de HQ dis mornin, no doubt de feckin focus groups would complain dat de result – 1-14 apiece – was indecisive. But 78,000 people didn't seem to mind.

TUESDAY

Slight differences have emerged between de Government parties over what to do wit de bird-watchers. My opinion – and I'm almost unanimous in dis – is dat it's solely a matter for de guards and de DPP. De PDs argue dat, while we don't have an extradition treaty wit Colombia, we should at least explore de legal option of puttin dem in a crate and sending dem back by Federal Express. Dis is a view strongly supported by de autorities in Bogota, where de home affairs minister, Enrique del Fascisto-Porco, is insistin dat we honour de findings of de independently-appointed Kangaroo Court dat found dem guilty. De White House is also leaning on us, and has offered help in flyin de men back to face justice. Apparently dey can smuggle dem trew Shannon in a US army plane.

WEDNESDAY

De Nordern peace process remains on hold, needless to say. But de positive side of dis is dat lately I've been able to devote me legendary negotiatin skills to udder international problems, like de Middle-East. It's just a way of keeping me hand in. Nuttin spectacular: a phone-call here, a phone-call dere, persuadin Ariel Sharon to evacuate de settlements – dat kind of ting. It's all on de QT, but I'm not worried about gettin de credit. De main ting is dat me plan for de Gaza pull-out is goin smoodly, tank God. Once dat's completed, I can move on to sortin out de West Bank. And if dat goes well, I'll do de East Bank sometime in de new year.

THURSDAY

On de udder hand, I had a call from Avril Doyle last night askin me to intervene behind de scenes in de Irish showjumpin crisis, and I just had to say no. As I told Avril, sortin out de Arab-Israeli conflict is one ting. But de opposin sides in de equestrian row are too entrenched, de hatred runs too deep, and de egos are way too big for any chance of a breaktrew soon. Even so, I didn't want to leave poor Avril widdout hope altogedder – she seemed so helpless. So I gave her George Mitchell's number and told her he was good, if she could get him.

FRIDAY

De Colombia Tree's decision to present demselves for interview by de guards has not made de situation any better. I tink de PDs were hopin de cops might find a reason to clap dem in a cell and lose de key. But of course de lads walked free again, in anudder blaze of publicity. Having now presented demselves for interviews to bote Charlie Bird and de Gardaí, hopefully dat'll be de end of deir public appearances for a while and we can get back to normality. Knowin de Shinners, dough, dey'll probably run dem for election instead. In de meantime, de rottweiler is strainin at de leash. He's been exercising heroic restraint on dis issue so far, helped by de fact dat he was on holidays in Wagga Wagga when de news of de trio's return broke. Unfortunately he's in de mood for bitin bums now. For all our sakes, I hope de Garda report on de matter will give him a bone to gnaw on.

SATURDAY

Good news from de national teater where, respondin to a suggestion from de movement's political leadership (Zero), de board has agreed to disband. It will hencefort exist only as an old comrades association and will not engage in activity dat trettens a revival of *The Shaughraun* – or anyting else dat would involve bombin in London – in de near future. *Shadow of a Gunman* and udder material will also be decommissioned. Zero says dis paves de way for a bright new future for de teater, which after careful examination of all de requests by Dermot Desmond – eh, I mean, of all de available options – will soon be taking up residence in de docklands. It seems like a happy ending: not something you're always guaranteed at de Abbey.

MONDAY

It's too early yet for de resumption of talks in de Nort, but tanks to de latest riots, we're a lot more optimistic dan we were. De gap between de two sides certainly seems to have narrowed. Grizzly is cock-a-hoop at de pictures of Orangemen expressin deir culture by attackin de police. Dat's de way republicans express deir culture too, he says: "I always knew we had more in common than the loyalists were lettin on." De fact dat unionist politicians refused to condemn de violence is just a bonus. Grizzly admits dat not all Shinners are ready yet to accept McDowell's recommendation dat dey "reach out" to deir loyalist bredren. But at least de hard-line republicans are now more entewsiastic about de prospect of joinin de PSNI, if it means dey can legally beat de crap out of Orangemen. As Grizzly says, it's a "win-win" situation.

TUESDAY

Of course, de riots also strenten our hand in negotiatin wit de DUP. We may even table a demand for de decommissionin of Orange Order weapons, just for de crack. By our calculation, de Order's arsenal includes tousands of ceremonial swords, which dey're prepared to use in a non-ceremonial way. Intelligence reports suggest dey also have de capability to make crude-but-effective petrol bombs (aldough de way oil prices are goin, dis is less of a worry dan it would have been). If nuttin else, it'll be an ice-breaker before de real negotiations begin. Peter Robinson says de horse sedatives are beginnin to work on Paisley. Barring a setback, we'll invite him to preliminary talks before Christmas.

WEDNESDAY

Off to New York, where tonight I will recommit Oireland to reachin de UN aid target by 2012. Of course, when we were runnin for a seat on de security council a few years back, I promised we'd reach de target by 2007. But den circumstances changed (ie, we got de seat), so we had to scale back dose plans. Recommittin ourselves now, when we're not runnin for anyting, shows we really mean it. Even so, de aid agencies have deir doubts. Dey'd like to see General de Chastelain oversee de recommittin process, in de presence of a couple of clergymen. Michael D Higgins wants photographs of de actual hand-over of money. But de hardliners in de Department of Finance say dat would amount to public humiliation: it's a deal-breaker as far as dey're concerned. So de critics are just gonna have to trust us on dis one.

THURSDAY

Me speech went well all tings considered, and despite our previous U-turn, most people believe we'll deliver. Kofi Annan himself came up to me afterwards and said

Me black arts are very powerful. Even so, dey're takin a while to work on de new British prime minister. I may have to learn a few Brown arts as well if I'm gonna make any headway wit dat dour Scotsman.

It's no exaggeration to say dat Michael McDowell is me new best friend. I've always been a cat man meself. But now dat I have a pet Rottweiler, I can understand what people see in dogs.

Achievin a handshake was obviously de first step towards any agreement. It was a historic moment. I tink I've shaken hands wit everyone in de Republic at least twice by now, and I'm hopin to do all dem a turd time before next June. But it's always excitin to break new ground.

De one real advantage of de mornin raid on de Aras was dat it was a chance to remind de electrit dat Enda Kenny is a Mickey Mulchie. In de immortal words of Albert Reynolds (words dat I got him back for eventually), people are entitled to know where deir Teeseach sleeps at night: de back end of Mayo bein de terrible trute in Enda's case.

Biffo has been like a rock – big, round, and hard-hittin – trewout dis campaign.

De decision of de *Oirish Times* to publish a cute photograph of me and de twins is yet anudder example of de personal vendetta against me in certain sections of de media. OK, I might have invited de paper to send a photographer around but I had no idea de picture would be placed so prominently. De fact dat I got a five per cent bounce in de polls as a result does not lessen de shock I felt at havin me personal life paraded in dis way.

I was very grateful when a group of friends – de Review Body on Higher Remuneration – got togedder recently and organised a bit of a whip-around for me, to de tune of €38,000 a year. Of course it's not just me dat has been remunerated. Evryone in de cabinet gets a dig-out of at least 25 grand. But de public can rest assured dat dere is nuttin untoward involved. De increase is not tied to promises of improved performance or any udder favours.

De hacks caught me off guard at a gig dis morning when I admitted under questionin dat de Oirish economony had a "hard year" ahead. Of course, even de dogs in de street know dat tings will be difficult in de short-term. As de sayin goes, when de US sneezes, de rest of de world catches a flyin snot.

I leave de economy in good shape. And I'm handin it over to Biffo just in time for de worst global recession since de Wall Street crash. Maybe dat's why, as I shut de office door last night, I taut I heard a ghostly laugh from inside and an old familiar voice. I probably just imagined it. But I coulda sworn it was sayin something like: "the most devious, the most cunning, the most ruthless of them all."

he trusts me like trusts his own son, which I taut was very touchin. Dis mornin, I unveiled a plaque at de site where Eamon de Valera was born, before him and his mudder came to Oireland as asylum seekers. Nowadays we'd have dem deported. Den it was off to de New York Stock Exchange wit Una, me special adviser, and a group from de American Ireland Fund. I got to ring de closin bell, which was a big trill for me (and for Una, who got to join me on de podium). We finished de session several points down, amid continuing uncertainty about where we were going to have dinner tonight.

FRIDAY

Had a quick meetin dis mornin wit Bill Clinton, on de margins of de so-called "Clinton Global Initiative". Dis is a kind of unofficial UN in which world leaders discuss issues of common concern and den each of dem pledges to do one ting to help de world (I pledged to light a candle). I briefed Bill on de latest violence in de Nort, which he agreed was progress of a sort. Now dat loyalists were attackin de crown forces, he joked, a united Ireland couldn't be far off. He looked forward to a time when Hillary was President and could invite loyalists and republicans to celebrate St Patrick's Day togedder and share deir riot stories. I said never mind dat, I was just lookin forward to a time when we could have a drink in the White House again.

SATURDAY

I was outta de country for de Fine Gael tink-in, mercifully. But apparently Enda has announced dat he's targetin turty extra seats at de next genral election. Dey're not all ours, of course. He's focusin on Liz O'Donnell's seat (aren't we all), for example, as a possible FG gain. But most of dem would be at Fianna Fáil's expense. Dis is all talk, of course. But our private opinion polls show dat, if dere was an election tomorrow, we could lose up to 20 seats. De good news is dat most of dese would go to Eddie Hobbs, who would emerge as de largest opposition party. De bad news is dat de "social capitalism" lark I've launched in Cavan dooon't seem to have caught on wit de punters yet. Our pollsters say I've confused de electorate, but dat's exactly what I was tryin to do. It's always worked for me in de past.

SUNDAY

De news from Berlin tells me I was right all along. Deir version of Mary Harney was supposed to become Germany's first woman chancer. Instead it looks like de electorate dere has recoiled from de PD agenda and stuck wit de status quo for anudder term. Dere are two big lessons for me in Gerhard Shredder's success. One is dat people want economic reform, but not at all costs. De udder is dat I should dye me hair. Dis would be a drastic move, obviously, and one dat I'd have to discuss wit de make-up people. But if I phased it in gradually, it just might work.

MONDAY

Seein Micheál Martin screw up in public is like watchin de English soccer team get beaten. When it happens too often, ye can't enjoy it properly. So I was less dan pleased to hear dat a €3million internet porthole ("portal" – Ed) he unveiled last year is in fact non-existent. He says it was only de "concept" he unveiled. But be dat as it may, dis is yet anudder waste of tax-payers' money. And apart from de law of diminishin returns vis-a-vis me and Micheal's public setbacks, dis sort of ting reflects badly on all of us. De opposition may have no big ideas – unlike dose of us who read bukes by American professors – but de idea dat de Government are a bunch of wasters might be enough to make Pat Smartarse Minister for Finance in 2007. Dat's why de porthole fiasco is not as entertainin as it could have been. Any more cock-ups from dat quarter and I may have to unveil de concept of Micheál Martin as a back-bencher.

TUESDAY

Needless to say, de PDs are gettin nervous about bein associated with de wholesale misuse of public funds. Harney has never forgiven me for agreein to make her Minister for Helt when she asked me to. Wit evry new scandal in Hawkins House, de deviousness of my strategy in givin her what she wanted becomes more clear. From now on, de PDs will exploit every chance dey can to distance demselves from Fianna Fáil and, if possible, find a poplar cause to bring de government down on. Hence Fiona O'Malley's save-de-salmon campaign. Personally, I have nuttin against a ban on drift nets. But Cap'n Birdseye (Pat de Cope) will not surrender on dis one. And as events elsewhere dis week remind us, Donegal Fianna Fáilers are very hard to turn around, even when dey're goin de wrong way up a dual carriageway.

WEDNESDAY

It's not very comfortin to tink dat we're dependin on de Department of Helt to prevent an epidemic of Avian flu here. We'll probably find out too late dat dey spent millions on de concept of a cure for de virus, but not on de actual cure itself. Maybe I should bring Joe Jacob back and put him in charge of the emergency plan, to reassure de public. Actually I taut de bird flu had struck already when I surveyed me back-benches durin Leaders Questions dis mornin. De turkeys were very scarce, despite de Chief Whip's efforts to round up a flock for de TV cameras. Tankfully, we learned dat none of dem had fallen to de Avian bug: dey were all just off somewhere else, gettin fat in de run-up to Christmas, as usual. Still, I told Kitt dat if we didn't have a better show next week, fedders would fly.

THURSDAY

Like evrybody else, I'm sick as a parrot over Oireland's failure to reach de World Cup. We were bankin on de feel-good factor next summer: it woulda been de sportin equivalent of de SSIA scheme. In fact, if de lads had made de quarter finals, de plan was for us to force a snap election in de autumn, by introducin special tax incentives for fishermen investin in new, bigger drift nets. Now dat's not goin to happen. Worse still, it looks like Brian Kerr is a goner. I have me own tauts about de job he's done. But as de manager of Team Oireland, it makes me nervous to see a fellow leader hounded out of office for squanderin his resources. Unlike Kerr, tankfully, I don't face competition from any of de top continental managers (which is just as well, now dat Gerhard Schroeder is out of a job). But de question for bote de FAI and de Oirish electorate is dis: given de sort of chancers who are likely to apply for de position, can we realistically hope to get anyone better?

FRIDAY

Me concerns over a Muslim national school in Cabra have nuttin to do wit de Icelandic *("Islamic!" – Ed)* religion itself. Muslims have evry right to instruct deir children in Icelandic beliefs. But I was gettin reports dat certain activities at de school bordered on transcendentalism *(er "fundamentalism"? – Ed)*, such as de alleged cancellation of a soccer match because dere were girls on de opposition team. Dat's why I asked Hanafin to monitor de situation. As I say, dis is not about intolerance of udders. On de contry, we're very open-minded here in Nort Dublin. We welcome people of all fates and culchures. All we ask is dat dey respect our culchure too, and dat dey don't seek to overtrow our way of life. But dat's enough about Mary Lou McDonald's plans to take de second FF seat here in de next genral election.

SATURDAY

Just when Paisley was respondin to medication, Fadder Alec Reid has stopped takin his. Jaysus. It must have been de pressure of spendin a week supervisin de destruction of arms dumps dat made him run amok, shootin his mout off left right and centre and mowin down innocent Protestant by-standers. Den, instead of just shuttin up, he goes and says he believes de IRA when dey claim dey didn't rob de Nordern Bank. I'm a Cattalic meself and I've always admired people wit a strong fate. I believe in one God, de fadder almighty, maker of heaven and ert, and all tings seen and unseen. But unlike, Fadder Reid, I draw de line at de Gospel accordin to St Gerry. As for de peace process, I also believe in de resurrection of de dead and de life of de world to come, amen. But dis certainly hasn't made it any easier.

MONDAY

"Oirishmen and Oirishwomen: In de name of God and of de dead generations from which she receives her old tradition of nationhood, Oireland, trew us, summons her children to de flag and strikes for her freedom ... " It was wit dese words I stood on de steps of de GPO dis mornin and announced dat we, de provisional Government of Oireland, were reclaimin de spirit of 1916. "... We declare de right of de people of Oireland to de ownership of de Easter Risin, and to de unfettered control of annual celebrations dereof, to be sovreign and indefensible *("indefeasible" – Ed)*. De long usurpation of dat right by a bunch of Shinners has not extinguished de right, nor can it ever be extinguished, except by de destruction of de Oirish people ..." By de end of de proclamation, dere was only one man and his dog watchin me. Dey bote applauded. Den I told dem to go home to deir famlies, because dere'd be trouble here soon.

TUESDAY

We know de Shinners have overwhelmin superiority in terms of resources. But for de moment, we seem to have caut dem by surprise. De mood in de GPO is good, and news from around de city is also encouragin. De Valera (Sile) is holdin Boland's Mills; Countess Harnievicz has set up a field hospital in Stephen's Green; Commandant Martin has hired a firm of consultants to advise him on de feasibility of seizin de Four Courts in de short-to-medium term; while Biffo and a small band of comrades are holed up in de back room of Doheny and Nesbitt's and are heroically resistin de attempts of bar staff to get dem out.

WEDNESDAY

Today I left Captain Dempsey in charge of de post office and led a raidin party to a big house in Kildare Street, where a group of Government back-benchers were pinned down by a speech from Baldy O'Caolain about Monaghan hospital. We got dere just in time. Baldy had been talkin for 15 minutes by dat stage and already sevral of our backbenchers were pleadin to be shot. We returned fire to de Shinners side, causin O'Caolain to pause once or twice and take a drink of water. We were soon leggin it down Moleswort Street, trilled to be breedin fresh air again.

THURSDAY

Conditions have worsened back at headquarters. Dempsey had been attemptin to reorganise de post office workers to face de challenges of competition. But he appears to have mishandled it, and now dey've taken de advice of de proclamation and have decided to strike for DEIR freedom too. Unfortunately dis means we cannot contact our udder garrisons by post, while de pigeon service has been grounded because of de bird flu. Also, de revolutionary new e-mail system pioneered by Comrade Cullen has been found to be unworkable.Countess Harnievicz has come under particular heavy fire and has had to take cover in de College of Surgeons. Luckily her field hospital was highly mobile – most of de patients were on trolleys – so it was no problem movin dem.

FRIDAY

We had hoped for support from de Citizens' Army in Liberty Hall. But de union leaders – possibly under communist influence – are refusin to discuss a new partnership deal. Meanwhile, de problem of looters has led to divisions widdin our ranks. Commandant McDowell favoured shootin dem all on sight. But Countess Harnievicz said dey were only followin her advice in shoppin around for value, and dis was an example of de free market at its freest.

SATURDAY

Terrible news. Our old Comrade Liam Lawlor has fallen: shot in de back by snipers in Abbey Street. Ar dheis de go raibh a h-anam. At de time of his det, he had been on a top-secret mission to raise support among our allies in Europe. Now, like Roger Casement before him, he has joined de panteon of republican martyrs. And just as wit Casement, our enemies have sought to blacken his good name wit baseless diminuendos about his personal life. Nuttin changes in de struggle of Oirish republicans. For various reasons, me recent contacts wit Liam had been via a 40-foot pole. Unfortunately, due to a subsequent engagement, I can't attend his funeral eider, or deliver de oration.

SUNDAY

Our situation is hopeless. De post office is collapsin around our ears. Our relationship wit Liberty Hall is in flames. De Shinners are rumoured to be sailin a gunboat (captained by Martin Ferris) up de Liffey. Meanwhile, a force led by Mary-Lou McDonald has surrounded our Dublin Nort garrison, where me old runnin mate, Diarmuid Fitzpatrick, appears doomed. Worst of all, de Shinners have deployed Baldy O'Caolain wit a loudspeaker in O'Connell Street and have trettened round-de-clock speeches unless we come out wit our hands up. In order to avoid unnecess'ry sufferin, derefore, I have decided to surrender. General Adams has ordered dat me and de udder leaders of de rebellion are to be shot in de mornin (by a photographer from Daily Oireland). I have no fear. Me 1916 initiative has attracted only derision. But I am confidant dat in de rerun of de 1918 election, due in two years, our sacrifice will be vindicated. Tiocfaidh ár Lá!

MONDAY

Ever since de Donaldson ting, we're all parannoyed about British spies. So when I rang Blair today to wish him a happy new year and he said he'd been expectin me call, I was immediately suspicious. He claimed he meant nuttin udder dan dat it had been a while since we spoke. If I hadn't a rung him first, he'd a rung me, he said. But I told Gerry afterwards to get de office swept for bugs, and he promised he'd call Rentokil first ting. Anyway, Blair agreed wit me dat it was time for anudder push on de Nort. Dis is his last term in office and, as he admitted, he's now tinkin about his "legacy to posterity". His posterior is a bit exposed in Iraq, right enough, and his back benchers are queuin up to kick it. De Nort is probably his only chance to feel de hand of history on his shoulder again, before he feels de boot of history somewhere else.

TUESDAY

Today I did an interview for de influential RTÉ arts programme *Prattlebag*, in which I had to choose me favrit records. Obviously I ran de list past de lads in Mount Street first, and it was a good ting too. One of me original picks was Simon & Garfunkel's 'De Boxer', but dey rightly pointed out dat dis might suggest we were backin Kevin "Boxer" Moran in de Longford-Westmead selection convention. God knows, we're in enough trouble wit Mammy already. So I picked 'Nights in White Satin' to represent me long-haired hippy period instead. From me childhood, I chose 'How Much Is Dat Doggy In De Window?' partly to show dat I was concerned about de issue of consumer prices before Eddie Hobbs had an arse in his trousers. I trew in a bit of Neil Diamond too of course. And finally, de modern era was represented by Westlife's 'You Raise Me Up' (which I hope will be de effect of de whole exercise on me poll ratins).

WEDNESDAY

As a Nortsoider, one of de highlights of 2006 for me personally will be de openin of de Dublin Port Tunnel. Dat's why I was very concerned at reports of a leak in de pipe. But I'm glad to hear dat de engineers are playin dis down as a routine problem – all tunnels have dem, apparently – which will not affect de openin in May. Dere's good news too from de Department of Justice, where de leaks from de minister have also been plugged, at least for de moment. De experts say dat, while dey may be cause for concern, occasional leakages from Mr McDowell are only to be expected. In fact, he wouldn't be able to function properly widdout dem. Neverdeless we're keepin de situation monitored.

THURSDAY

In deir different ways, de problems of Charles Kennedy and de fat lad in Israel highlight de unhelty lives politicians lead. I haven't had much dealins wit Kennedy so I didn't know he had a drink problem, even dough I always found him unusually cheerful for a Scotsman. But from me behind-de-scenes work on de middle-east peace process, I knew Sharon had a food problem all right. Recently he'd been tryin to give up eatin between meals, but obviously de damage was done. Still, at least he's left an example to udder hard men about de ability to change. He pulled out of Gaza and maybe, if he'd been given more time, he'd a pulled out de West Bank too. As I said to Grizzly recently, if only de Provos had pulled out of de Nordern Bank, we wouldn't be in de mess we're in now. But in terms of big men givin up deir hardline ways and makin peace wit deir enemies late in life, Sharon is an example for a certain DUP leader. I hope dis is not lost on de latter, despite all de sedatives Peter Robinson is slippin into his tea.

FRIDAY

De challenge facin Ariel Sharon's doctors is nuttin compared to de one facin dose of us tryin to get de Nort's institutions movin again. De assembly has been in a medically induced coma for tree years now, and de fear must be dat its mental faculties may have been impaired in de interim. Not dat it had much to lose in dat regard – I taut de Provos were bein optimistic in havin an intelligence gadderin operation at Stormont, personally. Anyway, my suggestion to Blair is dat a little bit of shock treatment might be in order. If he trettens to switch off de life support (ie de fat salaries dat de MLAs get for doin nuttin), de patient might start respondin. It's wort de risk, I reckon.

SATURDAY

Out to RTÉ again to record me interview for tomorrow's Dis Week programme. Dis is a New Year fixture at dis stage and de questions were fairly soft, tank God. Short of bein given anudder opportunity to play 'How Much Is That Doggy In The Window?' I couldn't have been more comfortable. On de way home, I decided to ring Mammy O'Rourke and wish her well in de convention tomorrow. She was in good form and fairly optimistic too, because as she said, her campaigners were "workin like Protestants". I told her I was glad to hear dat but, eh, assumin she won, I hoped she wouldn't put it in exactly dose terms in her acceptance speech. Ye know how politically correct de media are, I said, and we didn't want to offend protestants. She told me not to worry: "You know me, Bertie: I'd never be that tactless."

MONDAY

De decision to scrap de Westlink toll plaza shoulda caused de biggest celebrations since de fall of de Berlin Wall. People shoulda been climbin de toll boots and breakin pieces off a dem for souvenirs. OK, de Berlin celebrations woulda been more subdued if de end of communism had been phased out over two years and if de replacement was subject to traffic studies and EU procurement procedures. But still. De fact dat we were gettin rid of de plaza at all was a good news story. Den Cullen had to blab about de four new tolls on de M50. Worse still, he had to mention dat dere'd be electronic equipment involved, which comin from him was just askin for trouble. So now we're back in de doghouse. Sometimes I tink I sacked de wrong transport minister before Christmas.

TUESDAY

Of course dere'll be new tolls, but de people didn't need to hear dis for anudder 18 munts or so. De next genral election is a bit like de Westlink. De tailback starts here, and government promises will be bumper-to-bumper between now and den. But once we've crossed de bridge of pollin day, we'll be in open country again and we can do what we like. Meanwhile, tanks to Cullen, de opposition had yet anudder stick to beat me wit on Leaders Questions today. Joe Trotsky had a field day on de M50, sayin we were like warlords in Afghanistan chargin peasants for use of a mountain pass. If he was in power, de Oirish people WOULD be peasants, and dey'd have to swim across de Liffey because dere wouldn't BE a bridge, wit or widdout tolls. But somehow he gets away wit dis guff.

WEDNESDAY

An eventful Cabinet meetin yesterday. We agreed an immediate ban on magic mushrooms, while Dermot Ahern briefed us on de contents of de IMC report on paramilitary activity in de Nort. De latter wasn't as bad as it coulda been. But it wasn't good eider, and Biffo suggested dat de best hope of political progress in de talks next week would be if we gave magic mushrooms to all de participants. I wasn't surprised to hear dat de Provos are still gaddrin intelligence. In fact, when dat hotel was raided by de CAB de udder day as part of de investigation into Provo money-laundrin, dere was a major scare involvin Willie O'Dea, who often stays dere. De fear was dat bugs (listenin devices, dat is, not insects) might have been attached to his person when he wasn't lookin. An extensive search of his moustache, using metal detectors revealed nuttin. But you can't be too careful.

THURSDAY

When Dermot told me dat de makers of *Sesame Street* were plannin a series of programmes aimed at promotin tolerance in Nordern Ireland, I taut he'd been at de mushrooms himself. But apparently it's true. De producers have secured a million dollars from de American Oireland fund to produce 26 programmes featuring Nordern Oirish teems. I suppose anyting dat encourages political progress is wortwhile. No doubt de DUP will raise objections about Kermit bein green, and republicans will complain about bein portrayed as a bunch of muppets (controlled by unseen hands). But after eight years of stalemate, it's about de only ting we haven't tried. If de DUP ever sit down to talk to de Shinners, we might get Big Bird to chair de meetin.

FRIDAY

Compared wit de Nort, de talks on a new social partnership will be a doddle. Dis time I'm aimin for a ten-year-deal – partly just to stretch mesclf. De short-term agreemcnts aren't a challenge any more. I'm like Sonia O'Sullivan. After all dose 1,500 and 5,000 metre agreements, I'm steppin up to de marraton, just to see if I can do it. But at dis stage of me career I'm also tinkin in terms of a legacy to histry. I'll probably be in a nursin home before de Nort's finally sorted. So a ten-year partnership deal would be me personal monument. De statue in O'Connell Street can wait until after I'm gone.

SATURDAY

Good news from de DUP conference where, apart from attackin de president and sayin he'd share power wit Shinners when hell freezes over, if not later, Paisley was in conciliatory mood. He said dat part of de Good Friday Agreement was "in a Saducee's grave" – which apparently means it won't be resurrected, even on de last day – and he's now demandin de disbandment of de IRA as de latest precondition for power-sharin. But a careful readin of his speech shows dat he never mentioned Kermit de Frog anywhere. De DFA observers – it was de first time Iveagh House was invited to a DUP conference – interpreted dis as a positive signal. When we get Paisley on de mushrooms, anyting could happen.

SUNDAY

I'm glad de Independent Monitorin Commission wasn't compilin a report on today's game in Omagh, or de political crisis would be worse dan it is. Bote teams engaged in criminality, punishment heatins, targetin of suspects, and probably intelligence gadderin (ahead of de championship). It was de worst outbreak of violence in de Nort since de last Tyrone-Armagh match. But it just goes to highlight de need for proper community policin, by referees dat have de respect of de players. We obviously need to work sometin out before de marchin season – de big games in Croke Park, when teams parade around de pitch beforehand – when passions are runnin high. If we don't, tings could get really ugly.

MONDAY

For de parties in goverment, de week around Paddy's Day is like de climax of a genral election campaign, except of course dat in dis case, de whole world is our constituency. We have people in de four corners of de globe: knockin on doors, shakin hands, slappin backs, and genrally meetin and greetin de great Oirish diaspirin on which de sun never sets. All right, dere's no actual pollin day. But dis annual canvass serves a number of important functions. First of all, it gets us all outta de country on March 17th. Given de levels of drinkin and street violence, and de rise in gun crime – let's face it – we're a lot safer abroad. But more importantly, de contacts we make dis week will be vital in de year ahead. De teme of dis year's promotion is de "knowledge economy". So evrywhere we go, we'll be stressin de importance in Oireland of who ye know. If ye know us, will be de message, ye don't need introductions to anybody else.

TUESDAY

Willie O'Dea has heroically volunteered to remain behind for de week, to allay public suspicions dat de country can run itself widdout politicians. His duties will be two-fold. He will be actin Taoiseach in my absence – aldough I've warned him dat if dere are any important decisions to be made, he should put dem off indefinitely, which is what I always do. Secondly, he will be keepin an eye on Micheál Martin, who lost out in de Cabinet raffle for foreign destinations and is spendin de week in Cork. Of course, as head of de army, Willie will also have responsibility for restorin law and order if de Paddy's Day celebrations get outta hand. He's very excited about de prospect, obviously. But I've warned him again about pointin guns at people widdout reason.

WEDNESDAY

One ting we're always nervous of when de Government travels abroad is de risk of a coup. I had hardly landed in de States dis mornin when Willie rang me on de emergency mobile to report dat Kenny and Rabbitte had seized a Dublin city centre hotel and were clearly up to no good. On furder questionin, he admitted dat "seized" might be overstatin it: apparently dey booked de hotel in de normal manner, for some sort of press conference. But he wanted permission to round up all known Fine Gael and Labour sympatisers, anyway, just to be on de safe side. I urged caution, advisin him to keep de army in reserve for now, while monitoring events. It turned out de two Mayo lads were just launchin a joint policy document, and de only ting dey seized were a few cheap headlines. Before goin to dinner here, I formally downgraded Willie's state of alert from "red" to "orange". He was gutted, of course.

THURSDAY

Bit of a head on me dis mornin after de gig at de ambassador's place last night. As usual, dere was no expense spared, wit evryting from Ferrero Rocher to Bass on tap. We did it justice, needless to say. Today was a non-stop round of meetins on Capitol Hill. We discussed de immigration bill wit Ted Kennedy and John McCain, and we assured dem we were 100 per cent behind deir campaign to secure rights for illegal migrants (except de ones in Oireland). We also met Hillary C, who reiterated her sincere commitment to exploitin de Oirish vote in her run for de 2008 presidency. And we attended de annual lunch hosted by de speaker of de House of Representatives, Denis Bastert *(er "Hastert" – Ed)*. Apparently I got his name slightly wrong durin me speech. But apart from dat it all went very well.

FRIDAY

President Bush's intrest in Oireland grows greater evry year, a point underlined today by his gratitude for de traditional gift of shamrock. Aldough he referred to it as a "salad bowl" and said he'd get Laura to rustle up something special wit it later on, he said de present emphasised to him how "different" de Oirish were. "Everybody else brings me useful presents," he quipped. After dat, it was down to business. I impressed on him de need for more transparency in relation to CIA flights trew Shannon. He accepted dis, while impressin on me de need for more transparency in relation to Oirish illegal immigrants in America. "You give us their names and addresses, and we'll give you information about the flights," he said. We agreed to furder discussions on de subject. Den, remembrin de promotional aspects of me US tour, I asked him to remind de CIA dat Shannon currently has a special offer on Bailey's: two for de price of one, dis munt only.

SATURDAY

All in all, it's been a great week for de Oirish, bote in politics and in sport. Our ministers have gone around de world, like de early Christian monks spreadin de Gospel (dere's no word yet of any martyrs). Meanwhile, Oirish horses were winnin all before dem at Cheltenham. Ok, Zero informs me dat dey were de wrong horses, mostly. De knowledge economy went into recession on Wednesday, he says, and all de nags he backed since den are still runnin. Still, wit a record 10 wins, it shows our investment in elite sports stars wit four legs is payin off. Meanwhile, de two-legged stars are doin alright as well. Dere was a gold medal at de world indoor atlettics, of course, and den de rugby team won some sort of a plate in London. I'm not a rugger man, and I'm not sure what was so good about finishin second in the Six Nations. But apparently we won de British home championships again, so I suppose dat's a big deal. Anyting dat gets de crowd cheerin is OK by me.

MONDAY

Me keynote speech on de 1916 celebrations, delivered at de openin of de exhibition in Collins's Barracks at de weekend, was closely modelled on de original proclamation. But whereas Padraig Pearse summoned de children of Oireland to de flag to strike for deir freedom – which I tink was pitchin it a bit high for most of his audience – my speech aimed lower. I just called for a "great national conversation" on what it means to be Oirish. We should be able to achieve dat much, no bodder. Maybe Joe Duffy could hold it on his radio programme dis week. In de name of God and of de dead generations, ring de *Liveline* number now and tell us what you tink.

TUESDAY

Dere's been no reaction yet to de udder message of me speech, which was to brand de Risin – and evryting else dat was good in 20th century Oireland – as de work of Fianna Fáil. Like de IRB commandeerin key buildins in Easter week, I identified a number of strategically important dates in Oirish history – 1916, de '37 constitution, EEC membership, and de signin of de Good Friday Agreement (by, eh, yours truly) – and hoisted de FF flag over dem all. De "four cornerstones" of Oirish independence, I called dem. De Blueshirts will be up de Liffey in a gunboat any day now to shell our position. But until den we're stayin put. Up de Republic!

WEDNESDAY

Speakin of great national conversations, de word from our focus groups is dat I may have overdone it a bit wit de bowlin-alone, social-capital, kinder-gentler-Fadder-Seán-Healy crap dat I've been spoutin dis past year. De lads in HQ say I now need to reassure an important element of our constituency dat FF is still de party of get-up-and-go greedy-bastard capitalists. At de autumn tink-in dis year, we'll probably have Roman Abramovich or somebody like dat as de keynote speaker. In de meantime, I have to make a few speeches about – for example – how good it is dat Oirish banks are de most profitable in Europe, and how anybody dat says udderwise is a communist.

THURSDAY

You can talk all you like about 1916, but nuttin says "Rising" quite like de Oirish property market. Prices are still goin trew de roof, despite de warnins of de doom-merchants and de nay-sayers who predicted a hard landin two or tree years ago. De only hard landin has been for deir predictions, which fell flat on deir big fat faces! Now de financial services autority has joined de commie conspiracy to undermine confidence in de market, urgin banks and buildin societies to put more cash aside for defaultin mortgages. Claptrap! Dat sort of talk is for losers. Anyone who listened to de economists a couple of years back and held off buyin a house is now tousands of euro poorer as a result. Dat's why we say: Oirishmen and Oirishwomen, in de name of God and de dead generations, take out a 110 per cent mortgage now and grab yourself a slice of de action before it's too late.

FRIDAY

Inda has finally risen to de bait of me Collins's Barracks speech, accusin me of "airbrushin" Fine Gael out of Oirish histry. Apparently I forgot to mention de four cornerstone achievements of his party: takin a shillin off de old age pension in 1929, introducin fascism to Oireland in de '30s, attemptin to impose VAT on childrens' shoes in 1982 and, eh, I forget what de udder one was. Oh, yes, I remember: forcin a democratically elected president to resign after he was insulted by a Blueshirt minister for defence in 1975. Obviously dis was a big oversight on my part. Naturally, I'm happy to set de record straight here, and acknowledge de proud contribution of Inda's party to de development of de State.

SATURDAY

I don't know how people can call our 1916 parade divisive. De event is bein boycotted by bote Ian Paisley AND Gerry Adams, and dere's not many parades can boast dat. In fact, we hoped somebody from de DUP might come down for it. We reminded dem dat republicanism was part of deir histry too, tanks to de Antrim presbyterian Henry Joy McCracken and de United Oirishmen. Sadly, dey sent us back a note sayin dat we were Henry Joy McCracked if we taut dey'd fall for dat. But it was wort a try anyway.

SUNDAY

A great day for Oireland. De highlight for me was Kilmainham Gaol, where all de party leaders gaddered at dawn to honour de men who were executed dere in 1916. After a final cup of tea, I was taken out to de Stonebreaker's Yard and shot – but only by photographers, mind you – while layin a wreed. Den it was into de GPO to review de parade, which included armoured cars, scorpion tanks, anti-aircraft guns and a fly-past by de entire air corps. Dis was ostensibly ceremonial, but it also doubled in a security role. McDowell had requested maximum back-up for de Gardaí, in case de residents of de nort inner city rose again. I was a bit nervous in case some gouger trew a bottle and it sparked an air-and-ground assault on Seán McDermott street. Luckily, de event passed off peacefully and de defence forces returned to base widdout firin a shot.

MONDAY

It's 80 years since dat never-to-be-forgotten night when Fianna Fáil was founded in de La Stampa restaurant in Dawson Street *(er, the La Scala theatre off O'Connell St – Ed)*. To mark de great occasion, dis week I'm embarkin on a series of exclusive interviews wit everyone dat'll have me. Of course, as well as lookin back, I'll also be lookin forward. Because dis is also de first pre-anniversary of anudder historic occasion: de start of me turd term in office. I have secretly fixed de genral election for de eighteent of May, two tousand and seven, so de count-down starts here. As usual, our campaign will be mostly about me. Dat's why I'll be usin dis week's interviews to distance meself from issues dat have made de goverment unpoplar: decentralisation, Mary Harney, de canary yellow jacket I wore to de Azores summit, etc.

TUESDAY

Enda Kenny may be a more dangerous opponent dan we taut. For two days now, a crack team in FF headquarters has been goin trew his Ard Fheis speech line-by-line, searchin for any evidence of an idea. So far dey've found nuttin – not even a coded suggestion dat a Blueshirt-Labour coalition might increase public spendin. Anudder key plank of our election strategy is dat, sooner or later, FG will resort to hare-brained schemes – like de compensation for Eircom shareholders last time out – dat we'll be able to seize on as evidence of unelectability. De dreaded scenario is dat dey might take us on at our own game, wit Enda just bein nice, sayin nuttin, and lookin pretty. Already de signs are ominous. I could be wrong, but I tink he's wearin lipstick in some of dose billboard ads.

WEDNESDAY

We finally called de search off early dis mornin. I visited HQ last night and de exhausted team were already pleadin wit me: "Please don't make us read Enda's speech again". But I told dem dere could still be a live idea trapped inside, dependin on us to get it out. So, bravely, dey went back in and carried on until it was obvious dat dere were no signs of life anywhere. It was time for us to face de worst. We taut we might get away wit only 500,000 election posters of me. Now I've ordered de printers to make it a million.

THURSDAY

I used me exclusive interview wit Sam Smit today to raise de white flag on decentralisation. It was a noble aspiration to move all de civil servants in Dublin back to where dey came from, so de rest of us could get a drink at de bar easier.

Unfortunately de time frame was overly optimistic. It's a bit like de first world war. We taut de culchies would be home by Christmas. But den de f***ers started diggin trenches. Aldough Willie O'Dea genrously offered to use mustard gas to get dem out, I've decided we should just extend de time frame by anudder tree years. It'll be Biffo's problem by den.

FRIDAY

Off to Vienna for de EU/Latin America summit, where I was embraced warmly by de Venezualian president, Hugo Chavez, and de lad from Bulimia *(er, "Bolivia?" – Ed)* whose name I can't remember. Dey kept calling me "amigo", and sayin I was deir ally in de war against "Neoliberalism". "Neil Who?" says I. But Hugo just laughed and hugged me again and said dat, while we socialists were few in number now, our will was strong and soon we would sweep away de "old world order". "Viva la revolucion!" said de udder lad, kissin me on bote cheeks. De EU president, Jose Manuel de Rossa, took me aside afterwards and asked me why I was such a big hit with those "head-bangers". I told him I had no idea: "I tink dey mistook me for somebody else."

SATURDAY

I was back in Dublin last night in time for a few scoops in Fagan's, and dis mornin, I recorded an exclusive interview for RTÉ's Dis Week programme. Den it was off into de studios to rehearse me exclusive interview wit Ryan Tubridy tonight. De backroom lads said we could maybe have got bigger viewer numbers doin Podge and Rodge, but dey feared de questions might be too political. Dis will be a soft-focus job, and it's a chance for us to "hit a lot of different demographics" at once, as our PR people say. "Make sure and mention how you grew up on a farm in the middle of the city," they told me.

SUNDAY

It went like a dream. De audience loved de stuff about All-Hallows farm and, usin me experience from all dose years ago, I milked dem till dey said "Moo". De toughest question I had to face was whedder I'd like to see England win de World Cup. But somehow I struck a balance between de mature, post-Good-Friday-Agreement, all-friends-togedder-now answer (Yes) and de more truteful one (Anybody except England). Den still on de football teem, Ryan asked me who I'd like to "buy" from each of de opposition parties and I said Enda from Fine Gael. In fact, I'd be hopin to get him on a Bosman when he's out of contract next summer. More to de point, from Labour, I picked Brendan Howlin. He's small but highly mobile. And in terms of potential coalition partners, unlike his leader, he can still kick wit eider foot.

MONDAY

Tings seem to have taken a turn for de worst. De latest private polls for Dublin say we're in deep doo-doo. Seán Haughey is in danger of losin his seat – but it's not all good news. We could lose eight or nine udder ones as well, accordin to de figgers. Dis is on top of various newspaper polls showin dat de pact between Laurel and Hardy is gainin credibility as an alternative government. How de f*** did dat happen? Anyway, what wit de polls, and de pay talks stallin, and de decentralisation plan goin off de rails, me backbenchers are muttrin again. Dere's talk of me losin me touch as de Teflon Teeseach. People are askin whedder me non-stick finish can still cope if de s**te really does hit de pan.

TUESDAY

De importance of de social partnership is a bit of a mytt. It was a big factor in gettin de country goin back in de early '90s. But de economy is now steamin ahead at such a rate dat it's doubtful if even Laurel and Hardy could make a balls of it. De point is, dough, dat after 20 years of agreements, I can't afford to be de Teeseach dat presides over de break-up of de partnership process. It'd be one ting to lose me non-stick coatin. But to lose me reputation as de world's greatest deal-maker would be de last straw. Unfortunately, de talks parties seem to have finally copped on to me secret negoshiatin weapon (always agree wit everyone). Now dey're takin advantage of me good nature by demandin more and more. De gap between de sides is so big dis time, I don't know if even I can come up wit a fudge.

WEDNESDAY

It's partly because of de talks dat we're beatin a retreat from de decentralisation fiasco. Jack O'Connor wants it scrapped. But Jack is like one of dose lads who used to walk in front of a train wavin a flag. De train is de genral election, and de possibility of masses of disinfected *(er "disaffected"? – Ed)* civil servants votin against us. I'm not waitin around for dat to hit me. Of course it's not so much de civil service departments dat are de problem. De biggest mistake wit de scheme was includin State agencies like Fas, which is supposed to go to some one-horse town in Parlon Country. At de very least, we should have sent de Ordnance Survey dere instead, so dey could finish mappin de place. Dere's parts of Offaly dat are still virgin rainforest, I believe.

THURSDAY

Dere are no one-horse towns in Nort Kildare: dey're all multiple-horse towns. What dey do have a shortage of, unfortunately, is Fianna Fáil TDs. In fact, de constituency is currently a no-horse town, as far as we're concerned. Dis is a direct result of de decentralisation programme in which I moved de former Minister for Finance to Brussels, to ease congestion in de Cabinet. But tankfully, when I toured de area today on a whistle-stop canvass, nobody brought dis up. And de udder good news is dat, even dough she lost de by-election, we now have an established, high-profile candidate in Aine What's-her-name. Yes, I tink tings are definitely lookin up dere.

FRIDAY

I nearly forgot to mention, but dis week also saw an unforgettable occasion in de Dáil: an address to de House by de very carismatic prime minister of Australia, Ron Howard. Ron is probably better known for his former career, when he directed fillums such as *Titanic*. But if anyting he's been even more successful in his new career, in which he plays de leader of a supposedly unsinkable country dat's somewhere in de middle of de Pacific when disaster suddenly struck – but I better not give de plot away. Anway, he gave a very interestin speech about, eh, about … it'll come back to me in a minute. I'm only sorry for de independents who boycotted de occasion.

SATURDAY

It was typically opportimistic *("opportunistic"? – Ed)* of de Greens to expose de sensitive issue of me make-up bill, and to ask what Dev would tink of a Fianna Fáil leader dat spends 25 gees a year on cosmetics. I must admit, I prefer not to dwell on dis when I'm gettin powdered up in de mornin. But as John Gormless very well knows, we live in a television age and ye can't go on television widdout make-up. Or if ye do, ye end up lookin like Dev, after he died. When we saw de question on the order paper, I got our contacts in RTÉ to check if Gormless wears make-up himself during his TV appearances, and of course he does. But dis wasn't enough to make him back off, and of course he got loads of mileage out of de issue in de press. De way he went on about it, ye'd tink I was some kind of lady-boy.

SUNDAY

It's been a terrible munt, as far as de wedder goes. But de good ting about livin in a rainy climate is dat you save on moisturiser. De sun is very harsh on de skin: it can make your face look like shoe ledder. At least in a wet country, we don't have dat problem. OK, we look pale and unhelty. But dat's easily delt wit. I recommend a good foundation – someting from de Colour-Me-Beautiful range, preferably. Also ye need to exfoliate regularly with one of the better body scrubs. After dat, it's just a question of choosing eye-shadow, lip gloss, etc, dat suits your basic mood and goes well wit yer handbag.

MONDAY

De end of anudder Dail year, and not a moment too soon. Dis has been an anus horribilis, as Queen Elizabet would say. Worse dan dat, it's been a pain in de anus horribilis. Not even de fact dat de recent Fianna Fáil back-bench rebellion folded in de end, like a cheap deckchair, was much relief. Short-lived as it was, de rebellion distracted from de only good news on de horizon lately: de fact dat de PDs were tearin demselves apart in public. As I told de parliamentary party de udder night, we should been sittin back watchin de power struggle between beauty and de beast and havin a laugh, instead of competin wit dem for de front pages. But at least I was able to buy de rebels off cheap. Tank God dat Sile Dev's job will soon be vacant. I've lost count of de number of people I've promised it to at dis stage.

TUESDAY

In keepin wit time-honoured custom, de opposition are complainin bitterly about de lent of de summer holidays. Dey want to reduce de break from tree munts to a long weekend, or someting. One of dese years I'm gonna stand up and tell dem deir wish has been granted, just for de pleasure of seein de bastards' faces when I do. But I honestly don't tink I could look at dem for even anudder week, much as I'd enjoy de joke of seein dem unpack deir suitcases. Similarly, I'm tempted to grant de early election dat de Blueshirts and Labour have demanded in a motion. De only ting dat stops me is dat I believe de current Labour leader needs anudder 12 munts to reposition himself. His no-coalition-wit-Fianna-Fáil-until-hell-freezes-over stance hasn't left him much wiggle room. But as wit all former Stickies, I'm confident about his flexibility.

WEDNESDAY

After an argument, de cabinet has reluctantly decided to let ordinary people buy shares in Aer Lingus. Despite de Eircom debacle, apparently, de prospect of fools and deir money bein parted remains high. But de real reason we're lettin de genral public in on de deal is dat we have no choice: if we didn't, de feckers would tink dey were missin out on someting. It's an awkward one. All de advisors warn us dat airline shares are subject to turbulence and dat shareholders should keep deir sick-bags handy at all times. Like most investments, dis is one for de long-term. Unfortunately we have a genral election comin up in de short term, and we don't want a nose-dive in Aer Lingus shares causin de voters to trow up at de wrong moment. Dat's why we've pitched de minimum purchase at ten grand. Accordin to our market research, only PD supporters will be able to afford it.

THURSDAY

Fresh from makin crime levels in Kenya an election issue, Inda has pressed home his credentials as an international statesman by travlin to Belfast for meetins wit Paisley and udder leaders. Afterwards, he claimed de two goverments needed to "inject new momentum" into de peace process. I'm prepared to take a lot of guff from Inda. But after ten years of tryin to sort de Nort out, I'd inject me foot up his hole before I'll take lectures from him on de subject. I notice he brought his prospective Tánaiste to Belfast, to give de impression of a Government-in-waitin. So maybe dat's de secret Blueshirt plan to solve de Nordern problem. When all else fails, Inda will do de one ting dat I haven't tried, and pull a Rabbitte out of a hat.

FRIDAY

For de moment, I'm concentratin on a solution to de udder Nordern problem. Ever since de tragic events of 1970, it's been a priority for Fianna Fáil leaders to try and reclaim de fourt green field dat is Neil Blaney's Donegal. Now is de hour, and I tink I'm de man to do it. In fact, Charlie Haughey pleaded wit me on his det-bed to sort dis out. He always felt guilty about how Blaney was treated back den. So he made me promise dat I'd reunite de party (in return for his promise dat he wouldn't write his memoirs). Dat's why I've launched de Donegal peace process, despite de objections of de local grassroots. It might make me unpoplar. But as John Hume used to say, some tings are bigger dan de party.

SATURDAY

For me de big story of de World Cup was de revival of de French team. I'm writin dis de night before de final. But surely nuttin dat happens dere can change de beauty of what Zinedine Zidane has achieved. It was as if, at a certain point in de tournament, he just put his head down and went for it. De French are an inspiration to de current Government. After all, accordin to de critics, we also delivered our best performances back in de late 90s and we haven't done anyting wortwhile since. But de French have shown dat you can look tired and incompetent for five or six years and suddenly come good again just when it matters. Dat will be my hope when we get back from de holidays and start trainin for de crucial 2006/7 season. As for Italy, a team playin against de shadow of tribunals, court cases, and years of wholesale corruption, dere's no similarities between dem and Fianna Fáil, obviously.

MONDAY

I considered interruptin me holiday when de news came trew of a terrorist plot in England. Den I considered interruptin Willie O'Dea's holiday instead. But based on a combination of security briefins and de wedder forecast, I decided in de end dat neider of us was required in Dublin. It was a bit of a bluff on my part. I figgered it would have a calmin effect on de population if Mary Coughlan handled de press interviews, since de public would reckon dat if dere really was a problem, dere's no way she'd be left in charge. I tink de plan worked. In any case, a meetin of de national security committee set de national tret level at "code yellow". Dis is de mid-point of a scale where code green means dere's no tret at all, and code red means dat Jimmy McDaid is drivin de wrong way up de Naas dual carriageway again.

TUESDAY

When Dublin played Westmead in de All-Ireland Quarter final, however, it was clear dis was a genuine emergency of de kind dat required my immediate return to Drumcondra. Luckily, tanks to good intelligence work by Pillar Caffrey and de lads, a potential disaster was easily averted. Westmead's tret level was downgraded to "moderate" durin de pre-match kick-around. It was reduced to "completely harmless" after five minutes of actual play, and by half time de security assessment was dat de poor boggers were a danger to demselves. Dere was a brief scare in de second half when a couple of Westmead players attempted to board de pitch carryin "sports drinks", of de kind dat allegedly keep top atleets and terrorists goin for 33 per cent longer. Happily the lads involved bote tested negative for any atletic content and de alert was soon called off.

WEDNESDAY

I'm back in Kerry now, relaxin. But, of course, a world leader never really rests. Aldough I can't go public yet on my involvement in de middle east conflict, suffice to say dat I have been very busy on de telephone. De Lesbianese people have suffered enough, God knows, and I was only too glad to help dem. De trick was persuadin bote de Israeli and Hezbollix leaderships dat dey'd won de war, but I did much de same ting wit de Good Friday Agreement, so it was no bodder. Dis mornin I had Kofi on de mobile askin me for an Oirish input into de peace keepin force. I told him we would do our bit, as always, and de prospect of me succeedin him as UN secatry general – hint hint – had nuttin to do wit it. I've warned Willie O'Dea dat Sout Lebanon will be a very dangerous place for Oirish troops. But as he says himself, he has to canvass in Sout Hill regularly, so danger is relative.

THURSDAY

Maybe we should send de Oirish football team to Lebanon, instead of de Army. Not dat dey could defend de green line, or any kind of line. But after last night deir credentials as an international peace-keepin force are beyond question. De back four were neutral, de midfield was non-aligned, and despite severe provocation from de enemy de forwards refused to fire a shot. De commitment to non-violence was total. Arjen Robben in particular was just askin to be kicked, but dere was a demilitarised zone between him and de nearest defender all night. It was like he had a Red Cross uniform. I don't know. I tink I favour a unilateral Oirish witdrawal from de game against Germany next munt, to avert a humanitarian disaster.

FRIDAY

In de light of de latest Morris reports, it's now clear dat gardaí are a bigger danger to de State dan international terrorists. We knew de Donegal coppers were as bent as de road to Buncrana, but de judge says de problem exists right across de force. McDowell had dat crazed look in his eye again on de news last night. Dere'll be no stoppin his Ranelagh Reserve now. And I suppose we'll have to ram his new Garda code of ettics trew as well, even dough I was hopin to put it off to a more oppertune time (ie after de election). Between blue flu and bird flu, it could be a long winter. But, eh, on de plus side, if dere are any bad colds going, it should be de PDs dat catch dem.

SATURDAY

Good news on de security front, wit de intelligence people reportin dat de main tret to planes at Shannon airport is anudder lump hammer. Years of careful work by Bord Fáilte means dat most Icelandic fundamentalists have never heard of Shannon, or its famous security-free zone. Good news too from party headquarters, which informs me dat we have secured an Oxford professor and energy expert as our keynote speaker for de tink-in next munt. Energy is one of de most important issues facin us. Dere's a severe lack of it in de party at de moment. We remain heavily dependent on fossils like Seamus Brennan, and dese are fast runnin out. Of course, John O'Donoghue and udders have made great strides in de area of wind energy. Conor Lenihan could keep de national grid goin on his own sometimes. But we're hopin de Oxford man will point us in de direction of new renewable sources. Failin dat, we'll have to go nuclear.

MONDAY

Culchies. Dey come up to Dublin. Dey take our jobs and our women. Dey price us out of de housin market. And now, not satisfied wit all dat, dey take over de Hill 16 end of Croke Park for a pre-match warm-up against de Dubs. Is nuttin sacred? Under de city plan, dis part of Drumcondra has always been earmarked as a green space for local residents. So to see a bunch of boggers rezone it for agricultural use, and den establish a big, ugly warm-up session on it widdout plannin permission, was just not on. Of course, residents of de near-by terraces objected, and I had a quiet word wit Nicky Brennan meself to see if de offensive, large green-and-red structures could be removed forcibly from de site. Unfortunately, and unbelievably, it turned out dat dere was no law against dem bein dere. We could do nuttin except sit and watch. But mark my words: one of dese days, de culchies will push us too far.

TUESDAY

I know it was a good game and all, but I can't ignore de fact dat, at de start of an election year, de result was a very bad omen. De udder Mayo team – de one wit Indakinny and Willie Joe Rabbitte in midfield – has also looked impressive in de warm-ups, wit deir fancy interpassin and deir stretchin exercises. But until now I was confident dat when de campaign got under way, de only ting dey'd be stretchin was credibility. When de pressure built up, I taut, de Mayo talent for chokin on de big occasion would resurface. Rabbitte's lads would start goin on solo runs up de left, Kenny's Blueshirts would be huggin de right touchline, and de midfield would gradually fall apart. In de meantime, we'd just calmly pick off de scores. Den wit 20 minutes to go, we'd bring de Bomber Cowen off de bench wit his SSIAs, and it be all over bar de tree cheers for de born – eh, I mean gallant – losers. After Sunday, dough, I'm worried.

WEDNESDAY

De event cast a shadow over de first Cabinet meetin of de Autumn, wit Zero givin me lip about de Dubs' defeat. De slaggin was great down in Kerry durin de holidays and de day I left Parknasilla it was: "we'll see yiz in de final". But dat had gone a bit sour now. On de udder hand, de meetin also discussed de genral political outlook, which we agreed was positive. It had been a good summer – no big PR disasters and no massively poplar RTE series about rip-off consumer prices (last year we were moppin up for munts after de effects of Hurricane Eddie). So me mood had improved a bit by de end of de meetin, when I outlined priority legislation for de comin Dail session. Dis will include de emergency Hill 16 End Warm-Up (Exclusion of Culchies) Bill 2006, which will be rushed trew all stages of de house in October.

THURSDAY

Blair is also back from his holidays and he rang me today to discuss tactics for de fortcomin Nort talks. We know de IMC report will declare de Provos cleaner dan a presbyterian nun's knickers, but dis will still not be enough for de DUP. So as on previous occasions, we're gonna get de parties outta Belfast for a couple of days – maybe to Scotland – for what are called "Hot-house" negotiations. De idea is dat de participants are isolated in an enclosed environment, like rare plants, and fed large amounts of fertiliser, in de hope dat dey'll experience some sort of grote (if only emotional). Drink would normally be an important part of de process, but wit Paisley around, we'll have to improvise. We can only try, I suppose. Blair said he'd get back to me as soon as he found a venue remote enough from civilisation.

FRIDAY

De allegation dat a Fianna Fail councillor took cocaine is a serious issue and one dat I'm determined to get to de bottom of. De man is entitled to due process, of course (except in de view of me brudder). But I've seen de newspaper pictures in which Mr Kelly appears poised to snort a white powder-like substance up his nose, so I've appointed a committee to look into it (de matter, dat is, not his nose). If he's found guilty, we will take action reflectin de party's total abhorrence of dis sort of ting. Dere can be no room for ambivalence on drugs. But as I say, dere may be an innocent explanation. He might have had a load pints on him, for example, and not known exactly what he was doin. Sure plenty have all been in dat position at one time or anudder.

SATURDAY

De annual tink-in has taken on added significance dis year. Not only will we be de last before me attempt at an electral tree-in-a-row. But by havin it in Mayo, I can take revenge against de boggers for what happened in Croke Park. It's like we're seizin de psychological advantage by warmin up in front of Inda's own supporters (not dat dere'd be enough of dem to fill Hill 16 or anyting). Kenny and Rabbitte will again try to distract de media wit deir Mullingar sideshow. But I tink dat stunt peaked two years ago when dey lured Charlie Bird down dere, instead of Inchdoney where de rest of de world media had gaddered. Somehow, I tink de main focus will be on us dis time. After all, de public will want to know exactly how we plan to buy – I mean win – de genral election.

DE FULL FINANCIAL STATEMANT
OF A NORTSOIDE TAOISEACH
(Property of the Mahon Tribunal)

1956

De early 1950s were not a difficult time for me. Despite dis, for sevral years runnin, a man I only ever knew as "Santa" left unsolicited gifts for me under de Christmas tree every December. I believe dere may have been a number of elves involved as well, aldough I never knew deir names. It always happened at night and I never met Santa. But I made inquiries around Drumcondra and discovered he had an address c/o de Nort Pole. So in 1956 I wrote to him to try and regularise de situation. I knew de tax law: I was gonna be an accountant. I told him I could not accept his presents except as a debt of honour, to be repaid eventually at tree per cent per annum. Den I asked him for a bicycle. I never did anyting for Santa in return. I accept now dat he only gave de presents on condition dat I was "good", and dat I may have acted unwisely in takin dem. But de way I saw it at de time, I was good anyway, so no ettical issue arose.

1958

De late 50s were a dark period in me life. Me teet were fallin out, one after anudder, and aldough new teet gradually replaced dem, I suffered a significant dental shortfall for a time, especially during de winter of 1958. I heard from one of me friends – probably Tony Kett – dat somone called de "Toot Fairy" could give me a dig-out. It wouldn't be in de form of new teet, he said, just a few bob to tide me over de crisis. When I said I might be intrested I was told to leave me old teet under de pillow and de money would "appear" in deir place. I did dis, but I also left a note for de Toot Fairy sayin dat I regarded de monies as loans, repayable eventually at tree per cent. I knew de tax law. Unfortunately dere are no documents available. De fairy kept me letter.

1959 (A)

At de time of me first Communion, I found meself financially embarrassed. I had a simple lifestyle. I was still wearin short trousers, even dough all me friends had long ones. But even de basics of life – penny toffees, chewin gum, gob-stoppers, and so on – cost money. So de day of me communion, a group of friends organised a whip-around. To de best of me recollection, de group included me fadder and mudder, aunties and uncles, and a few neighbours. Paddy de Plasterer might have been involved as well. Naturally, I refused to take de money unless it was repayable. At my insistence, we agreed a fixed compound annual rate of 3.75 per cent, wit de first payment due in 2059. De adults were impressed wit me figgers. "Mark my words," me uncle Tommy said: "Dat lad'll be runnin de country some day."

1959 (B)

Around de same time, I had me first confession. Of course, I had nuttin to tell. As far as I was concerned, I had broken no codes – tax, legal, ettical, or udderwise – and I told de priest so. He was a bit puzzled. Ye must have done someting wrong, my child, he said. I said, no fadder, I lead a simple life and have no intrest in ertly tings. So de priest – Fadder McDowell his name was – said I should offer an act of contrition anyway to take de bad look off it. He gave me an Our Fadder and tree Hail Marys. I said I'd only take dem if he considered it a loan.

1963

When I was 12, me and de udder boys in de class were invited to join someting called de "army of Christ". Ye had to buy yer own uniform, dough, and dere were a lot of udder expenses. So de day of de confirmation cermony, anudder consortium of friends came togedder, unsolicited, and gave me a dig-out. I believe dere were 11 equal donations of two and sixpence, while Paddy de Plasterer gave five bob. De money was handed over after a function in de local church. I don't recall speakin at dis function, aldough I did participate in a short question-and-answer session. A man identifyin himself only as "de Bishop" asked me who died for my sins. I said I didn't know, but whoever it was must have been mistaken, because as far as I was concerned, I hadn't committed any. I accept now dis may have been unwise.

1972

At the time of me 21st birtday, a group of close friends and famly members tried to present me wit what dey said were de "keys of de door". After legal advice, I refused to take dem, widdout knowin where exactly de door led. Instead dey organised a whiparound of cash so dat, as me fadder put it, I could afford "a proper hair cut". I tink I did make a speech on dis occasion, but I can't remember.

1976

Some time shortly after dis, to de best of my recollection, I received an education from de London School of Economics. I can't remember de exact amount, and I have no documentation. Neider has de school apparently.

1987

It was at about dis time dat a group of friends known collectively as de "GAA" started invitin me to big games as a VIP. I made it clear dat I would attendin not as a VIP, but in me own right as a private citizen. Dey said OK, but I might as well sit in de VIP section anyway because all de udder seats were gone. I always made a point of payin for me own travel between Drumcondra and Croke Park. Also, I derived no pleasure from most of de games I attended, because de Dubs were shite by den and it was always coulchies winnin de All-Ireland. After seein Mead win four times in de 80s and 90s, I feel dat any debt I owe has been repaid at a high rate of intrest.

MONDAY

De payments scandal has been so poplar wit voters dat de lads in party HQ are desprit for more of de same. Me focus group approval ratins are trew de roof, and in private pollin, me personal popularity is higher dan Mudder Teresa's ever was. So de handlers have asked me to rack me brain and see if dere's anyting else from de dark period of me life dat we could leak to de *Oirish Times* to keep de scandal goin. Dere's two skools of taut here. One is dat we should leak someting big enough to bring down de opposition now. De udder is dat we should have a slow, drip-drip of allegations about me, which would allow Fine Gael and Labour to limp on, more and more damaged, until June. I tink dis is de smart move meself.

TUESDAY

Me plan to ditch de PDs before de Budget has been less successful, unfortunately. When dey didn't walk over Paddy de Plasterer, we taut dey would definitely go over Mick de Bus Driver. But our tinkin was based on de belief dat dey still had some shame left. It turns out dat Mick de Barrister is me best friend of all: he just can't bear de prospect of life widdout me. It woulda been nice to have a nine-munt run-in to de election on our own, complete wit de, eh, caring Budget dat Fianna Fáil have always wanted to bring in, if only our hands weren't tied by mean coalition partners. But de PDs obviously did de sums and decided dat nuttin short of me bein implicated in de Nordern Bank robbery would be grounds to quit government. Dey must have focus groups too.

WEDNESDAY

It's no exaggeration to say dat Michael McDowell is me new best friend. I've always been a cat man meself. But now dat I have a pet Rottweiler, I can understand what people see in dogs. He's very loyal and – contry to what people say about de breed – affectionate. Too affectionate sometimes! Dere was a moment at de end of de joint press confrence de udder day dat I taut he was gonna shag me leg. But he's great for breakin de ice wit people. Whenever I take him for walks around Government Buildins or Leinster House, we're always running into backbenchers dat I shafted at some stage. Normally dis would make for tense situations. But now Mick distracts dem by rollin over and lettin dem tickle him. Den evrybody goes away wit smiles on their faces. Of course he's very good at fetchin tings too.

THURSDAY

In retraspect, dough, it wasn't de wisest ting for me to start dose rumours about a Cabinet reshuffle. I taut de PDs were gone at de time. So I told Willie he was de new Minister for Justice, and I dropped a hint to Sean Haughey dat if he baut anudder new suit, dis one wouldn't be wasted. De poor hoor was off to Louis Copeland's like a flash. Now I've had to put him on hold again. He wasn't de only one disappointed. De look on Jim Glennon's face will haunt me until Christmas. MJ Nolan was de only one relieved to hear he wouldn't be promoted. I had planned to reward him for his loyalty durin de payments crisis by makin him junior minister at de Department of Helt, wit special responsibility for trolleys, de winter vomitin bug, and meetins wit de Monaghan hospital protest group. I'll have to tink of anudder way to reward him now.

FRIDAY

In all de times I've met Ian Paisley, he had never yet shook me hand. Achievin a handshake was obviously de first step towards any agreement, so we exchanged a number of position papers wit de DUP in recent weeks. We made certain suggestions – dat he could wear gloves, dat we could have a "proximity" handshake trew an intermediary, and so on – and de DUP came back wit counter proposals. Eventually we agreed to a carefully coreographed sequence in which we would shake in de normal manner, but den Paisley could have a shower. It was a historic moment. I tink I've shaken hands wit everyone in de Republic at least twice by now, and I'm hopin to do all dem a turd time before next June. But it's always excitin to break new ground.

SATURDAY

Once dat was out of de way, de draft agreement was a formality. De Dupes and de Shinners now have until November 10 to sign up. Den dere'll be a carefully coreographed sequence of events includin elections, restoration of de executive, de Shinners joinin de policin board, and a major breaktrew in de Nordern Bank investigation. Crucially de whole ting will have to be underpinned by a massive financial package. I don't know if de Oirish Exchequer can afford to contribute at a time when we also have an election to buy here. But dis has been a dark period for de Nort. I'm sure Paddy de Plasterer and de lads in Manchester will not be found wantin.

MONDAY

De Goverment is like de Oirish rugby team dese days: winnin evry week and goin from strent to strent, albeit against crap opposition. De only worry is dat we might have peaked a year too early. De Blueshirts are like England: dey can't possibly get any worse. Also we have to remember dat conditions in de Dáil at dis time of de year are very windy, which suits our sh*t-kickin game. Take Jim O'Keeffe's suggestion de udder day dat armed criminals should be able to dump deir guns in churches, wit no frensic tests. Dat was extremely windy – gale force, at least – which is de sort of ting we trive on. Next June, conditions could be a lot calmer, because de opposition will probably have talked demselves out at dat stage. Still, I'd radder be where we are now, wit a 10-point lead in de polls, dan where dey are – dat's for sure. All we have to do is wait, while de fat lads up de front – Biffo in particular – keep winnin de ball. I'll just kick evryting to touch, same as always.

TUESDAY

Of course rugby is only for knobs. I still prefer de Gah, especially because Mayo people are so bad at it. Dat's why I wasn't really sorry to see de back of Jim Glennon in Dublin Nort. Not when we could replace him wit Dubs goalkeepin' legend John O'Leary. Now dat Gay Mitchell has decided to commit himself to Europe (what did Europe ever do to deserve dat?), de chances of Fine Gael gettin a result in Dublin are slimmer dan Kylie Minogue. But just in case Inda turns into Kieran McDonald on a good day next June, or Willie Joe Rabbitte rolls back de years wit a solo run, it's as well we have an experienced goal-keeper to call on. I've assured John dat he is definite junior minister material if we get a turd term. Den again, I tell dem all dat.

WEDNESDAY

De pre-budget submissions are comin in tick and fast. But if Biffo plays his cards right, dere'll be a post-budget submission too: de one where de opposition finally trow de towel in. De tax revenue is arrivin in lorry-loads and, basically, we can do anyting we want wit it. We can widen de tax bands to benefit de poorer off (de so-called "broadband roll-out" option), but we can also cut de top-rate to appeal to de greedy bastard vote, which is crucial to de PDs. I still have to pretend to be grateful to McDowell for supportin me durin de dig-out crisis, even dough we secretly hoped he'd pull de plug at de time and give us a solo run to de election. But anyway, de former Rottweiler is such a patetic sight dese days, I'm nearly embarrassed for him. We might trow him a bone in de budget, for old time sake.

THURSDAY

Bad news from de Nort where, accordin to de DUP reformers, Paisley's sedatives are wearin off, just as Stormont is about to reconvene. Dey had new stuff for him – very strong – dat someone got from a former KGB agent, but dere's been no chance to slip it into his food. Some fool arranged to meet him in a sushi bar, apparently, and he got suspicious and increased his security. De split in de DUP, between de mad mullahs and de progressives, was bad enough. Now dere's a split in Paisley, wit de voices in his head evenly divided as to what to do tomorrow. It's a sorry situation when we're dependin on Big Ian to prevail over de bigots in his party. But de point is, dey are in his party, and what he says still rules. Trimble always had to look over his shoulder at de DUP. At least de DUP don't have to look over deirs, because dere's nobody more extreme dan dem on de loyalist side.

FRIDAY

I spoke too soon. Michael Stone, de most famous member of de ULF (Unhinged Loyalist Force) has made a comeback, launchin a gun and bomb attack on Stormont. Police said his device was crude and amateurish in design. But you could say de same ting about de St Andrews Agreement and de shadow assembly, so I wouldn't knock him for dat. Stone should probably have been sent back to jail earlier, on a technical charge (possession of a pony-tail 15 years after it was fashionable, maybe). But we hoped dat hard-line loyalists like him had developed de same way as de Provos did. We were wrong, obviously. Dey'll have to send him back now and trow away de key. At least he'll get a chance to finish his PhD in body-buildin.

SATURDAY

Good to see anudder peace process comin togedder, dough. Last night's historic handshake between Roy and Mick points de way forward for udders, and I take a certain amount of credit meself. Back at de time of Saipan, I made meself available as a mediator between de two men, urgin dem to resolve deir differences and meet half way. Unfortunately Roy was in Manchester at de time and Mick was in Korea, so halfway would have been somewhere in Iran. De meetin didn't prove feasible at de time. But de seeds we sowed back den finally came to fruition in Molyneux last night. De handshake was followed by a carefully coreographed sequence in which Wolves scored first, as a confidence-buildin measure, and den Sunderland equalised. By de closin stages of de game, dere was parity of esteem: it was obvious to everyone dat bote sides were shite. And of course de whole ting ended in stalemate. No wonder people are callin it de second Good Friday Agreement.

MONDAY

When I heard dat de Blueshirts were embarkin on an American style negative electioneerin campaign, it never occurred to me dat Enda Kenny would be de first target. So it was like a late Christmas present when de Fine Gael yoot wing attacked de leadership from de rear. OK, John Deasy has a bit of pedigree in dis area. When it comes to leadership heaves, he's a chip off de old shoulder. But de udder lad, English, is supposed to have a bit of cop-on. Ye'd tink dat when journalists placed him in a hole and handed him a shovel, he'd have added two and two togedder. But no. OK, he was on a skiin holiday at de time and he may have had his guard down. In fact, I hear he was on de piss *(er, "piste" – Ed)* when he gave de interview. Dat would certainly explain it.

TUESDAY

Criticism of a sittin Fine Gael leader – whoever it is – is always welcome, of course. Just so long as dey don't get rid of him too soon. Dis was my big fear in 2002: I was worried sick dey might ditch Baldy Noonan before de electrit got a go at him. Tank God he lasted as long as he did. And come to tink of it, tanks to Baldy, de list of potential replacements for Enda is not very long, if dey did move against him now. De current FG front bench makes de cast of Celebrity Big Brudder look like celebrities. Which reminds me: de Blueshirts' official opinion poll ratins are bad enough. But deir worst poll result was de one a while back where a clear majority of Gay Mitchell said he'd prefer to stay in Europe radder dan come back and fight de genral election. Say what you like about Gay: he always knew which way de wind was blowin, long before de wedderman.

WEDNESDAY

It turns out dat Fine Gael has also launched an American-style negative electioneerin campaign against de Government. I must have missed it amid all de coverage of deir internal rebellion. Apparently, de idea is to feature pictures of McDowell, Cullen, and Mickey Martin on billboards, wit sarcastic slogans. Dey're not targetin me, funny enough. It was obviously too much of a risk to put photos of yours truly up all over de country (which is of course de main plank of our election strategy). It wouldn't matter how sarcastic de slogan was: people would just gaze into me big, round, trustin eyes and vote Fianna Fáil in spite of demselves. To tell de trute, we were radder hopin de FG campaign might save us a bit on poster costs. As it is, it looks like we'll have to print de full two million copies of me self-portrait out of our own budget.

THURSDAY

As PJ Mara proudly reminded me de udder day, we pioneered dat whole negative electioneerin ting (aldough of course dis won't stop us expressin disappointment at de Blueshirts' tactics). "Zero Tolerance" – O'Donoghue's campaign against de den justice minister Nora Owen – is still regarded as de standard text for anyone studyin dis technique. When we were in opposition, evry time a bicycle was stolen anywhere, Zero would be on his feet in de Dáil, claimin dat Oireland had tipped over into anarchy while de minister did nuttin. He also presented himself as a Dirty Harry-type, who was ready to clean up de streets his way. It was a very successful tactic and soon, sure enough, Zero had replaced Nora in de Department of Justice. It goes widdout sayin dat de his record in combattin crime is one of de main reasons why he is now such a respected Minister for de Arts.

FRIDAY

As anudder new year begins, de situation in de Nort is still uncertain. It's very hard to read what's goin on in de DUP. We know de party is split between liberals and fundamentalists. But what adds to de confusion is dat Ian Paisley is split too: between a modernisin tendency, on de one hand, and a hard-line rump. Which group his brain belongs to changes from week to week. His actual rump, meanwhile, is sittin on de fence. De Shinners are a worry too as dey prepare for de special Ard Fheis on policin. Grizzly is even more cautious dan me: he never consults his membership about anything widdout first consultin dem to see what dey'll say when he consults dem. Normally de mere fact dat an Ard Fheis was takin place would mean de result was a forgone conclusion. But Grizzly swears dat dis time, it's not a done deal. If dis is true, and de Shinners really are turnin democratic, we're in worse trouble dan I taut.

SATURDAY

Still, I can't complain, especially when I consider de fate of udder leaders wit whom I have shared de world stage: Saddam Hussein, for example. De genral outlook for 2007 is rosy and, barrin a miracle, me historic turd term is already in de bag. Ye never know, even an overall majority might not be outta de question. What wit de Oirish rugby team maybe trouncin England at Croke Park, de last of de SSIAs, and den Georgina havin a baby, I could be campaignin on a wave of public affection come June. De sun will be shinin and we'll all be plasterin ourselves wit feel-good factor 40. On de udder hand, if I come up short of de 83 seats, dere's always anudder coalition. I'll have more potential partners dan a millionaire in a brottel. Except for de Blueshirts and Joe Higgins, nobody has ruled out sharin power wit us (Pat Rabbitte doesn't count, or so I'm hearin). I suppose a hung Dáil is de most likely outcome, all tings considered. But dat's ok by me. Dere's nuttin wrong wit a hung Dáil, just so long as it doesn't involve a rope.

MONDAY

Our tour of Arab states is not all about money, whatever de cynics tink. Sure, we're hopin to cut a few deals here and dere. But de main objective of de trip is to spread westrin values. Engagement is always a positive ting (as Celia used to say, before she went blue in de face). By exposin de Arabs to Oirish ways, we hope to show dem dat dey have nuttin to fear from democracy, and dat even lettin wimmin drive cars is not as scary as it first sounds. In short, de plan is to continue de "greenin of de desert" policy dat began 20 years ago under CJH. Tanks to his visionary scheme of sellin passports to sheikhs, dere is a bit of Arabia dat is forever Oireland. Our aim is to find dat bit, and build on it.

TUESDAY

Of course, as advised by de protocol people, we're takin a softly-softly approach to de mission. At de formal welcome dis mornin, I was about to introduce Mary Hanafin to de Saudis' top man, Crown Prince Rashid Bin Liner. Den, before I could get de words out, he pointed to her and Mary Coughlan and complimented me on my excellent choice of "wives". I meant to correct him. But instead I heard meself sayin: "Tanks very much - I've anudder couple at home." At which point, Hanafin nearly broke me ribs wit a dig. "Tell him the truth," she hissed. "Later," I whispered, rubbin me side, "Remember what de Iveagh House lads told us: we mustn't embarrass our hosts."

WEDNESDAY

As promised, durin a quiet moment, I put de Saudis straight about Hanafin, tellin dem dat she was me "secretary". Dis allowed her to attend today's meetin (albeit sittin at de far end of de sofa) wit de education minister, Sultan Khalid Al-Uminium - a cousin of Rashid - at which we signed a deal for de live export of a tousand Saudi students. Den it was on to a meetin wit Khalid's brudder-in-law, Sheikh Yermiki Al-Fresco, de man in charge of de new national development plan. I was gonna raise de Saudis' bad human rights record wit him. But, eh, he mentioned dat de NDP had a budget of 500 billion euro and said he would need lots of overseas help in spendin it. So I taut we'd do de human rights ting later.

THURSDAY

De great ting about engagin wit people is dat ye always find common ground. As we left Saudi Arabia today (dere was no time to visit Nordi Arabia, unfortunately), I realised it was a lot like Oireland. A few families control evryting, for example, and it's all about who ye know. Den again, dere's tings dat we could learn from de Saudis - like deir approach to de planning process. I'm not sure which is de most excitin ting about deir development plan: de 500 billion budget or de fact dat dey don't have An Taisce tellin dem what dey can't do wit it. No wonder dey were able to build de pyramids. As for crime - sure, dey still flog people. But if dis trip proves anyting, it's dat in Oireland, people are about de only ting we don't flog. Which reminds me, I clean forgot to raise de human rights issue. Feck! I must e-mail de Crown Prince about it when I get home.

FRIDAY

We arrived in de United Arab Hemorrhoids yesterday, wit a few sore heads on us after all de parties in Riyadh. Officially dere's no alcohol in Saudi but, eh, dey didn't call it de "Enterprise Oireland" mission for nuttin. As I told guests one of de nights, "de minerals are very strong here". Anyway, de second leg of de trip is also goin well. For a Fianna Fáil Teeseach, arrivin in Dubai is like dyin and goin to heaven - it's just one massive buildin site. Evrywhere ye look dere's cranes. It's just as well I don't live here, because I'd never get anyting done wit all de openin ceremonies I'd be doin.

SATURDAY

I wouldn't mind - but dere's nuttin in Dubai, except sand, and yet dey're turnin it into dis tourist Mecca. As Sheikh Maktoum explained to me, de attitude is: "Build it and dey will come." I told him dat in Oireland, de attitude is: tink about buildin it, and some smelly f***er wit sandals will object and chain himself to de nearest tree. De Sheikh nodded sympatetically and said dat democracy must have its ups and downs. But de more I tink of it, de less entusiastic I am about spreadin westrin values. If Abbotstown was in Dubai, after all, I'd've had me national stadium years ago.

SUNDAY

Engagement is a two-way ting, of course, and as I arrived back in Oireland last night, I realised I had taken some eastrin values home wit me. When I heard dat my sworn enemy, Sheikh Khatfeed Al-Reynolds, had criticised me over de payments saga, I wished I had Sharia law to deal wit him: only he has so many offendin parts I'm not sure which I'd lop off first. I was also disturbed to hear dat Joe Burke is on his uppers and may have to sell his gold Mercedes if I don't renew his contract as Sultan of Dublin Port. After all de publicity about de dig-out, dough, dat'll be awkward. But it's not all bad news. De Blueshirts have been forced to abandon deir attack campaign, I'm told, and Rabbitte has been tyin himself in knots about his post-election plans. So as I was sayin to me brudder de junior minister dis evenin, I have more in common wit de Saudi crown prince dan ye'd tink. After all, neider of us has to deal wit a meaningful opposition.

MONDAY

When I first heard de proposal to lay a wreet at Croke Park before de Oireland-England rugby game, I was all for it. A gesture like dat would give people closure, I taut. What I had in mind was a simple, dignified cermony in which John Delaney would express regret for de killings made by de FAI out of de openin of Croker. He would apologise to de famlies of dose who had laid down deir 80 quid a ticket for de Wales and Slovakia matches. Den he would walk forward and laid de wreet at a specially designed "tomb of de unknown gouger". Dat was de way I saw it happenin, anyway. I was a bit disappointed to discover dat, actually, it was only de Brits who were suggestin an apology, over de events of de first Bloody Sunday. I taut we already had closure on dat, to be honest. In fact, if I was Peter Hain, I wouldn't have even mentioned it. Now dat he has, de Shinners will be lookin for anudder public inquiry.

TUESDAY

A very emotional day in de Dáil. First we had de Stardust relatives holdin a vigil outside to mark de 26th anniversary of de fire and support deir demands for a new inquiry. I appreciate dat dey need closure on dis and believe me, wit an election comin up, so do I. We just can't seem to agree terms, so far. But today was doubly emotional because I also had to make me formal statement about de Moriarty report, which of course rapped me on de knuckles over signin blank cheques for CJ.

Naturally, it wasn't de criticism – or de opposition's jeers – I was worried about. It was havin to relive dose terrible moments when I first realised dat Haughey had betrayed my trust. As an accountant, I would never a signed a cheque for him if I'd suspected for a moment dat he was anyway dodgy. De day I heard he was on de take – excuse me while I compose meself here – ye coulda knocked me down wit a fedder. In a way, I was a bigger victim dan Brian Lenihan. At least Brian got his liver transplant, despite CJ pocketin de funds. But I lost me innocence den. And even in America, dere's no operation to replace dat. Dis is why today was so important for me. I needed closure.

WEDNESDAY

Dick Roche was updatin de Cabinet on de cost of de Mahon Tribunal, and dere was a lotta grumblin about it around de table. So I just happened to remark, from force of habit, dat we needed "closure" on de issue of planning corruption. I was speakin in de psychological sense of course. But suddenly McDowell picked up de ball and ran with it. "I couldn't have put it better myself, Taoiseach," he said: "Let's shut the damn thing down." Dick Roche weighed in with a complaint about de size of de lawyer's "brief fees". Whereupon Biffo quipped dat if de tribunal was still chargin brief fees after 10 years, he shuddered to tink what deir long-drawn-out fees would be like. Suddenly de whole Cabinet was in favour of achievin closure, as soon as possible. It wasn't what I wanted, exactly. But, eh, wit de Quarryvale module comin up, a pre-election appearance in de dock at Dublin Castle is not what I want eider. So I said nuttin, except: "Any udder business?" I knew McDowell and Roche could be relied on to go out and run de idea up de nearest flag-pole. We'll see if people salute it, I taut.

THURSDAY

De media reaction to de suggestion has been so hostile dat I've had no choice but to distance meself and assure de public I have no attention of shuttin de tribunal down. De chairman even sent a snotty letter to de Dáil today advisin us dat de inquiry will cost a mere tree hunderd million, not de one billion Baldy suggested. He also says his public hearins will be wound up next year – a fact he claims he informed Dick Roche about only a couple of weeks ago, before de minister apparently forgot. Feck it, anyway. Now dat we've got his back up, Mahon will be in even more of a rush to do Quarryvale. Meanwhile, McDowell is ticked off wit me for not supportin him. I explained to him dat it was his own welfare I had in mind. If de polls are correct, his ministerial career will have achieved closure by May. De good news, I said, is dat de tribunal will still need lawyers.

FRIDAY

I may also have to distance meself from Biffo's comments in which he claimed de Government would not engage in "auction politics". It's a matter of principle, he says. And of course, I admire his stand. But, eh, Fianna Fáil has done pretty well so far widdout principles and I don't tink dis is de time for tryin out a new policy. De fact is dat Pat Rabbitte has caut us on de hop wit his tax-cut, and de PDs have already outbid him. It's all very well talkin about "auction" politics, but when de electrit comes under de hammer in May, I don't tink we can afford to sit on our hands. If Biffo persists in dis attitude, I might have to make a few gestures – de old scratch of de ear, maybe – to catch de auctioneer's eye behind his back. We're talkin about me historic turd term, after all. I'm not gonna let de Blueshirts pick it up cheap.

SATURDAY

De Brits have wisely backed off de idea of a gesture before de England game at Croke Park. De event will be highly enough charged widdout addin to it. I know dat many Shinners still regard de idea of rugby in Croker as an atrocity, and would like an apology for dat, never mind Bloody Sunday. But even moderate nationalists may not be prepared for de spectacle of de Artane Boys Band playin God Save de Queen in front of de Hogan Stand. It'll be a tense moment when dey raise deir trumpets and trombones and open fire indiscriminately on de crowd. I just hope dere are no reprisals.

MONDAY

Even now, more dan a week later, I'm still buoyed up by dat historic result in Croke Park. Me big fear beforehand was dat de weight of histry – all de stuff about antems and wreet-laying, not to mention de eighty tousand people watchin – might affect de performance. But I held me nerve, and when de chance came, I took it. As soon as McAleese got widdin a couple of feet of me, I just grabbed her. Den, after checkin dat de TV camras were on us, I planted a smacker on her cheek. It was de first big tackle of de night, and de crowd in de stadium responded wit a mighty cheer. PJ Mara texted me afterwards to say it was wort at least two per cent in de polls. But Paddy de Plasterer, who was sittin beside me at de match – and who, no more dan meself, is not a rugby man – summed it up best. "I think that's called a converted try," he said.

TUESDAY

It's top secret for de moment – I haven't even told Biffo yet – but de genral election will be on May de 24th. I don't have to call it till June and, in dis as in all tings, me instinct is to put off de decision as long as possible. But May 24th is de last Friday before middle class voters start takin deir kids out of school early for de first of de two summer holidays dey can now afford tanks to us. And of course de school exams begin a week later too, so realistically dat's as far was I can push it. We use some of de exam halls as pollin stations, after all. In fact, when ye tink about it, de Government is in de same situation as many second-level students. We're bote awaitin de verdict on five years of hard work. De only difference, I suppose, is dat one of us is hopin not to get de Leavin Cert.

WEDNESDAY

De udder part of me calculation is to balance de afterglow from me ardfheis speech later dis munt wit de onset of de good wedder. I haven't even started work on me speech yet, so I don't know what'll be in it. But at least Biffo has clarified his opposition to so-called "auction politics", explainin dat Fianna Fail will only cut tax rates if and when de time is right for de economy. By a happy coincidence, he tinks de time should be right at 8.45pm on March 24th, when I'll he half way trew my televised address. De effects of dat should be good for two munts afterwards, by which time de bounce dat Labour, de Greens, and de Shinners got from havin early-spring confrences will be well forgotten. It's a bit like de Gaelic football season. De little teams are always leppin outta deir skins in February. We're concentratin on de championship.

THURSDAY

Paddy's Day is on de way. Which means it's dat time of de year again when, like de Wild Geese, Oirish politicians must take to de skies and bring our carbon emissions to de four corners of de globe. I'll be goin to Washington, of course, to rub shoulders wit evryone from de president to de great Democratic hopeful, Barack Alabama. In keepin wit tradition, Zero will be visitin de Oirish consulate in Cheltenham. As usual, however, dere is intense competition for de more exotic destinations. Like a German puttin his beach-towel on a deck-chair, Cullen snapped up San Francisco first ting. Biffo bagged Chicago. But as usual, half de Cabinet wants to go to Sydney, so we're holdin a raffle for dat after next week's meetin. De second prize is Buenos Aries.

FRIDAY

As a gesture to de Kyoto Photocall, dough, we'll be keepin Micheál Martin at home in Cork. Dis is partly to reduce our carbon footprint, but mainly because of private polls dat suggest we could lose tree seats in de county. In light of de findings, I have ordered Micky to increase his ledder footprint on doorsteps over de next couple of munts. I spent today down dere meself, and got a bit of a rollickin over de airport issue. Still, I survived me tour of de county in one piece – which, as Michael Collins might say, is all you can hope for – and I made it back into de second city tonight for a gala dinner. Needless to say, I didn't eat any of de food: ye never know how dey'd get you.

SATURDAY

De turbalence in de stock markets is a big worry, especially at dis time, when de Government's free-money scheme is nearin a climax. People who put deir SSIAs on deposit are OK. But for dose dat chose riskier investments, it could be like havin yer money on de leader of de Grand National and seein it fall at de last fence. I wouldn't mind so much if I wasn't de one ridin de horse. Biffo says it proves de old sayin dat when a butterfly flaps its wings in China, it can cause an ertquake on de udder side of de world. I never heard dat before meself: if it's true, de Chinese must have big fuckin butterflies. De udder problem, meanwhile, is dat de arse has finally fallen outta de property market. Hopefully, dere won't a complete collapse. But eider way, it looks as if, for de first time since I became Teeseach, de boom is not gettin boomer.

MONDAY

All dis talk about tax cuts and policies must be very confusin for voters. Dat's why we want to give dem a simple choice when dey go to de polls in May: namely whedder dey tink me or Enda Kenny would be a sexier Teeseach. Dis is a serious decision, and I hope people will reflect carefully before doin anyting rash, like not votin for me. Yes, Enda has a full head of hair, which is not someting ye could say for his predecessor, Baldy Noonan. And yes, unlike John Brutal, he also has a smile dat doesn't scare babies. But voters have to ask demselves: is he as cuddly as me? Has he shaken hands wit evrybody in de country while lookin dem in de eye for two seconds and makin dem tink dere's a connection, like me?

Of course, it's not all about looks, eider. Voters should also ask demselves: does Enda sound like someone dey can trust? Most of us live in greater Dublin dese days, and tanks to de success of de Government's decentralisation policies, dere are more arrivin here evry day. Dis is a new, confident, urban Oireland. And de question people in it must ask is: after a decade of havin a Dub as Teeseach, are dey really now ready to endanger our prosperity by electin a lad wit an accent?

TUESDAY

Dis strategy also explains why Paddy de Plasterer is such a key member of me electral team – not just in de constituency, but nationally as well. Basicly, de whole plan is to plaster pictures of me all over de country, wherever we can find a wall. Paddy's professional experience is vital in dis task. But I also value his input on policy matters. Before de Ardfheis, for example, dere was a debate among me advisers as to how far I should go wit de spendin promises. Some people taut I should exercise an element of restraint. But Paddy argued dat I should "lay it on wit a trowel". It was his advice I went wit in de end.

WEDNESDAY

Mini Brennan is still in a huff over me speech in Citywest. And ok, I may have reassured him and de rest of de Cabinet beforehand dat dere would be no reckless spendin promises. But it's not my fault dat he went around doin his Mudder Teresa impression for de media, lamentin de crass materialism of de opposition parties. Biffo is partly to blame, for given de impression dat we were serious about de no-auction-politics line. When he took over from McCreevy, I told him to push de social conscience ting for a while, until de polls improved. But I tink Biffo really enjoyed himself on de moral high ground. No Fianna Fáiler had been up dere for years and de view was lovely. Unfortunately, elections are usually fought nearer sea level, and Biffo is findin it hard to come down again. He's a bit ticked off over de Ardfheis speech too, but he'll get over it. De early-season altitude trainin will stand to him in May. He'll be flyin den.

THURSDAY

Like de tax cuts, me conversion to environmentalism is a tactical move, designed to nullify de effects of opposition promises so dat voters can concentrate on de real issue: how cute I look in dose posters. I still suspect dat Trevor Sargent's speeches are de real reason for de hole in de ozone layer. But voters seem to like him at de moment, which is why I need to carve meself a piece of de eco-warrior action. I'm searching evry tree in Nort Dublin again, dis time lookin for one I can chain meself to. So de situation wit de Galway water supply could not be worse-timed. Well, eh, maybe it could. If it happened in July, it could wipe out de entire Fianna Fáil fundraisin operation. But it's still bad, even now. Dat's why I've sent Dick Roche down to tour de affected area and disburse millions in emergency relief. Even if he doesn't solve de problem immediately, it'll be an opportunity for him to talk to de people of Galway. And after dey have to listen to him for a few hours, diarrhoea won't seem quite so bad.

FRIDAY

I don't know if dere's any votes in it at dis stage. But de agreement in de nort is nonedeless welcome, especially since Paisley postponed it to de first week of May, just when I'll be formally announcin de election. De pictures of me shakin hands wit de protagonists will look good, especially if we can find a way of keepin Mary Lou McDoughnut outta dem. We all need closure on de Nort. I feel like I've spent half me life in de negotiations, aldough I'm still in better shape dan Blair. He was de one dat felt de hand of histry on his shoulder a few years ago when we taut we had a deal. Little did he realise he'd be feelin de boot of histry up his hole before it was finalised. Like I say, dere's probably no votes in it. But sortin out de Nort was never about personal gain. It was just someting I had to do. If I get de Nobel Peace Prize, dat'll be a bonus.

SATURDAY

Biffo needn't be worryin himself about auction politics. If de latest ESRI forecast is accurate, de next government won't be able to keep de promises anyway. Wit economic grote expected to drop to 1993 levels, de only Celtic Tiger left next year will be de one in Dublin Zoo. Hopefully dis sober news will concentrate de electrit's mind on de real issue – whedder me or Enda looks better on de posters. Havin said dat, I note de Fine Gael leader's solemn pledge not to seek re-election if he fails to deliver his programme. And in keepin wit me election strategy, I'm prepared to match dis. I hereby declare dat if de next Fianna Fáil-led government fails to do everyting I said it would widdin de first two years, I will not seek retirement, as originally planned. I will carry on as Teeseach, and Biffo will be on a one-way ticket to Brussels, de same as his predecessor.

SUNDAY

Me original plan was to announce de dissolution of de Dail on Tuesday de furst. But tanks to a combination of de *Oirish Times* poll and de tribunal, I had no choice but to dissolute it a couple of days early. Once de back-benchers got word of de poll figgers, dey were as nervous as a lorry-load of pigs in a meat factory. As dey fled squealin for de constituencies at de weekend, I knew dey wouldn't be back. Den I realised dat de Mahon tribunal had sprung a leak, and even if we could close de Quarryvale module before it opened it was already too late. So makin de best of a bad job, I rang McAleese on Saturday night and told her to be on stand-by at dawn. On de plus side, dis meant dat we forced a bunch of journalists to get up at six am on a Sunday for de first time in deir lives. I hope some of dem went to mass afterwards. But I felt like de bleedin milkman sneakin into de Aras at dat hour. It was just as bad down at headquarters where we had a short campaign launch – no questions afterwards – before de tribunal damage limitation team sent me back into hidin. As PJ said grimly: "It's no-show time, folks".

MONDAY MORNING

De one real advantage of de mornin raid on de Aras was dat it was a chance to remind de electrit dat Enda Kenny is a Mickey Mulchie. In de immortal words of Albert Reynolds (words dat I got him back for eventually), people are entitled to know where deir Teeseach sleeps at night: de back end of Mayo bein de terrible trute in Enda's case. We were hopin dat he would have to make his first televised statement of de campaign somewhere deep in Mulchieland. But fair play to de Blueshirt press office, dey got him back up to de big smoke in time to pull dat P45 stunt outside Leinster House, and by Sunday afternoon, he was campaignin on me own doorstep in Nort Dublin. I suppose it's our own fault for spendin so much money on infrastructure. De west is not cut off anymore. Still, dey can't do anyting about Enda's accent. And de good ting about de polls showin dat he would be Teeseach if dere was an election now is dat voters have a full tree and a half weeks to come to deir senses.

MONDAY AFTERNOON

When you're in a hole, as I appear to be at de moment, de first ting to do is stop diggin. Dat's why I've put me pick and shovel to one side for de moment and gone to ground. Unfortunately, de Mahon tribunal has hired a fleet of JCBs, which are at work under me even as I speak. Dey'll find nuttin in relation to Owen O'Callaghan, no matter how deep dey dig. But de worry wit all dat ert-movin goin on around me is is dat someting else might stick. For de statement to de lawyers, I had to go into me personal finances again which, in de early 90s, were messy to say de least. Presented in a certain light, some of me arrangements might look as dodgy as a tree-pound-note. And de problem is I won't get into de witness box to give my side of story before de election. In fact, probably de only way I can explain meself fully would be in a tearful interview wit Brian Dobson. Our media people are workin on dis as a matter of urgency.

MONDAY EVENING

If anyting, McDowell is more alarmed at de apparent collapse in FF support dan I am. But of course, he's as dependent on us as a new-born lamb is on its mudder. His only prospect of ever seein de inside of a State car again is if bote de Government parties hold most of deir seats. De words "snowball", "chance", and "hell" come to mind here. Dis probably explains his proposal – in a top-secret memo which I was instructed to eat after readin – dat if de polls do not improve in de next fortnight, we should consider declarin a state of emergency. Dis might involve postponin elections "for a year or two," de note added. But it would be in de national intrest, "to prevent the opposition throwing away all we have achieved". I ate de memo, as instructed, and told McDowell to leave it wit me for a couple of days, until we saw how de tribunal ting panned out.

MONDAY NIGHT

De reason I'm not hittin de panic button just yet is dat – unlike de PDs – Fianna Fail can afford to take a kickin from de electrit and still end up back in Government, probably wit Labour. When voters realise dat Enda as Teeseach is a real prospect – someting we'll be remindin dem about a lot – hopefully it'll be deir turn to panic. And we have a few udder cards de play too. Even if we can't swing anudder Dobbo interview, de good news, media-wise, is dat we're gettin Tony O'Reilly's papers back on board. To consommate dis relationship, I gave de editor of de Sunday Indo an exclusive eve-of-campaign interview. And I don't know how it was for him, but I felt like smoking a cigarette afterwards.

TUESDAY

Den dere's de Nordern settlement. What wit de return of Stormont, followed by Paisley's historic visit to de Boyne, not to mention me address to de British joint houses of de Oireachtas, de next few weeks will be one long lap of honour for yours truly. Dis will help clarify de choice facin de electrit on May 24th: between a proven international statesman on one hand and, on de udder, a lad who sounds like Miley from Glenroe. De opposition can complain all dey like about me politicisin de agreement. But de peace process is my personal SSIA scheme. I've been savin it up for 10 years, trew tick and tin. Now it's time to cash de cheque. And nobody is gonna tell me how I spend it.

TUESDAY

It's been a bitter tree weeks, wit accusations flyin from de start and an unprecedented level of animosity between de two sides. But dat's enough about de Fianna Fáil campaign in Longford-Westmead, where I spent de second-last day before pollin. Supporters of Mammy O'Rourke and Donie Cassidy announced a tempry ceasefire for de walkaround in Atlone, and it was fairly well observed, aldough you could still have cut de tension wit a meat-cleaver. I decided to avoid de usual visit to a butcher's shop, just in case. Me task for de day was to appear impartial. But since de two of dem clung to me like a pair of shoulder pads trewout, dis wasn't hard. Word on de ground is dat Mammy is well ahead, and dat her and Donie will be swoppin places when de Dáil and Seanad return. I'd check under me seat if I were eider of dem.

WEDNESDAY

Of course it's nuttin like dat in Dublin Central, where me two partners on de ticket, Cyprian and Mary, are just committed to de challenge of maximisin de Fianna Fáil vote. Dis is a bigger challenge for Cyprian, obviously, whose support is currently runnin at about minus five per cent in de polls. Natcherly, I'm completely neutral about de result, despite de fact dat one of de candidates is me fateful right-hand man and I don't get on wit de udder camp. De point is, I always stand up for de underdog. Which is why we sent letters out to evry house in de constitchency dis mornin recommendin dat people give Cyprian deir second prefrences. It's part of de Fianna Fáil commitment to help de marginalised. We knew Mary would understand. But we took de precaution of not tellin her beforehand, anyway.

THURSDAY

If PJ Mara is right, me historic turd term is in de bag. Dere's a last-minute surge to Fianna Fáil, apparently, and even Cyprian's figgers are now in de plus column, just. Still, I was as nervous as a kitten castin me vote dis mornin. I was even more nervous when PJ said dat, win or lose, he was retirin from politics after de election. But I relaxed a bit when he told me not to worry: he wouldn't be publishin his memoirs while any of us were still alive. Meanwhile, me visit to de pollin boot reminded me of de number one priority for any new FF goverment: draggin Oirish elections into de 21st century. I'll get rid of dose stupid oul' pencils yet, if it's de last ting I do.

FRIDAY MORNING

It was all over before breakfast. I was just about to have me Weetabix when Mara rang me wit de exit poll figures. "Forty-one-point-six!" he said, before breakin into a version of de old Lionel Ritchie song: "You're once, twice, three times a Taoiseach." I tanked his for all his work, bote in dis campaign and down de years. "Don't forget who your friends are," he quipped. "And you don't forget not to write dat buke," I said back. Normally I just have de two Weetabix for breakfast. But to mark de occasion, I awarded meself an historic turd one, den I hit de sack for a while.

FRIDAY NIGHT

After I woke up I could start enjoyin de results. Cyprian got a whoppin 939 first preferences, in de end. If his vote hadda been a baby, it would have been in an incubator for weeks. As it was, me transfers dragged him trew eventually. Who says de trickle-down economy doesn't help de less well off? At de udder end of de spectrum, Biffo and Willie O'Dea polled 19,000 each. De only ting more remarkable dan O'Dea's figgers was de fact dat he didn't bring in tree seats. I know he always claims dat it's not a Fianna Fáil vote he gets – "It's a Willie O'Dea vote." I do have a similar problem in Drumcondra, come to tink of it. But when he's badgerin me again for de Department of Justice next week, I'll have to remind him dat it's not a Willie O'Dea ministry. It's a Fianna Fáil one.

SATURDAY

Speakin of Justice, I was sorry to see de end of McDowell. I know he was a bit mad, but he was entertainin to de last. His performance in de junior leader's debate was a bit like a suicide bomber – he blew himself up and took everyone in de studio wit him. In fact, he probably won de election for me dere and den. I just hope dat de 72 virgins arc waitin for him in paradise. It must be a great consolation to Michael dat, tanks to de success of his short time in charge, Mary Harney is now de only one left who can lead de party. Eider way, I'm plannin to leave her in de Department of Helt if she's willin. If dat doesn't finish de PDs off, nuttin will.

SUNDAY

It looks like it could be de Greens' turn to experience de special joy of bein Fianna Fáil's junior partner in Goverment. But I don't know. Some of deir people are flakier dan a Cadbury's Flake ad. In de unlikely event ye survived a full term wit dem, it'd put more dan five years on ye. On de udder hand, buyin even a second-hand Labour Party (slightly used, one previous owner) off de Blueshirts might be expensive in terms of Cabinet seats. We'll spend a few days talkin to de independents first, in any case. If nuttin else, as Biffo says, it'll soften de udders up until dey're gaggin for a deal. Biffo has been like a rock – big, round, and hard-hittin – trewout dis campaign. Dat's why I'm puttin him in charge of de negotiatin strategy. Sure, Dermot Ahern and Mickey Martin have done well too. But Biffo has proven himself as my wordy successor when de time comes. Ye could almost say he's de most cunning, de most devious, de most rootless of dem all.

MONDAY

De decision to anoint Biffo as me long-term successor was partly a way of sayin "Tanks, big fella" for de part he played in de election. Aldough he's a few years younger dan me, he was like an older brudder. When de bullies had me cornered in de playground, it was Biffo who came to de rescue, beatin de shite out of anyone who looked at me crossways. Now I'm de king of de skule yard, because dey're all scared I'll set Biffo on dem again. So I wanted to reward his loyalty wit a public endorsement. But, eh, as usual, dere were udder considerations too. I've learned from Tony Blair's mistakes. By namin Biffo publicly as me chosen heir, I'm buyin his future loyalty. He can't afford to shaft me any time in de next five years. And as for de udders who fancy de job, dey also know dat dere's no point in tryin to get rid of me early, because Biffo is de real problem. By rewardin a loyal servant, derefore, I have also shifted all de heat onto him. I'm so devious, sometimes, I scare meself.

TUESDAY

Never mind George Lee and de udder merchants of doom. De economy is still boomin, whatever dey say. OK, de property market is stagnant, construction has slowed, and inflation is risin fast. But de country is still experiencin double-digit grote in key areas. Take de size of de goverment, for example. Economists taut de number of junior ministers had reached saturation point at 17. Dey were wrong. De latest figgers – which I'm about to release – show dat de number of junior ministers will rise to 20 for de turd quarter of 2007: a whoppin 18 per cent increase! Dis means dat, contrary to de economists' predictions, Dick Roche will experience a soft landing, and it also means I can give Trevor Sargent a job widdout causin a recession on de Fianna Fáil back-benches. Oireland will now have de biggest government in Europe, per head of population. And to tink dat some people say I'm mismanagin de economy!

WEDNESDAY

De new coalition's first Cabinet meetin was dominated by de stamp duty bill. Basically dis was just de Fianna Fáil election policy. De Greens are still so excited about bein in power dat dey rolled over and said "Woof!" Meanwhile, de PD watchdog didn't have to roll over, because it's still prostrate after de visit to de vet last munt. Wit Fido and Rover so cooperative, Biffo got away widdout even trowin dem a bone. As he told me afterwards, his "minimalist" stamp duty reform is de cheapest round possible. Dere was a giddy mood at de meetin. De Greens were still a bit wet behind de ears: litrally, because dey were after cyclin to Government Buildins in de rain. But deir entoosiasm is touchin. On "any udder business", Eaman Ryan suggested a debate on de issue of nuclear power. Whereupon Biffo countered by proposin a debate on de issue of where we were havin lunch. His motion was carried unanimously.

THURSDAY

Wit John McGuinness bein promoted to junior minister, dere was always gonna be a vacancy for de job of most disinfected *("disaffected" – Ed)* back-bencher. Sure enough, no sooner had I announced de new line-up dis mornin dan Seán Ardagh was off to de media to apply for de position. Not dat I blame him. As Seán "new suit" Haughey proved, de squeaky wheel does get greased, sooner or later. Anyway, I rang Ardagh afterwards and explained dat de decision to pass him over dis time, painful as it was, was forced on me by de sheer richness of embarrassments – eh, I mean embarrassment of riches – on de backbenches. I also dropped a hint dat if he bought himself a new suit between now and de mid-term reshuffle, it wouldn't go to waste. He was off to Louis Copeland's like a shot.

FRIDAY

Me apparently casual remarks about Beverly – which involved sayin dat she woulda been in line for a junior minstry if her legal affairs had been sorted out first – was in fact a pre-prepared script agreed in negotiations last week. I felt a bit like an American hostage havin to say dat Allah was great while some lad stood over me wit a Kalashnikov. But I tink I got de words out all right. Dis was de first part of a carefully coreographed sequins dat will involve Beverly settlin wit RTE, endin her Supreme Court challenge, and callin off de hunger strike for justice dat she had planned later dis year. De next step after dat will be to persuade de grassroots in Mayo to take her back into de party. Den in two years time, come de reshuffle, I'll swallow hard and, eh, give her de job I promised to Seán Ardagh.

SATURDAY

De summit in Brussels was an emotional occasion for two reasons. First I was sayin farewell to me old friend Tony Blair, at least from de world leader circuit. And second, I was sayin goodbye to me EU constitution: de one I slaved over for de whole six munts of de Oirish presidency. Not dat de document is changed substanshally. Dey're only tinkerin wit it, so dey can sell it as someting new to de French. But I hate to see udder people's fingerprints on me masterpiece. Blair told me dat one of de first tings he's gonna do after he leaves Downing Street is become a Cattalic. Understandably for a man who's made as many big mistakes as him, he's very attracted to de Cattalic approach to absolution. He tinks if he'd had de practice, he might have tried a televised confession of his sins, like de one I made wit Fadder Brian Dobson in St Lukes, and den he'd have got away wit invadin Iraq, give or take tree Hail Marys. I tink he's coddin himself dere. But I wished him well in his conversion.

MONDAY

De Star Chamber has rejected me lawyer's submission dat public hearins should be stopped. Dis means dat de AIB can start givin evidence about me personal finances today, and dat me show trial will go ahead next week. Of course, I could still appeal to de High Court and postpone it for a year. But Rambo and Liam Lawlor gave dat sort of ting a bad name. Besides which, maybe de best ting at dis stage is for me to go into de witness box and, eh, clear evryting up. Viewed in a certain light, me financial dealins are about as plausible as de plot of de latest Harry Potter novel. But if JK Rowling can make her stuff believable, I can too. In a confrontation between me and de evil Lord Voldemahon, dere can only be one winner. I'll use de magic powers dat I have perfected for years in Hogwash Castle – or Leinster House as it's usually known – and cast de tribunal under a spell. If dey tink dey're confused now, wait till I'm finished wit dem.

TUESDAY

Speakin of spells, de one I cast on Ian Paisley shows no sign of wearin off yet, tank God. De real DUP leader has been trapped in anudder dimension – somewhere near Cullybackey – ever since I presented him and Eileen wit dat piece of so-called "ancient bog oak from de site of de Battle of de Boyne" (Ha, Ha, Ha!) for deir 50th weddin anniversary. Today's British-Irish council meetin passed off widdout incident, I'm glad to say, just de usual photos of a beamin Paisley chattin with Martin McGuinness. And aldough she must have her suspicions, not even Mrs Paisley seems to have copped dat she is now livin wit a changeling. Me black arts are very powerful. Even so, dey're takin a while to work on de new British prime minister. I may have to learn a few Brown arts as well if I'm gonna make any headway wit dat dour Scotsman.

WEDNESDAY

Today it was de turn of de Nort-Sout Council to meet in Armagh. I warned de lads to leave de State cars at de border dis time, and get a bus de rest of de way. De UUP never forgave us for de stunt we pulled at de inaugural meetin, when de whole Cabinet turned up in Mercs. It looked like a Mafia funeral, and sure enough, it helped to bury David Trimble, even dough he wasn't dead yet. But we've learned de importance of sensitivity in de meantime. Anyway, dose nordern roads are shite, so it might be as well to leave de cars in de Sout and avoid de unnecessary wear and tear. In fact, we're givin de Stormont executive 400 million to bring deir motorways up to standard. But we should be able to claw back some of dis on de project designed to link de Ulster Canal wit Lough Erne. If it keeps rainin de way it has been, de two waterways should be linked by de middle of August, at no cost to eider goverment.

THURSDAY

De Armagh car ban was also a sop to John Gormley who, as expected, has beaten Luna Lovegood in de competition to lead de Hogwash Castle "green" team for de foreseeable future. Luna got a bigger vote dan expected, perhaps reflectin de confusion widdin de Greens at deir magical transformation from a bunch of losers to a party of power. But I'm confident our partners now have de firm leadership dey will need durin de difficult days ahead: days like next Tuesday, for example, when me and Lord Voldemahon have our long-awaited showdown. Meanwhile, de udder goverment partners have postponed deir leadership election till next year, by which time it is hoped dey may have acquired a few voters.

FRIDAY

I'll miss de Sopranos. I didn't always get to see it because of de early start time. I'd still be in de office at 10pm most days, of course. But when I did see it, its portrayal of de life of a New Jersey mob family was uncannily reminiscent of de Fianna Fáil Nortsoide operation. De rows over territory. De importance of famly. De Feds tryin to pin financial regularities on us. It's all dere. And of course dere's a similar level of rutelessness involved in de two organisations. When Mary Fitzpatrick had to be whacked durin de election campaign, for example, nobody was more upset dan me. But as I explained to de lads down at de Bada Bing – eh, I mean Fagan's – de night after, it was nuttin personal – just business. Tony Soprano would have understood.

SATURDAY

Of course, he's not de only Tony whose record-breakin run has come to an end recently. In fact, I had to launch a buke about de udder one – De Blair Years by Alistair Campbell – dis week. It's a back-handed compliment to Blair dat dey chose Dublin for de party. Baghdad was outta de question, I suppose, and London is nearly as hostile to de former PM dese days. Oireland was de only ting dat didn't turn pear-shaped on him in de end. But anyway, I did de needful for de buke. Dere was a certain amount of mutual back-scratchin, of course. I said what great lad Alistair was, how he never told a lie in his life, and how comparisons between de dossier on Iraq and de work of JK Rowling were completely exaggerated. Meanwhile Alistair said I was one of de greatest world leaders of me generation: up dere wit Clinton and Mandela and John Paul II. So at least one of us was tellin de trute.

MONDAY

I'm writin dis in an air raid shelter under Parknasilla, where I've been hidin since de war over Shannon started last week. Like evrybody else at de time, de event took us all here by surprise. We were upstairs in de hotel bar when Aer Lingus dropped de first bombshell. De place shook so much I nearly spilt me pint. But since den, we've been livin safely underground, where we have little or no contact wit de outside world (and more importantly, it has no contact wit us). De war is just a distant rumour here. Evry night we can hear de drone of de Aer Lingus Luftwaffe as dey attempt to blow Shannon off de map. Sometimes we can also hear a diffrent sound: a kind-of high-pitched whine, which we tink is Willie "Biggles" O'Dea takin to de air-waves to defend de airport single-handedly. Mostly dere is only silence. Except, dat is, from Nicky, who is keepin our spirits up with his constant renditions of Westlife's greatest hits.

TUESDAY

Life is very basic here in de shelter. Apart from de silence, de worst ting is de darkness. It wouldn't be so bad if I could pass de time wit a good buke – or even one of Cecelia's. But bright lights would betray de Government's whereabouts to de enemy. So we have to make do wit candles. Also, de rations are beginnin to run low. I'm down to de last two kegs of Bass now. Luckily, Nicky is still entertainin us wit assorted classics; aldough dat said, Fadder and Son can get a bit wearin after de first turty times ye hear it.

WEDNESDAY

Worryin news from de aerial war over Shannon, where dere has been an exchange of friendly fire between Goverment forces. De incident happened last night when Biggles took off as usual, intendin to engage de enemy and defend de Shannon-Heetrow route. Apparently he was expectin ground cover from Noel Dempsey. But instead, Dempsey opened fire on his tail-plane and under-carriage, forcing Biggles to return to base for repairs. Dempsey has offered me his apologies over de incident. But I told him not to worry: dat in times of conflict, bad tings sometimes happen. Tonight, for example, I had to order dat Nicky be taken outside and shot. War is hell.

THURSDAY

De battle over Shannon has taken a surprise turn, wit Michael O'Leary joinin de resistance. At first I taut it was an air-raid siren. But den I realised it was even louder dan an air-raid siren, so it could only be one ting: a Ryanair press conference. O'Leary has offered to combine forces wit de Government and de Aer Lingus pilots in defendin de Heetrow route. But wit allies like him, who needs enemies. In his entusiasm for targetin Aer Lingus, he has been firin left, right, and centre. Some of de flak is now landin uncomfortably close to me bunker. If dis continues, I may be forced to come out in de open, which is just what O'Leary wants.

FRIDAY

De Bass has run out, and so have my hopes dat de LRC would hold peace talks and save me havin to take sides. In a communique dat arrived today by express pigeon from de Algarve, General Biffo argues dat we can no longer avoid saying someting. O'Leary's cunning offer of support means dat if we really wanted to, de Government could force Aer Lingus to back down. But of course dis would amount to a vote of no confidence in de board, and we can't do dat. Biffo recommends a two-pronged approach: first we issue a short statement sayin how it would be inappropriate for de Government to intervene in a commercial decision. Den, in a diversionary tactic, we set up a govermental committee to study "all de options" at Shannon. I have agreed wit his recommendation by return pigeon. We have chosen a member of de Women's Corps, Major Hanafin, to issue de first part of de statement: on de understandin dat if she is captured, she didn't get it from us.

SATURDAY

Sad news from de front, where Biggles has gone down in flames. We heard him take off yet again last night, his high-pitched whine even higher dan normal. Den, his engines started splutterin. Dis was followed by an eerie silence, and we knew he had run out of fuel. He could still have saved his credibility by pressin de Cabinet ejector button. But instead, he issued a press release sayin dere was nuttin to be gained for de Sout-west by him givin up his seat on de plane. He would remain on board, where he could be more influential, he said. After dat we just heard a crash. De silence in de air raid shelter is now even more deafenin dan before, which is really sayin someting.

MONDAY

It seemed like a good idea at de time. But in retraspect, de goverment's 25 per cent share-holdin in Aer Lingus is about as useful as tits on a bull. De trute is, we can't interfere wit de company's commercial plans. On de udder hand, because of de golden share, we could. So I can't do me usual ting when asked about a difficult issue in de Dail: which is to pretend dat I have no power to change it, dat I'm tired telling people to do de right ting, but dat dey just won't listen to me. De man-in-de-street act has always served me well on de helt service (even dough we have a 100 per cent share-holdin in dat). But dis Aer Lingus ting could be de det of me. I could end up wit a 25 per cent stake trew me heart.

TUESDAY

De worst ting is dat it's not just about an airline. Dis also has de potential bring down de whole social partnership dat I've spent me career buildin up. What happens at Aer Lingus could determine de future direction of de country. It's as if de Government is sittin helpless in de back of de plane, while de pilots and de management wrestle each udder for control of de cockpit. De nervous passengers don't know whedder we're goin to Boston or Berlin, aldough at de moment we'd settle for gettin to eider destination safely. De risk is dat, if de unions get pissed off and pull de plug on partnership, we could all be in for a hard landing.

WEDNESDAY

Biffo calmed de nerves a bit at de Cabinet meetin, insistin dat de pre-budget economic forecast will be better dan de ESRI's predictions. Even so, he's aimin for a grote rate of only 3.5 per cent dis year, which is well off what we had in de election manifesto. I tink we can kiss any budget cut in de top tax rate goodbye. Today's meetin also discussed gangland crime, and dere was a bit of banter over Willie O'Dea's role in certain recent incidents. Noel Dempsey suggested dat de Minister for Defence would need a projected grote rate of at least 3.5 per cent per annum if he was going to continue pickin fights with six-footers. Whereupon Willie told him to "sod off", or "hump off", or words to dat effect.

THURSDAY

I'm still not sure what Biffo and O'Dea were doin drinkin togedder in a pub in Limerick in de first place. Maybe I'm bein paranormal *("paranoid"? – Ed)* here. But country and western alliances make me nervous. De official explanation – dat dey were after attendin de openin of an art exhibition – is all me eye. I've attended a fair few openins meself over de years, but I draw de line at art exhibitions. And I'd be fairly culchered, compared to dem lads. I just hope Biffo has learned someting from de recent experience of his role model, Gordon Brown. Incidentally, de fiasco over de UK's election dat wasn't highlights de wisdom of me strategy in always goin de full term. But I might go anudder if Biffo and his pals try to force me out early.

FRIDAY

It's too early to say yet whedder Dunphy's intervention in de Mahon tribunal amounts to a dangerous tackle. He certainly had a few studs showin, but I'm not sure about de question of intent. One teery is dat he was exactin revenge for an earlier off-de-ball incident in which his team-mate Frank Connolly was taken out by Michael "Bites-yer-legs" McDowell. But McDowell has since been shown de red card, so I don't see why Dunphy should pick on me. Den again, his evidence to de tribunal seems to be a game of two halves. I'll bide me time on it for a while to see what he's really sayin. If necessary, I'll do an Alf Inge Haaland on him in due course.

SATURDAY

Griim news from East Cork, where de search for former junior minister Ned O'Keeffe – who went missing in stormy conditions earlier dis munt – has been called off. Dere have been numerous reported sightins, includin one in de Dail carpark de day of de confidence motion. But it obviously wasn't Ned, or he'd have voted for me, because he was never a man to let personal rancour get de better of him. Ar dheis De go raibh a hAnam. Tankfully dere's better news from Mayo, where de way hao been cleared for de prodigal daughter to rejoin de party. De fatted calf has been slaughtered, as has any internal opposition to de move; aldough dere's little enough of dat, because widdout de Flynn corporation, Mayo Fianna Fail is a mess. I know some commentators will question what has changed since Beverley was trown out of de party. But, eh, it's basic bankin practice, really. She was expelled on a matter of principle. Now she's bein readmitted on a matter of compound interest.

MONDAY

It's been anudder dark period in me life of late, what wit de onset of winter and de clocks goin back. So I was very grateful when a group of friends – de Review Body on Higher Remuneration – got togedder recently and organised a bit of a whip-around for me, to de tune of €38,000 a year. I didn't ask dem or anyting: dey just took it upon demselves to do it, outta generosity. Dis has been de story of me life. Strangers keep givin me money for no reason (aldough try telling dat to de tribunals). At €310,000 a year, I am now Europe's best paid leader. In fact, at dis rate, I may have to review me plan to hand over to Biffo when de new EU president job becomes available. Blair is gaggin for dat position too, so dere's no guarantee I'd get it. But I don't know if I could afford de pay-cut, anyway.

TUESDAY

Of course it's not just me dat has been remunerated. Evryone in de cabinet gets a dig-out of at least 25 grand. But de public can rest assured dat dere is nuttin untoward involved. De increase is not tied to promises of improved performance or any udder favours. I can state categorically dat de donors have neider asked for nor will be given anyting in return. On de contrary, dere's an important point of principle here. De usual level of government incompetence must continue, despite de salary increases. Udderwise, people might tink dey could buy us.

WEDNESDAY

De debacle over learner drivers proves de point. As Minister for Transport, Noel Dempsey is clearly a danger to himself and udder motorists. Obviously I should give him a J-plate (for Junior Minister) and force him to re-sit his test for full Cabinet membership. It's not just dat he attempted to punish learner drivers for de State's failure to reduce de test backlog, and dat he's now bringin de law into disrepute by sayin de cops won't enforce it anyway. I've pulled a few u-turns meself from time to time, but dat's de equivalent of a 180-degree handbrake-assisted skid across de meridian on a dual carriageway. De point is, even before dis, Dempsey had form. Dere was his role in de Aer Lingus saga. Dere was his attempt to reintroduce college fees too. And of course he was de one dat first landed us in de shite wit e-votin. So obviously I should at least demote him at dis stage. But to sack a minister now – just after de a pay-rise – would send out de wrong message. Dat's why I have no choice but to promote him instead, as soon as de opportunity arises.

THURSDAY

Meanwhile, de economic down-turn continues. Wit tax-take fallin dramatically, next munt's budget will have to be tough: especially since – accordin to all de economic forecasts – dere is absolutely no chance of an election next year. It is time, derefore, for us all to tighten our belts. Well, eh, not us all exactly. But I hope dat Jack O'Connor in SIPTU doesn't start makin comparisons between my pay and dat of de workin man, generally. Because if he does, I'll have no choice but to say to him, "Eh, I'm all right, Jack."

FRIDAY

De construction industry may be slowin down, but dere is one sector where job creation is still in full flow. I refer of course to de lucrative politics business, in which de boom shows no sign of relentin. Today I announced 23 new Government committees, all of which will require a chairman, a vice chairman, and a whip. Dat's a whoppin 69 jobs, many of dem targeted at depressed areas, such as de opposition back benches. When ye add in ministers, junior ministers, members of de Oireachtas commission and whatever you're havin yerself, it means dat 130 of de 166 TDs will soon be toppin up deir 100k salaries wit some perk or udder. Dáil unemployment rates have never been lower. Of course dere will always be hard cases who fall trew de net. Maybe Combat Poverty would consider setting up a programme for de 30-odd TDs who miss out on de gravy train. But when you consider de success story dat is Leinster House, how de political correspondents can talk about doom and gloom in de economy is beyond me.

SATURDAY

I see de Mahon Tribunal has me return to de witness box scheduled for December 20. First dey mess up me summer holidays. Now dey're determined to ruin me Christmas as well. Feck dem. But I suppose de choice of dat date is appropriate in a way. It can only be a matter of time now before dey drag Santy Claus in to make a statement on de series of donations he made to me in de 1950s, durin yet anudder dark period in me life.

MONDAY

I know now what Alex Ferguson means when he complains about de lack of noise from his home supporters. When someone leaked me communications wit Revenue officials to de *Daily Mail* – a new low in Oirish life – dere should have been howls of protest from de Fianna Fáil equivalent of de Stretford End. Instead, dere was a deafenin silence. No doubt de backbenchers are too busy eatin prawn sandwiches, now dat deir Dáil season tickets are safe for anudder five years. Not dat de people in de posh seats – me so-called Cabinet colleagues – were any noisier. I suppose I should be grateful dat dey haven't started a Mexican wave yet, or a chant of "Cheerio, Cheerio, Cheerio". But I'll have to watch me back even more carefully dan usual over de next few weeks, in case de party tries to ship me out durin de January transfer window.

TUESDAY

After de dig-outs, now comes de dig-in. It was in enough trouble when it was only de Tribunal pokin round me bedroom, but wit de taxmen goin trew me drawers as well, I'm dubbly vulnerable to a heave. Not dat Biffo will move against me. I tink he has a genuine sense of loyalty, God love his innocence. It's Biffo's supporters I'm worried about. Wit de economy goin down de toilet like a bad curry, dey need to get him out of de Department of Finance before de next budget, which is liable to make Ray MacSharry's cutbacks look like de Teddy Bear's picnic. Luckily for me, Biffo's rivals will be just as anxious to keep him where he is for anudder year or two, which is de only chance dey have of matchin his approval ratins. So if I can continue to play dem all off against each udder, I might just see out 2008.

WEDNESDAY

De main plank of me survival strategy is de speech on Capitol Hill. Me enemies can't really shaft me before dat, so trick will be to put it off as long as possible. Mansergh sent me a first draft of de script last week and it was so good I had tears in me eyes – genuine tears, not like de ones in de Bryan Dobson interview – readin it. Even so, I've told him to cut back a bit on de Yeats quotations and to add in a few sports analogies. De odd joke wouldn't hurt eider, I said. But I've assured him dere's no rush wit de final draft. March 2009 will be time enough, if I have me way. De udder ace in me pack, meanwhile, is de EU referendum. De party can't be changin leaders before such an important vote, which I intend to turn into a referendum on me continued stewardship of de country. Provided we win, dat is. If we lose, I intend to turn it into a referendum on Dick Roche's performance as Minister for European Affairs.

THURSDAY

As part of de dig-in, obviously, I need to clarify me tax position, insofar as dis is possible. Basically, it is my belief dat I am fully compliant, which is not quite de same as sayin dat I really am fully compliant, but a nod's as good as a wink to a blind horse. I look forward to hearin from de horse, or de Revenue Commissioners, or bote, in due course: aldough, as wit de Mansergh's final draft, dere's no rush. I have also taken de opportunity of clarifiyin a statement to de Dáil in which I said dat, vis a vis de dig-outs, I had consulted de "tax autorities". I meant Des Peelo, who's de greatest autority on tax I know. Unfortunately, certain people took de phrase "tax autorities" to mean de Revenue Commissioners. Dese people included de Revenue Commissioners, who wrote me a snotty letter seekin an explanation. I hope I have now cleared dis up, and dat I can tink of a new way to restore de confusion as soon as possible.

FRIDAY

I'm not big on New Year's resolutions. But if dere's one ting I'm givin up in 2008, it's bein Mister Nice Guy, especially where de Mahon tribunal is concerned. Dis was de teem of an exclusive interview I did today for dis weekend's *Sunday Independent*: one of an exhaustive series of exclusive interviews I'll be givin over de next few weeks. In particular, I want to highlight de tribunal's unwarranted invasion of me privacy: de way dey drag me personal life into everyting, for de benefit of a grateful media. I hasten to say dat it's not for my own sake dat I'm doin dis. It's de integrity of public life in genral I'm tryin to protect.

SATURDAY

Take de decision of de *Oirish Times* to publish a cute photograph of me and de twins on de front of deir post-Christmas edition: yet anudder example of de personal vendetta against me in certain sections of de media. OK, I might have invited de paper to send a photographer around and, yes, maybe I posed for de camera wit Jay and Rocco on me lap. But I had no idea de picture would be placed so prominently, in a position occupied tree days earlier by a stained-glass portrait of de Holy Family. De fact dat I got a five per cent bounce in de polls as a result does not lessen de shock I felt at havin me personal life paraded in dis way. Again, it's not Bertie Ahern I'm worried about – I'm big enough to take dis sort of ting. It's future Taoisigh, whose grandchildren may not be as good-lookin as mine.

MONDAY

De more I hear about him, de more I realise how much me and Giovanni Trapanpony have in common. All right, he has more English dan I do. I wouldn't be surprised if he has more Oirish as well. But he's a proven winner, just like me. And, just like me, despite all his success, he still has critics who accuse him of bein too conservative, especially wit his mid-term reshuffles. Yes, he once took off Del Piero in a world cup match, replacin him wit de little beardy lad who kicks people, and – as a direct result – lost de game. But everybody's entitled to de odd mistake. De fact is, I know exactly how Trapanpony tinks. After all, I'm de man who brought back Mary Wallace while leavin me flair players (such as dey were) on de bench. Ultra-cautious tactics have served us bote well, on de whole. If Trap can keep his head here, dere's no reason he can't get us to de World Cup. And if I can keep mine, dere's no reason I can't qualify for Europe next year, when de presidency job becomes available.

TUESDAY

Dat, in a nutshell, is de tinkin behind me High Court challenge to de Mahon Tribunal. I'm not lauchin an all-out attack on de tribunal team, no more dan Trapanpony would. No – dis is a defensive strategy, to prevent de tribunal from attackin me. I'm settin out me lawyers in a 4-5-1 formation. And de plan is not so much to score – dat'd be a bonus – as to play for extra time. Me intention is to prevent Mahon from publishin his report before de middle of 2009: by which stage I may well be President of de EU and I won't have to give a shite what any tribunal in Dublin says about me. De result of de court challenge won't matter den eider. I'll be de winner, anyway – on de golden-goals rule. In de meantime, like any good continental football manager, I'll use whatever delayin tactics I can: takin de ball into de corner, lying down pretendin to be hurt, etc.

WEDNESDAY

Of course, de udder big ting me and Trapanpony have in common is dat we are bote recipients of independent financin by welty businessmen. De Oireland soccer team could never have afforded a manager as good as him widdout turd-party help. And you could say de same vis-a-vis me and Oireland in genral. Remember John Bruton? No, you probly don't. I tink he went to America in de end: to de so-called "major league". (Ha, ha!) But anyway, in his time here, he was de political equivalent of Steve Staunton. Incredible as it is to tink now, he was de Taoiseach immediately before me. Den, after a string of embarrassin results, de Oirish electrit finally decided to get serious and pick de best candidate, no matter what it cost. De ting is, dey might never have got me were it not for de generosity of certain individuals who realised dat de paltry ministerial salary den on offer could not support someone of my calibre. If it wasn't for deir financial assistance, I might have been forced to take a better-paid job in de private sector. But tanks to dem, I was able to become manager of Oireland for a record-breakin tree terms in a row: durin which – of course – we became de economic champions of Europe.

THURSDAY

Like Trapanpony, I'm a great believer in closin de opposition down. I just wish dat was legal here. In de meantime, I have to put up wit Enda Kenny and Eamon Gilmore givin cheek to me on Leaders Questions twice a week. But it could be worse. It used to be tree times a week until I cut a deal wit Labour a few years ago, whereby I got to curtail me Dail appearances and dey got to hold on to de last shred of deir dignity by bein allowed to continue speakin ahead of de Shinners and Independents. Evry Tuesday since den, I give tanks for dat arrangement, which leaves me more time to tink about de udder tactical challenges I face as Oireland manager: like how I can close down de tribunal widdout anybody noticin.

FRIDAY

Not for de first time, Eamon Dunphy has tackled me from behind, off de ball. But skooled as I am in de ways of professional soccer, I can deal wit it. Accordin to Dunphy's evidence at de tribunal, Owen O'Callaghan once told him dat I reneged on support for a development in Atlone despite havin been "looked after" or "taken care of". Dis last bit is true, as it happens. I remember de day well. I was havin a meetin wit O'Callaghan about de development, and I had a very bad cold. So at one stage, he opened his briefcase and said: "I have something here that'll sort that out." He took out a sachet of "maximum-otient" Lemsip, which I'd never heard of at de time. Den he went outside and boiled a kettle for me himself. I took de drink and sure enough it perked me up no end. But I still objected to his development and voted against it. Which is obviously what he meant when he told Dunphy I had been "taken care of". Now dat, in soccer parlance, I've treaded a slide-rule explanation trew to him, I expect Owen to run wit it at de tribunal in due course.

MONDAY

De hacks caught me off guard at a gig in Fairview dis mornin when I admitted under questionin dat de Oirish economony had a "hard year" ahead. Normally I try to stress de positive. And I wouldn't mind only de whole reason I was dere was to open anudder European headquarters of some finance company. But as usual de meeja seized on de bad news. Now dey're reportin it as if I officially launched de recession: promisin a roll-out of new dole offices all over de country by de end of the year. Of course, even de dogs in de street know dat tings will be difficult in de short-term. As de sayin goes, when de US sneezes, de rest of de world catches a flyin snot.

TUESDAY

De fact remains dat de indicators are not all bad. Take two sets of figgers released today. Yes, on de one hand, de CSO shows a sharp increase in unemployment last munt, which confirms de slowdown in construction. But I prefer to dwell on de latest statistics from de Dáil register of members' interests, which tell a far more positive story. Dere's certainly no sign of a slow-down in Frank Fahey, for example. On de contry, Frank is goin from strent to strent: buying apartments from Galway to de Gulf. De sun never sets now on his property portfolio, which is like a beacon in de gadderin gloom. Havin done our own modest bit for de property sector, we at de St Luke's Buildin Society salute Frank's achievements.

WEDNESDAY

Today was de last cabinet meetin before de break, and in keepin wit tradition, we had de crystal bowl for de White House shamrock on display. It's still empty, of course; so, as usual, we passed it around and got evrybody to put deir name on a piece of paper in it. I drew de winners of de Paddy's Day Trip raffle meself. Noel Dempsey won first prize: Australia. But dere were no losers, really, because even de short junkets have special extras: like de €1600 a night apartment in Rome, and so on. After de main raffle, we had a separate mini-draw for de Greens, who can only go to places dat are reachable by train, ferry, or bicycle. Not dat dey have a monopoly on concern for de environment. To demonstrate Fianna Fail's eco credentials, we will be offsettin our entire carbon footprint by plantin Willie O'Dea at home in Limerick for de week. De hope is dat he will harness his natural wind capacity to generate so much media coverage dat nobody will notice de rest of the Cabinet is missin.

THURSDAY

It's a pity about Paisley all de same. I was hopin he might last anudder year, at least, but it wasn't to be. And to tink I used to worry dat de horse sedatives we had him on would wear off before de executive settled in. Me big fear, always, was dat he might regain consciousness in de middle of a press conference, realise he was power-sharin wit de Shinners, and start beatin Martin McGuinness over de head wit a Bible: live on Sky. Instead, it was de side effect of de drugs – de uncontrollable chucklin – dat we couldn't control. De vets warned us about it from de start. But reducin de dosage was always too much of a risk. Peter Robinson was very insistent on dis, even when he know how unpopular de chucklin was wit DUP grassroots. As I said to Peter on de phone last night, it's sad dat de big man should have become a victim of his own sense of humour in de end. "Yes, it's tragic," agreed Peter, adding: "Ha, ha, ha!"

FRIDAY

Blair gone. Paisley going. Eddie O'Sullivan's four-year-contract sleepin wit de fishes. Dere's a end of an era feelin around suddenly. And now I hear dat Joe Lennon – me government press officer back in de good old days – has left de HSE to join Biffo as special advisor. Joe was a big part of de reason dat de meeja used to like me. And even dough he'll have his work cut out groomin Biffo, I'd say he's still up to de task. As if tings weren't bad enough for me, I have to fly to Washington dis weekend and meet Dubya for de last time: dereby runnin de risk of catchin Lame Duck virus off him, if I haven't got it already. No wonder I'm prevaricatin over de date of de Lisbon referendum. It's one of de few aces I still have in me pack: if only because de team can't get rid of an experienced manager goin into such an important fixture

SATURDAY

I've finally settled on June 12 for de Lisbon referendum, wit de replay if necessary in October. Here's me cunning plan. Nobody can shaft me before de first vote, which I tink we might lose. But dey can't shaft me den, eider, what wit de crisis dat will follow. De future of de EU will be at stake. So de entire continent will trow its weight behind de campaign to reverse de decision. Meanwhile I'll be even more important, and high profile, dan ever. Den – hey preoto! – Oireland will vote Yes at de second time of askin. And yours truly will be de hero of Europe, just as de member states are preparin to elect a president. Blair can eat his heart out. De tribunal can go and jump. And as for Biffo, he will have my full blessing to take over as Teeseach, just in time to deal wit de full-scale recession.

TUESDAY

What wit de tribunal and evryting, I was at a bit of a low ebb when Biffo dropped into St Lukes for the post-Easter briefin. So he tried to cheer me up wit stories from his recent Vietnamese trip. "You think your reputation is bad," he said: "Their prime minister's name is Dung – literally!" Den he launched into one of his funny impressions, as a grizzled Vietnam veteran remembrin de war against "Charlie". Unfortunately, dis was a bit close to de bone for comfort. As a Fianna Fáil Taoiseach, de spectre of "Charlie" haunts evryting ye do. He lurks behind evry tree (especially in Nort Dublin) and bush, ready to jump out at any moment and cut yer trote. Or so ye end up tinkin, after a few years in de jungle. It's a big strain on de nerves. So all in all, Biffo's attempts to cheer me were about as successful as his last diet. "I'll see you later in the week," he said on the way out. "I hope you're in a better mood then."

WEDNESDAY

It's a dirty war dis. De tribunal will stop at nuttin to get me, and nobody's safe from de crossfire. Even so, in retraspect, I shoulda done someting when I realised dey were holdin Grainne Carroot hostage. I shoulda burst into Dublin Castle shoutin, "Take me, and let de wimmin and children go!" De problem is: I would den have had to account for de sterling lodgements, on de spot. And unfortunately, I needed time to tink up someting good. I couldn't risk anudder short-term explanation, like de "dig-out": I've already dug meself furder in dan an eco-warrior on de M3. Also, I hoped de Grainne episode would rebound on de tribunal lawyers. Time was – when I was still de Teflon Taoiseach and before I turned into Premier Dung – it would have been dem dat got de flak for upsettin a female witness. Now, of course, dat's all changed. Suddenly it's like I'm de one dat made her cry.

THURSDAY

As if I didn't have enough wimmin problems already, Fiona O'Malley has called on me to make a statement. Apart from de immediate embarrassment dis causes, it's yet anudder unwelcome parallel with CJH, who had his fair share of O'Malley problems. At least de PDs had a mandate back den. As Biffo says, deir current leadership contest is like two bald men fightin for control of a comb. But her comments still have de potential to destabilise de whole government. Natcherally, John Gormless is callin for a statement too. And now dat lame-duck shooting season has been declared open, some of me back-benchers are probably reaching for deir guns.

FRIDAY

Eoghan Harris dropped in again today, sayin he was goin on de Late Late Show – to debate de tribunal – and needed to do some research. "Don't mind me, Taoiseach," he said; "I just have to look into your heart for a few minutes. You can carry on workin." I still haven't got used to dis, to be honest. But I behaved as normally as I could – takin phonecalls, writin memos, etc – while Harris sat dere gazin deep inside me and makin notes. Finally, he got up and tanked me for my cooperation. "I have all I need," he said: "I believe I know exactly what you were thinkin when you told the tribunal what you thought was the truth." Unfortunately I couldn't watch his performance tonight, in case anyone else on de panel accused me of committin perjury at de tribunal, in which case I might have to comment. But I'm sure he was very good.

SATURDAY

Hard to believe it's ten years since de Good Friday Agreement. And what tanks have I got for bringin peace to Oireland? None, dat's what. At de rate tings are goin, de Drumcondra Mafia will be disbanded before de IRA. And unlike dem, we won't even be able to organise one last big bank robbery before we go. Unlike dem, too, we'll be answerin questions about our fund-raisin activities for years to come. I hope we'll at least be allowed to continue meetin as an old comrade's association, evry Friday night in Fagan's. But I wonder what's de chances of an amnesty for de On-De-Runs?

SUNDAY

De feelin of gloom was not helped any by tonight's De Week in Politics, on which Mary Coughlan repeatedly refused to say whedder she believed me evidence. After she denied me for de turd time, I taut I heard a cock crow. But it was just de new ring-tone on me mobile phone. Biffo was checkin in wit me to see how I was. "Sorry about de brudder," I told him. "Well it just shows that none of us are above the tax laws," said Biffo. "Tell me about it!" says I. He asked if I was watchin Coughlan, and I said I was, aldough I was nearly afraid to turn on de television dese days, because I never knew when "me Nighthawks moment" would come. Biffo assured me dat, whatever happened, histry would not judge me as harshly as Haughey. "Let's face it, you're nuttin like Charlie," he said. "Tanks, big fella," I replied

MONDAY

De leadership of Feena Fail is like de Olympic Torch. Ever since Dev first lit it in 1926, it has shone like a beacon in de darkness: leadin de Oirish people forward to a better life. It has been my honour to carry de flame some of de way. But now, de time has come for me to hand it on to anudder generation. Like Dev, I have anointed me successor in advance, ensurin dere will be no repeat of 1979, when de torch transfer was fumbled, causin first-degree burns to bystanders and long-term smoke damage to Des O'Malley. No, dis time it will be a smood transition, guaranteein de party's future stability. It's a case of one long-distance runner passin de baton to anudder. I know it's a big stretch to imagine Biffo as a runner of any kind. But we can't all be built like Greek gods.

TUESDAY

Not everybody in Drumcondra is happy about me handin de flame back to de party's country-and-western wing. In fact, some Nortsoide separatists have vowed to attack de torch relay en route to Offaly, in protest at human rights abuse by Culchies. As one protester said in Fagans last night: "Dey come up here and take our jobs, our houses, and our wimmen. But dey'll never take our freedom!" De drink was flowin at de time. And after anudder few pints, a group of local Buddists (so called because of deir use of de phrase "How'ye bud") set out from de pub wit a plan to ambush de torch carriers at de M50, usin fire extinguishers. Biffo's local cumann has responded by enlistin de services of de Offaly GAA to act as "guardians of de flame" and escort it into Tullamore tomorrow. But de situation remains tense.

WEDNESDAY

De torch has reached Tullamore safely, despite a few scuffles, and Biffo has been confirmed as Teeseach-designate. Until de last minute, some of de more hardline Buddists were hopin dat my old anorak would be reincarnated in time to retain supreme power in St Luke's. But, God knows, we've tried it on Cyprian Brady often enough and it doesn't fit. Even de fanatics have now accepted dat de Dalai Bertie may have to skip a generation. I have urged me followers to remain calm.

THURSDAY

It was wort resignin if only to see de look on Enda Kenny's face at Leader's Questions dis mornin. He wouldn't have been half as entoosiastic about urgin me to quit if he taut I'd do it. Today, Biffo's regular slot deputisin for me was a taste of tings to come. Kenny and Gilmore looked like a team of second-rate tag wrestlers: dey were still congratulatin demselves on gettin rid of me, when Giant

Haystacks climbed into de ring and sat on dem. I winced as Enda tried his old cupla focal gambit on Biffo. It always worked on me. But by de time Biffo is finished wit him, Enda will be focalled front, back, and sideways.

FRIDAY

Beverly's return to de party could not be better timed. In case builders are gettin nervous over de tribunal stuff, it sends out de message dat it'll be business as usual durin de party's transfer to new management. On de udder hand, I was relieved today when John Gormless's application for FF membership was quietly witdrawn. Apparently, it was anudder side effect of dat embarrassin accident de day of me resignation speech. I was just after takin delivery of de last batch of illegal horse sedatives for Paisley, to keep him quiet until he steps down. As usual, dey were labelled "multivitamins", pendin dispatch to our friends in de DUP reform wing. But what wit de emotion of de occasion, I just left dem on me desk. And when Gormless was in, wishin me well, he picked up a couple and swallowed dem. Den before anyone could stop him, he was behind me durin de speech (where Donie Cassidy normally goes): peerin over me shoulder like Long John Silver's parrot, and nodding constantly.

SATURDAY

As I begin de sad task of clearin me office in Government Buildings, I'm not sure whedder to take down de picture of Padraig Pearse, or leave it where it is. Biffo will probably want Seamus Darby up dere instead – I must ask. Of course de important ting about de picture for me personally was dat – like all Pearse's portraits – it only showed him from de side. Dis always reminded me of de key to me success in politics. Goin back to de days of CJ and Rambo and Liam Lawlor, I always knew how to look de udder way, when necessry. If Paddy Hillery – God rest him – had learned dat lesson, maybe he could have been leader too.

SUNDAY

I wonder what Pearse would make of me time in office. I didn't unite Oireland, it's true. But I united Feena Fáil, which was an even bigger challenge. And pendin de return of de Nort, I transformed de Republic into one of de world's most successful countries: albeit wit a bit of help from dat Kildare fella whose name I've forgotten. So aldough I'm sad to be steppin down, I'm happy too. After all, I leave de economy in good shape. And I'm handin it over to Biffo just in time for de worst global recession since de Wall Street crash. Maybe dat's why, as I shut de office door last night, I taut I heard a ghostly laugh from inside and an old familiar voice. I probably just imagined it. But I coulda sworn it was sayin something like: "the most devious, the most cunning, the most ruthless of them all."